Children's Hospital

by car   by skate board   by coach   or by spaceship.

administrator's   visitors   and lots of other children.

tummy   foot   ear   or wing?   No

horse's   or bunny rabbits.

make you all better.

The
Royal Belfast Hospital
for Sick Children
A HISTORY 1948–1998

HAROLD LOVE

THE
BLACKSTAFF
PRESS

BELFAST

EDITORIAL NOTE

All illustrations in this book are the property of Media Services (Photography),
The Royal Hospitals, unless otherwise stated.

Illustrations on title page and dedication page
by John Kindness, contributor to the integrated art works project, 1998,
on the complex of new buildings at the Royal Belfast Hospital for Sick Children.

First published in 1998 by
The Blackstaff Press Limited
3 Galway Park, Dundonald, Belfast BT16 0AN, Northern Ireland
for the Royal Belfast Hospital for Sick Children
with financial assistance from
Macartney and Dowie Financial Services Limited
and
The Ladies' League (Royal Belfast Hospital for Sick Children)

Typeset by Techniset Typesetters, Newton-le-Willows, Merseyside

Printed in Northern Ireland by W. & G. Baird Limited

A CIP catalogue record for this book
is available from the British Library

ISBN 0-85640-621-X

To my grandchildren

Benjamin

Stephen

Amy

Joshua

Felicity

Charlotte

and

Hannah

Without history, a man's soul is purblind,
seeing only the things which almost touch his eyes.

THOMAS FULLER
The Holy State and the Profane State (1642)

in this house
whether I be born or unborn
struggle or be still
I am cradled

whether I speak or do not speak
see or do not see
I am seen and heard

should I hear or not hear
I can feel, touch
and know that nothing preys on me

be motherless fatherless
breathe in the breath
of the merciful

STEPHEN POTTS

CONTENTS

ACKNOWLEDGEMENTS

I am most grateful to my colleagues at the Royal Belfast Hospital for Sick Children who asked me to write a history of the Hospital, where I spent the bulk of my professional life. As honorary archivist, I have been privileged in having access to Hospital reports, records and minutes. More importantly, flesh has been put on the dry bones by the contributions of numerous friends, both retired and contemporary, who so readily supplied either written or oral personal memories. In particular, my thanks are due to Dr Gerry Black for his constant encouragement and meticulous scrutiny of the manuscript. For any remaining errors of omission or commission, I plead *mea culpa*. My secretary, Vicki Graham, coped with repeated drafts of the manuscript with patient good humour, despite the pressing demands of other duties; I am most grateful to her. My wife Nora endured disruption of family routine with commendable equanimity. My thanks are also due to Mark Tierney of Medical Services (Photography) for his expert production of many of the illustrations. Finally, I wish to thank all the staff at Blackstaff Press, whose expertise in production and presentation was of the highest standard.

H.L.

PREFACE

THE PERIOD 1948–98 IN THE HISTORY of the Royal Belfast Hospital for Sick Children has been one of change and challenge. In 1948, after seventy-five years as a voluntary institution sustained solely by public beneficence, the Hospital became part of the Belfast Hospital Management Group under the control of the Northern Ireland Hospitals Authority. In 1973 its administration passed into the hands of the North & West Belfast District of the Eastern Health & Social Services Board. This regime remained until 1993, when the Hospital was incorporated in the Royal Hospitals Trust.

In parallel, there have been the remarkable advances in all areas of child care. New drugs and the application of sophisticated technology have brought untold benefit to the sick children of Northern Ireland – but at a price. Dedicated staff have faced the challenge to develop and maintain a centre of excellence 'cribbed and cabinned' in outdated buildings, while endeavouring to solve the well-nigh insoluble: how to meet the insatiable clinical demands with resources of limited capacity. Furthermore, no other children's hospital in the British Isles has been forced to withstand the pressures of working in a deprived urban area under the constant threat of street violence and terrorist activity.

Therefore this book is not simply a record of a series of historical events deserving of public notice but, rather, it is a story of the internal tensions and outside pressures which have moulded the character of the Hospital over the past half-century. Above all, it is an account of a children's hospital which has served, and will continue to serve, the children of Northern Ireland with dedication and skill, maintaining the Hippocratic standards of caring, of sagacity, of humanity and of probity.

> It happens to us as it happeneth to wayfaring men, sometimes our way is clear, sometimes foul, sometimes uphill, sometimes downhill, we are seldom at a certainty and the wind is not always at our backs . . .
>
> John Bunyan, *The Pilgrim's Progress*

HAROLD LOVE
JANUARY 1998

The Belfast Hospital for Sick Children,
Queen Street, 1889–1932

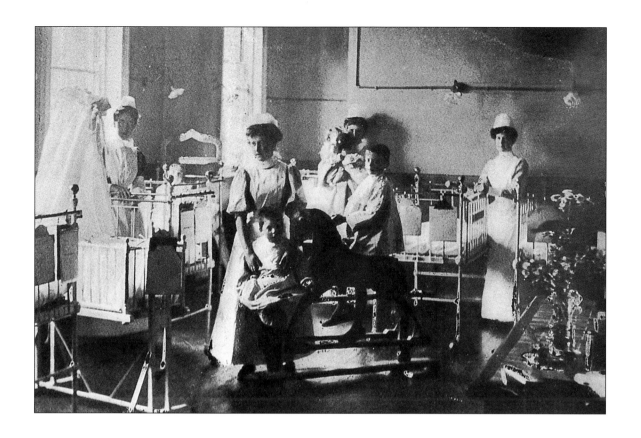

1

BEGINNINGS

The early history of the Royal Belfast Hospital for Sick Children, 1873–1948, has been faithfully recorded by the late H.G. Calwell in his book *The Life and Times of a Voluntary Hospital*, published in its centenary year, 1973. The present study covers the period from the beginning of the National Health Service in 1948 until 1998. Nevertheless, throughout the book, for the sake of continuity and comparison, reference will be made to certain events prior to 1948.

When the Hospital moved from Queen Street to the Falls Road in 1932, a booklet was issued, entitled *The Belfast Hospital for Sick Children (Incorporated)*, being a brief record of its foundations, history and activities. Reproduced here in full, the booklet states clearly the high ideals of the Hospital and lists members of management and Medical Staff, many of whom would continue to serve in a new era under state control, some sixteen years later.

Above:
A surgical ward in the Belfast Hospital for Sick Children, Queen Street, *c.* 1900. Wards were named O'Neill and Darbishire after Lord O'Neill (president of the Hospital) and Herbert Darbishire (honorary secretary)

Left:
The badge of the Belfast Hospital for Sick Children (Incorporated)

In 1907 the hospital was incorporated and the property of the Trustees then became vested in the body, viz. The Belfast Hospital for Sick Children (Incorporated).

OBJECTS OF THE HOSPITAL

The objects of the Institution have been similar throughout its existence and are as follows:

a) To provide for the reception, maintenance, and medical treatment of the children of the poor during sickness and to furnish advice and medicine to those who cannot be admitted into the Hospital.

b) To promote the advancement of medical science, with reference to the diseases of Infancy and Childhood.

c) To diffuse among all classes of the community, and chiefly amongst the poor, a better knowledge of the management of Infants and Children in health and during sickness.

It is worthy of note that poor children, from all parts of Ireland, are continually admitted without distinction of class or creed.

On 15 May 1873, at a meeting held in Belfast, it was unanimously resolved that an institution taking for its model the Children's Hospital, Gt Ormond Street, London, should be established. The Extern Department was inaugurated on 2 June 1873, at 25 King Street, Belfast, and in the interval between that date and 31 December, 1,617 patients were treated. The Hospital was opened for the reception of Intern patients on 4 August 1873, 103 cases being admitted to the wards during the remainder of that year. Eighteen beds were then available for patients between the ages of 2 and 10 years.

The Belfast Hospital for Sick Children

Front cover of *The Belfast Hospital for Sick Children*, a booklet published in 1932 to mark the opening of the new hospital on the Falls Road

EARLY BEGINNINGS

The following year, 1874, showed a great increase in the activities of the Hospital, 317 Intern patients and 5,408 Extern patients being treated and the Extern Department considerably enlarged. From that time the work of the Hospital grew so steadily that, in 1877, it was patent that the original building was altogether inadequate for the needs of the City and Province. A new site was accordingly purchased in Queen Street, Belfast, and a hospital erected at a cost of over £5,000. This building was erected on lines which at that time were considered most modern and adequate. It had a large Extern Department and wards for 45 beds, and was opened for the admission of patients on 24 April 1879.

The first Matron of the Hospital, Miss Lennox, was a pupil of Florence Nightingale's famous school. It was largely due to her efforts that the difficulties encountered in the early years of the Hospital were successfully overcome.

During the first year in Queen Street – 1880 – 294 Intern and 6,831 Extern patients passed through the hospital. These figures make an interesting comparison with those of the last full year in Queen Street – 1931 – when there were 799 Intern admissions and 13,251 Extern patients, totalling 44,050 attendances.

This great increase is indicative of the growth of the City of Belfast, and the added demands upon the Institution made a further extension of the Hospital accommodation imperative. Even had it been desirable, it was impossible to extend the premises in Queen Street. The Board of Management gratefully accepted on very favourable terms from the Belfast Corporation the offer of a high, sunny and airy site of approximately five acres in extent in the old Asylum grounds, Falls Road, adjacent to the Royal Victoria and the Royal Maternity Hospitals. The foundation stone of the new Hospital was laid by Mrs Harold Barbour on 5 June 1929. The administrative wing, the Extern Department and two Ward Blocks with space for 74 beds were completed at a cost of £115,000, and so generous was the response of the charitable public that the new building was erected and equipped with the latest Medical and Surgical appliances, the opening ceremony being performed by Her Grace, the Duchess of Abercorn, on 24 November 1932.

The façade of the Falls Road Hospital in the 1930s

PLANS FOR THE FUTURE

The complete plans provide for two additional ward blocks, which when erected will increase the Intern accommodation to 150 beds. The construction and equipment of these blocks will entail a further outlay of £33,000.

3

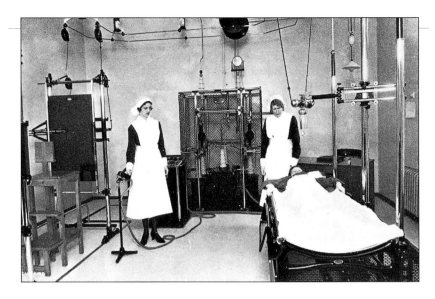

The new X-ray Department, 1932

Until this extension has been accomplished, the full potentialities of the Hospital will not be realised. As, however, their anxiety is divided between the necessity of meeting the running costs and the wish for the completion of their plans, the Board of Management cannot attempt the further extension until a considerable fund has been accumulated. Fears were expressed that the removal from Queen Street to a more distant site might militate against the usefulness of the Extern Department, but that these fears were groundless is proved by the astonishing total of 55,792 attendances in the Extern Department alone during 1933, the first complete year in the new hospital. To give adequate attention to this vast number and to maintain the

The Light Department, 1932; forerunner of the Physiotherapy Department

Intern with its subsidiaries, the X-ray, Massage and Light Departments, entails an annual expenditure of between £7,000 and £8,000. It will thus be realised that every possible effort will have to be made to increase the voluntary subscriptions if the Institution is to be kept free from debt. Until the Board of Management is assured that this income is forthcoming, the need for the additional wards must remain unsatisfied, as apart from the cost of construction, still further increased running expenses will be inevitable.

Subscriptions earmarked for the new wing will be gratefully received.

By its proximity to the Royal Victoria and Royal Maternity Hospitals and the Pathological Department of Queen's University, the Children's Hospital forms part of a Medical School of which any community may be proud. It will have marked and beneficial results not only on the health of the community, but on those medical students who have the advantage of study and instruction within its walls.

OUR ULTIMATE AIM

One factor which helps this Hospital is the natural response which human sympathy makes to the cry of a child in pain. Our organisation is a means of directing this feeling into channels of practical effect. This booklet is not simply a sentimental recital of childhood's troubles: it is a definite appeal for help to carry on a beneficent work which divides into two main heads:

a) the maintenance of the present efficiency, and

b) the addition of ward blocks necessary to complete the original plans for a hospital large enough to meet the needs of the sick children in this community.

In considering the question of sending donations and subscriptions which will enable the Hospital to reach this essential capacity for usefulness, please remember that it is, to-day, the only one throughout Northern Ireland devoted exclusively to the work of caring for ailing children under 12 years of age.

The first meeting of the Medical Staff in the new Falls Road Hospital was held in the Staff library on 20 April 1932, at 5.00 p.m. T.S. Kirk was in the chair, and the following were present: Dr Brice Smyth, Dr Rowland Hill, Dr F.M.B. Allen, Dr T.H. Crozier, H.P. Hall, Ian Fraser, Dr I. McCaw and P.T. Crymble (honorary secretary).

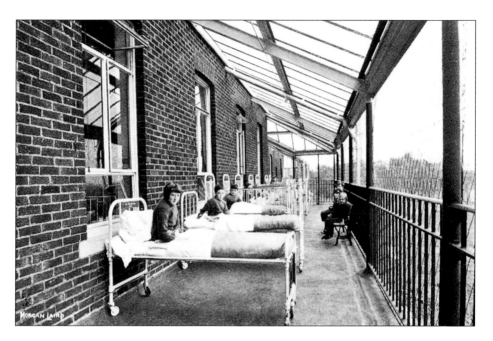

The Musgrave Ward
(medical) verandah, 1933

2

A NEW BEGINNING
5 JULY 1948

'No person need lack health for lack of means'

from Rita Duffy's mural,
Welcome to the Children's Hospital

A COMPREHENSIVE NATIONAL HEALTH SERVICE (NHS) was
one of the great plans of Winston Churchill's wartime
coalition government. A provisional scheme had been drawn
up during World War II with all the political parties agreeing
that something must be done to rid society of the stigma
that only the wealthy and the pauper could hope to receive
the best medical care. Sir Lionel Whitely, the incoming
president of the British Medical Association (BMA), stated
that the changes in medicine itself had tended to increase
the cost of medical treatment so that most people could no
longer afford to be ill. In 1942 Sir William, later Lord, Beveridge had
presented his historic report, in which five giants obstructing the path of
social progress were identified: Want, Disease, Ignorance, Squalor and
Idleness. Subsequently, statements were made in parliament about the
future of hospitals and other health services, to be followed by a White

Paper in 1944 and the National Health Services Act in 1946. The Northern Ireland Health Services Act did not receive the royal assent until February 1948.

With the defeat of the Conservatives at the post-war general election in 1945, it fell to Clement Attlee's Labour government to carry the concept of a National Health Service to fruition. Minister of Health Aneurin Bevan, in a notorious speech in Manchester, dismissed the Conservative Party as 'lower than vermin' and declaimed that 'people would come from all over the world to this modern medical mecca to learn in the twentieth century, as they had learned in the seventeenth'.

The National Health Service came into being against a background of worldwide unrest and social and financial difficulties at home. The British mandate in Palestine ended on 14 May 1948, to be followed by the Arab–Israeli conflict; an airlift was in operation supplying goods to a beleaguered Berlin; India and Pakistan were at war over Kashmir; and there was insurrection in Greece. Attlee warned that Soviet Russia threatened the welfare and way of life of the other nations of Europe. Many objected that Britain was not paying its way. With the cost of imports rising, a prolonged dock strike unresolved, petrol rationing in operation and food still scarce, how could a health scheme so comprehensive be justified? Two other dangers were envisaged: namely, the possible tendency of the public to become so welfare-minded as to regard health care as a right and not something to be earned, and the loss to productive industry of thousands of new officials who would be needed to administer a scheme of this magnitude.

There were some strident calls for militant action from the medical profession. For example, a meeting of doctors, called under the auspices of the BMA in January 1948, resolved to refuse to work under the National Health Services Act, describing it as 'so grossly at variance with the essential principles of our profession that it should be rejected absolutely by all practitioners'. The statement continued: 'The Minister has banged the door in the face of the profession and is determined to go on with the Act in spite of having failed to secure what he, himself, stated to be indispensable, namely, the co-operation of the doctors.'

Two months later the doctors gave what they declared was their final 'no' to Bevan, in what they perceived as a life and death struggle 'for freedom and independence'. This bluster went unheeded and, in the same month, March 1948, the names of the members of the new Northern Ireland Hospitals Authority (NIHA) were published in the local press. The list included two doctors from the Staff of the Children's Hospital, F.M.B. Allen and Muriel Frazer.

The prolonged and sometimes acrimonious negotiations with the government had ended with doctors reluctantly accepting the inevitable, divided and defeated as they were by a series of alternate blandishments and threats from the minister. Cynics were of the opinion that the doctors

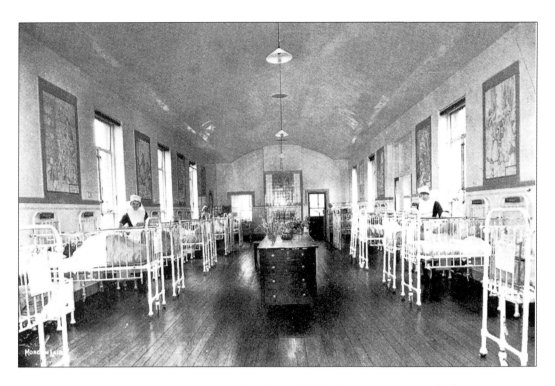

The Barbour Ward (surgical) in the 1930s

sacrificed their profession on the altar of filthy lucre. Dentists and chemists were last to bow.

In Northern Ireland there was less opposition to the new Health Service scheme than in Britain, although F.M.B. Allen spoke for many of his colleagues when he complained that the Health Service scheme was too ambitious: the resources of hospitals were limited, there were insufficient numbers of trained doctors and nurses, yet the public expectation would be of unlimited supplies of health service facilities. At this early stage, Allen had put his finger on the imbalance between supply and demand, a perverse ratio which has bedevilled the provision of health care throughout the life of the NHS.

As far as the Belfast Hospital for Sick Children was concerned, the financial situation in 1948 certainly would not have inspired confidence in the future of the Hospital as a voluntary institution. Between 1876 and 1916 the books balanced with a small credit, but by 1936 there was a debit balance of £1,166, rising over the next decade to £6,527. These figures did not include capital expenditure. The number of beds rose from eighteen in 1876 to ninety-seven in 1947. The Board of Management could not fail to recognize that further growth would be impossible and that before long there would have to be curtailment of service, or insolvency. As H.G. Calwell records, 'the State's intervention was timely'.[1]

On 5 July 1948 the Belfast Hospital for Sick Children passed from voluntary to state control, vested in the Northern Ireland Hospitals Authority. Henceforth, it would be administered by the Belfast Hospital Management Committee, responsible for a group of hospitals comprising also the Royal Victoria, Royal Maternity, Belfast Ophthalmic, Throne, Benn Ulster Eye, Ear and Throat, and the Claremont Street Hospital for Nervous Diseases.

These arrangements were communicated to the members of the Board of Management less than one month prior to the changeover date. The NIHA asked existing hospital committees to undertake duties as temporary committees; these would continue to manage the hospitals until the end of February 1949.

The Medical Staff, like the Board of Management, were concerned at the possible fate of the Hospital's Endowments (Free Funds), now controlled by the new Belfast Hospital Management Committee. There had been some question as to whether the provisions of the new Act fulfilled the promise that each hospital would retain its invested funds, although an assurance had been given by the chairman of the NIHA, Dr F.P. Montgomery, that such funds would be held by the Group Committee solely for the benefit of individual hospitals. A headline in the *Northern Whig* of 6 March 1948 struck an optimistic note: 'New Health Act welcomed at the Annual Meeting of the Belfast Hospital for Sick Children'. J. Morton McAuley (honorary treasurer) is quoted as saying that 'the Government would take over the hospital as a good solvent concern, entirely free of financial encumbrance: £125,000 would be handed over to the new Board of Management in cash and securities'. The Staff had obviously overcome, in some measure at least, their misgivings as to the fate of the Free Funds, and the Medical Staff Committee minutes reveal no strong antipathy to the prospect of working under state control. There were some efforts made to purchase particular items of medical equipment prior to the changeover, but little else was done against the uncertain future.

The first Annual Report of the Belfast Hospital Management Committee in 1948 shows that local management did not approach the new scheme unprepared. The development of the hospital service under the National Health Services Act was, to a considerable extent, anticipated by the Boards of Management of the Royal Victoria Hospital, the Royal Maternity Hospital and the Belfast Hospital for Sick Children. The Boards had met on a number of occasions with a view to the centralization of supplies and services and, consequently, the transition from the old method of hospital administration to that required under the Health Services Act was an evolution of projects already approved:

> The temporary Committees which were appointed to manage the hospitals until the statutory Committees could be set up, directed their attention to these developments, so that they would be at a stage where definite action could be taken by the New Belfast Hospital Management Committee as soon as it took over the administration of the hospitals within its group.

The Committee was anxious that the autonomy of the hospitals should not be compromised. However, it was agreed that while the new scheme was not ideal, every effort should be made to support the Hospitals Authority in its difficult task of taking over and co-ordinating the hospital services of Northern Ireland.

The Belfast Hospital Management Committee saw as one of its primary aims the setting up of hospital committees, each to administer its own Endowment Funds and to mobilize its own particular groups of voluntary helpers, thereby emphasizing the autonomy of the hospital concerned. Unhappily, some people who had previously given generously of their voluntary services had to be told that their services would be no longer necessary, owing to the constitution of the management structure under the new arrangements.

The widespread concern expressed that in a National Health Service there would be no humanizing touch between officialdom and the patient was shared by the Belfast Hospital Management Committee and its constituent hospital committees, including that of the Belfast Hospital for Sick Children: 'Before 5 July 1948, these services rendered in the interest of the patients were restricted solely by the financial ability to provide these services. However, the introduction of the new method of administration, involving the carrying out of many regulations, tended to cut down the time available to consider the needs of the patient.' This statement has echoed down the decades.

The NIHA Annual Report for 1948 began with a quotation from Benjamin Disraeli: 'Change is inevitable. In a progressive country change is constant.' The Authority endeavoured to highlight the human face of the new administrative structure and to counter the charge that the change from voluntary to state control would mean that medical care would become less human. It was at pains to point out that the Health Service legislation was 'not merely an exercise of the transfer of financial burdens from the individual to the community' but was designed 'to promote the health and thereby the happiness and prosperity of the people of Northern Ireland'. The report continued:

> It is easy to forget this fundamental aspiration in the struggle through the maze of administrative detail and the labyrinth of routine which appear to be inseparable from large scale endeavours in the modern world. How fatally easy it is to decry the high purpose and expectations of the whole scheme because the impatient cannot wait until Rome is built or because, by reason of the imperfections of human nature, a relatively small number of people abuse the scheme and gain undue and widespread publicity for their anti-social behaviour. Yet, if the main object is not kept in mind and is not resolutely and courageously pursued by all who have a part to play in the administration of the new scheme, the end will be failure and the road to it will be strewn with lost hopes, disappointment, discord and discontent. Many long and weary hours have been spent on matters which seemed remote from the sick patient in the hospital bed, or the hopeful or fearful patient visiting the specialist's diagnostic clinic. The tasks undertaken in those hours have been a tax on patience and enthusiasm which was endurable only through the hope and the belief that the work of those who directly minister to the needs of the sick or the injured will be lightened, facilitated and supported by a sound but not rigid or inflexible system.

The Authority saw as a major task the work of building for the future, concomitant with the maintenance of existing arrangements and standards. It recognized the immense labour necessary to keep the hospitals going and to meet the greatly increased demands imposed since 5 July 1948, and it acknowledged the achievements of medical, nursing, administrative and other staff of the hospitals, as well as the many citizens who served as members of Temporary Committees and in other capacities.

The last meeting of the outgoing Board of Management of the Belfast Hospital for Sick Children (Incorporated) was held in the boardroom of the Hospital on 29 June 1948. It was announced that the NIHA had confirmed the appointment of a Temporary Committee, consisting of twenty-one members, to carry on the work of the Hospital until a permanent committee assumed office. A highlight of the meeting of the Temporary Committee of 12 August 1948 was the announcement that, by command of His Majesty King George VI, the title of the Hospital should henceforth be the Royal Belfast Hospital for Sick Children. This recognition was largely due to the good offices of the Countess Granville, sister of Queen Elizabeth (now the Queen Mother), who wished the honour to be granted during her husband's tenure as Governor of Northern Ireland. This was not the first occasion on which the 'Royal' appellation had been sought; the Board of Management, at the instigation of Dr John McCaw, had petitioned for it in 1900 – coincidental with a visit to Ireland by Queen Victoria – but without success. However, in 1948, the Temporary Committee, while grateful, like Oliver Twist asked for more, approaching Earl Granville for royal patronage. Their request was turned down on the grounds that patronage for an individual hospital was deemed inappropriate.

As the new era dawned, the Board of Management and the Medical Staff of the Children's Hospital could look back over seventy-five years of caring for sick children in premises in King Street, Queen Street and the Falls Road. The Staff put on record their stated aim to continue the work of caring for sick children under the new regime as under the old. They were certain that the same devoted care would always be bestowed on sick children who needed it: 'more they could not give and less they would not offer'.[2]

The stark figures on the first page of the Annual Report of 1947 do not reveal the skill, compassion and dedication of all connected with the Hospital in its first three-quarters of a century.

Beds	97
Intern Patients (1947)	2,882
Extern Patients (1947)	31,405
Attendances (1947)	85,595
Intern Patients since 1873	58,302
Extern Patients since 1873	1,058,697

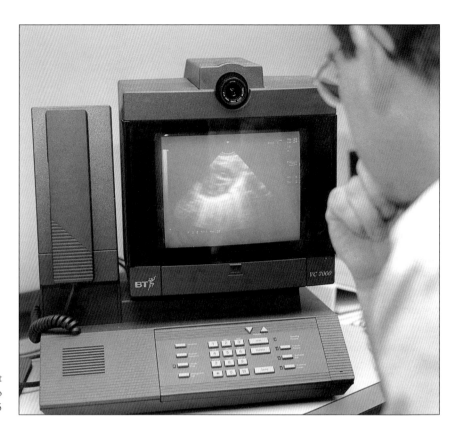

Paediatric cardiologist
Frank Casey with televideo
equipment, 1995

3

MEDICINE

IN 1948, ON THE ESTABLISHMENT OF THE NHS, the physicians on the Staff were F.M.B. Allen, Ivan McCaw, T.H. Crozier, Muriel J.L. Frazer and Rowland Hill. They were joined over the following year by J.M. Beare, Violet St G. Breakey, W.A.B. Campbell, A.A.H. Gailey, A.C. Stevenson and Joan Logan. Beare, Campbell and Gailey had been working in the Hospital following discharge from the armed services, prior to their formal admission to the Medical Staff.

THE DEPARTMENT OF CHILD HEALTH

The standing of paediatrics during the 1940s, in relation to other medical disciplines, was of concern to the Medical Staff. At that time, paediatric medicine was something of a sideline to physicians who earned their daily bread attending to adults: both F.M.B. Allen and T.H. Crozier retained control over adult wards in the Belfast City Hospital (BCH), in addition to their paediatric work. A career in children's medicine had few financial inducements and low prestige. It was not until the new system of a structured salaried service was introduced with the NHS that a fresh incentive was given to doctors who wished to make a career in paediatrics.

Nevertheless, during World War II, the management and Medical Staff of the RBHSC took the first steps to improving the standing of the Hospital as an academic institution. In May 1942 it was decided to apply to the Examining Board of the Royal College of Physicians (London) and the Royal College of Surgeons of England for the addition of the Hospital to the list of those approved for the Diploma in Child Health, a request granted by the Royal Colleges. Four years later, in June 1946, Medical Staff received a letter from the secretary of Queen's University Belfast enquiring what facilities the Belfast Hospital for Sick Children would grant to a Professor of Child Health. The Staff responded positively but with some conditions, namely: i) if a senior member of the present Staff were to be appointed, he should retain the existing full facilities of teaching, treatment and discharge of patients, ii) if a junior member of Staff were appointed, he would be given a substantial share of the beds; the exact number was not specified, although one-third was suggested, and iii) if the new incumbent was not a member of the present staff, he would be offered facilities consistent with his seniority in the hierarchical tree. At that time not all honorary consulting physicians and honorary attending physicians held higher medical qualifications; consequently, the Staff recommended that the qualifications required for physician candidates should be the MRCP (London) or such other qualification that the Board might, with the advice of the Staff, determine.

In March 1948 the chairman of the Board of Management suggested to the Staff that the Hospital should associate with a projected University Clinical Block which would provide fifty beds each for medicine, surgery and paediatrics. These beds would be additional to those then available in the Hospital, and the new building would be of a semi-temporary type. The functions of the paediatric component would be clinical teaching, especially of postgraduates, and research. The unit would be under the control of the Professor of Child Health; members of Staff could investigate any special problem subject to the professor's approval. The clinical material would be obtained by selection from the Hospital outpatients, as routine admissions would interfere with postgraduate teaching.

Muriel Frazer dissented, on the grounds that the collection of a series of cases was not in the interest of patients, since it tended to prevent each child being treated as a separate problem. She argued that the training of postgraduates on such highly selective clinical material would be inimical to the formation of a balanced judgement and a grasp of day-to-day paediatric problems such as are seen in routine outpatient and ward work. Moreover, she maintained that, since four physicians currently shared so few beds, to place such a disproportionate number of beds at the disposal of one individual (the Professor of Child Health) could not fail to create alarm and despondency in the minds of existing and intending paediatricians. With this one exception, the Staff agreed to commend the proposal to the Board of Management but nothing further came of it. The Staff were in two minds; on the one hand they wished to see the advancement of their speciality, and on the other they were fearful of professorial control.[1]

F.M.B. Allen, first Nuffield Professor of Child Health, Queen's University Belfast, 1948–62

In June 1948 Frederick Martin Brice Allen was appointed the first Nuffield Professor of Child Health in Queen's University Belfast. Twenty-four years earlier he had been elected honorary attending physician in charge of outpatients at the Belfast Hospital for Sick Children. The new chair was funded by the Nuffield Foundation, and the nucleus of a paediatric library was established through a gift to the university of £1,000 from Messrs Cow & Gate, the baby food manufacturers. (Cow & Gate continued to support the Department of Child Health by an annual subvention of £100 for travel to scientific meetings. Eventually this lapsed, only to be resurrected in another form by Professor J.A. Dodge. There is currently an annual Cow & Gate prize for final year students.) From this modest beginning the Belfast Hospital for Sick Children was to become the focal point of paediatric teaching in Northern Ireland.

In 1952 the Department of Child Health acquired its first consultant/senior lecturer, O.D. Fisher. He remained until 1956, when he took up a post at the Medway Group of Hospitals in Kent. Another lecturer in the Department of Child Health in the 1950s was R.D.G. (Des) Creery, subsequently deputy medical officer of health, States of Guernsey.

On assuming the chair of child health, one of Allen's first proposals was that new outpatient clinics were necessary to deal with increasing specialization, a suggestion not universally welcomed by his colleagues. Some felt that cases should be referred to these special clinics only after they had been seen in the ordinary Outpatient Department. In spite of these initial reservations, special clinics gradually appeared. Among the first, in 1947 and prior to Allen's appointment, was a Rheumatism Clinic, under the supervision of Dr A.A.H. Gailey, then a registrar appointed under the special scheme for ex-servicemen. Other clinics established included one for diabetic children and an Enuretic Clinic, started by Dr W.I. Forsythe in 1957, became a Joint Genito-Urinary Clinic with B.T. Smyth in 1959.

With the retirement of T. Howard Crozier in 1951, there was much discussion and some tension regarding the reallocation of the beds he had controlled. The majority view was that, in accordance with previous practice, his beds should be taken over by the next senior physician, Muriel Frazer. Consequently, Allen's strongly expressed opinion that his personal allocation of beds was insufficient to carry out the work of the Department of Child Health came as a considerable shock to his colleagues, to whom it appeared that Allen was demanding not only access to but control of a large number of beds already in the keeping of Frazer and her more junior colleagues. The Staff interpreted 'professorial control' to mean not just the professorial name on all patients' charts, but an entitlement to impose protocols of treatment.

Frazer eventually agreed to Professor Allen taking over Crozier's beds, but her colleagues continued to oppose the move. They did acquiesce to a temporary transfer, provided the contingency aspect was duly emphasized and honoured. In this decision, they were at pains to preserve the expectations of the younger paediatricians, who they believed had every right to gain access to more bed accommodation by normal succession. Their unanimous opinion was that Frazer should not waive her claim to beds but could make a loan to Allen if, and when, more beds became available and an equitable distribution had been made to those holding a few beds only. In January 1954 Frazer wrote that she had now been given beds in the Ava Hospital (the children's department of the Belfast City Hospital) and would be willing to relinquish her five beds in the Children's Hospital medical ward if she could continue to admit an occasional case requiring special investigation. The Staff immediately decided that these vacated beds should be at the disposal of the junior physicians.

Events elsewhere brought about Muriel Frazer's change of mind. Dr Samuel Armstrong had turned sixty-five and was expected to retire from the charge of the Ava Children's Hospital. He maintained that his original contract with Belfast Corporation, made in the days of the Belfast Union Infirmary, contained no fixed age of retirement, and he resolved to remain in post. As a result, a new appointment to Ava had to be delayed. An impasse was reached when the NIHA refused to recognize his position while he continued to visit the Ava Hospital regularly and sit in his office. The day-to-day management of Ava began to devolve on Dr Frazer – quite appropriately, in view of her position as consultant paediatrician at the City Hospital's Maternity Unit in the Jubilee Hospital. Eventually, Dr Armstrong's 'sit-in' was overcome and Dr

MURIEL JOSEPHINE L. FRAZER MBE was the first woman to be appointed to the Medical Staff of the BHSC (1939–76). She was a brilliant student and followed her BA degree with an outstanding postgraduate medical career, passing the MRCP examination in 1938 and the FRCSI a year later. Articulate and dogmatic, she was an excellent lecturer and bedside teacher. She organized the resuscitation and blood transfusion service within the Hospital in 1941, the year of the massive German air raids on Belfast. Fiercely independent, Frazer fought passionately for what she believed in, and she had a considerable influence in shaping the course of paediatrics in Northern Ireland. Her dedication to her patients was equalled only by her devotion to her church.

C.M.B. Field was appointed consultant to the Ava Hospital. He immediately and generously gave twelve beds to his senior colleague, with the result that the disputed beds at the RBHSC ceased to hold any charm for Muriel Frazer.

Dr Frazer's connection with the Children's Hospital was not completely severed. She was chairman of the Medical Staff in 1965–7, and continued her outpatient clinics until her retirement in 1976.

In November 1962 F.M.B. Allen retired from the chair of child health and from the Staff of the RBHSC, having been a member for thirty-eight years. He contributed greatly to the local advancement of hospital paediatrics and during the fourteen years of his professorship did much to raise the stature of the Children's Hospital to that of a major centre of paediatric medicine. Fred Allen's interests ranged well beyond the purely clinical sphere. He played an important part in the establishment of the Child Guidance Clinic (the first in Ireland), the Speech Therapy Department, the laboratory services, and a special unit at the Royal Maternity Hospital for the care of premature babies – one of the first of its kind in the United Kingdom. Well known outside Northern Ireland, he was a founder member of the British Paediatric Association, and its president in 1955.

His most significant addition to the medical literature was the textbook *Aids to the Diagnosis and Treatment of Diseases of Children*, the original author of which was Dr John McCaw, father of Ivan McCaw. The first edition had appeared in 1893, and Allen was the author of the sixth edition, in 1927. It ran to an eleventh edition, published in 1962, which he wrote jointly with I.J. Carré.

In view of his manifold contributions to paediatric medicine in Northern Ireland, it is regrettable that Allen often failed to establish amicable working relationships with some of his colleagues. He was stern of mien, somewhat aloof and dictatorial. This attitude led to conflict, not only with fellow paediatricians but with those colleagues engaged in adult medicine, and the Children's Hospital gained a reputation which had an adverse effect on the recruitment of good junior staff.

On a lighter note, Sir Ian Fraser recalls an example of Allen's early difficulties with interpersonal relationships. His senior colleague Rowland Hill, for reasons best known to himself, wrote the patients' notes in shorthand, so that Allen could not understand them. Undaunted, he went to night classes to learn to read shorthand, but then discovered to his chagrin that he had acquired a knowledge of Gregg's instead of Pitman's, or vice versa.[2]

Off duty, other facets of Allen's personality were displayed, as R.S. Allison recalled in an obituary for his friend and colleague: 'Fred, supported by his wife Eve, was at his best when receiving friends and overseas visitors into their home and all who had the pleasure of joining them on these occasions will remember their generous and elegant hospitality.[3]

During his life Allen was no stranger to adversity. He suffered from severe generalized psoriasis, the constitutional symptoms of which led to him being confined to bed for varying periods, an affliction he bore with commendable fortitude. In April 1956 his brother-in-law, Cecil A. Calvert, a highly respected and distinguished neurosurgeon, was killed in a motor accident in which Ivan McCaw and Allen were injured, Allen more seriously.

In October 1965 Allen's professional work was formally recognized when he was appointed an honorary governor of the Royal Belfast Hospital for Sick Children. The citation read:

> whereas Professor Frederick Martin Brice Allen served as a member of the Staff of the Royal Belfast Hospital for Sick Children for a period of 40 years, was a pioneer in the field of child health in this province and in the United Kingdom, contributed greatly to the research and literature of his subject and played a unique part in developing the scope and teaching of paediatrics and whereas the outstanding services so rendered by the said Professor Frederick Martin Brice Allen merit the gratitude of the Management Committee and the people of Northern Ireland.

F.M.B. Allen died on 10 January 1972 at the age of seventy-three and in December the Medical Staff heard with pleasure that it was the intention of Eve Allen to donate a gift of £10,000 to the Hospital in memory of her husband. Trusteeship of the fund would be vested in the governing body of the RBHSC for the benefit of doctors, nurses and paramedics. The fund would be administered by a subcommittee consisting of the dean of the Faculty of Medicine of Queen's University Belfast, then Peter Froggatt, the head of nursing services at the RBHSC, Miss M.H. Hudson, the chairman of the Medical Staff Committee, J.M. Beare, and one other member of Staff co-opted at their discretion. At present, the fund is administered from within the Hospital, to be used for travelling expenses and the purchase of appropriate equipment such as aids to teaching.

THE ALLEN MEMORIAL READING ROOM

The Hospital library was established in 1948 with the gift of £1,000 from Cow & Gate. The room was the site of the first Medical Staff meeting in the new Hospital, on 20 April 1932, and continued to be used for this purpose for many years.

The word 'library' implies a borrowing facility, which never officially existed; the only borrowing was unauthorized. Valuable books disappeared on a regular basis, many never to return. In 1955 F.M.B. Allen wrote to the chairman of the Medical Staff threatening to withdraw the library to the Institute of Clinical Science 'as it appears impossible to prevent some individuals from removing books and journals without returning them'. This drastic action was never carried out. Instead, deposits of £2 10s were levied, rising to £5 – a measure which failed to check the determined pilferer – and the more precious volumes were chained to the shelves.

In 1973 the library, now called the Allen Reading Room, moved to a new location near the lecture theatre, and in 1990 it relocated to the third

Allen Memorial Library, 1948

floor of the Hospital, where readers must obtain a key at a nearby office. Its material is aimed largely at the specialist reader and includes a collection of tape/slide programmes and a cassette player. A CD-ROM with access to Medline, acquired in 1994, has proved an added electronic attraction. The first librarian of the new room was Kathy Jackson, followed in 1992 by Anne Levi.

In 1993 some textbooks which had been replaced by new editions, and other duplicates, were dispatched to a young paediatrician in Romania. By the mid-1990s the 'loss' of books had finally shown a marked reduction, and several volumes have been returned from other hospitals, one missing for more than four years.

F.M.B. Allen's successor in the chair of child health, in 1963, was Ivo John Carré, born in Guernsey. Educated at Emmanuel College, Cambridge, and St Thomas's Hospital, London, he held junior appointments at St Thomas's and at the Children's Hospital, Birmingham, before coming to Belfast in 1956, as lecturer in child health. His MD thesis of 1957, entitled 'A Clinical Study of the Partial Thoracic Stomach in Children', foreshadowed his later major research interest. Carré's stated aim on assuming the chair was to establish an active clinical department based at the RBHSC and the Royal Maternity Hospital (RMH), while at the same time developing a regional referral service for particular sub-specialities. At first he was hindered in this by the lingering adverse image of the Hospital among aspiring paediatricians. Nevertheless, from the outset Carré embarked upon a full programme of undergraduate and postgraduate teaching. He and other members of the university department travelled the length and breadth of Northern Ireland giving postgraduate lectures and partaking in day courses, seminars, and so on. The general public were informed about child health by weekly ten-minute contributions on BBC Radio Ulster, many of which were made by John F.T. Glasgow.

Over the years, Carré was successful in gaining approval for the establishment of lectureships in line with the trend towards sub-specialization. For example, a joint appointment lectureship in neonatology was established in 1973, based at the RMH, to which Dr Garth McClure was appointed. (A joint appointment had two components: the university and the NHS.) In 1980 a lectureship was created in nephrology, a post taken by Dr J.M. Savage. At the time of Carré's retirement, lectureships with sub-speciality interest in community paediatrics, respiratory disease and cardiology were projected. Throughout his tenure, an important aspect of the work of the department was the prosecution of research. In addition to his own field of gastroenterology, subjects studied by other members of Staff were many and varied. Grants were awarded by the Medical Research Council, the Cystic Fibrosis Research Trust, the Department of Health & Social Services, RBHSC/RVH fellowships, the Children's Research Fund, Liverpool, and the Birmingham Children's Hospital Centenary Research Fund, augmented by smaller contributions from Imperial Chemical Industries, Cow & Gate and the Hospital's own fund-raising bodies, such as the Ladies' League.

In 1978 Christopher Green was appointed consultant lecturer in child health. During his two years on the Staff, he made a considerable contribution to the activities of the Department of Child Health and the life of the Hospital. He organized weekly clinical meetings, including conferences on morbidity and mortality, sat on the Northern Ireland Council for Orthopaedic Development, and represented the RBHSC on a committee concerned with non-accidental injury. An impression made on a visit to Australia in 1976 led to an invitation to take charge of the Child Development Unit at the Royal Alexandra Hospital for Children in Sydney, where he has become a media celebrity. He features regularly on Australian television and radio, giving mothers assurance and advice on the rearing of their offspring. His books include *Babies! A Parent's Guide to Surviving (and Enjoying!) Baby's First Years* and *Toddler Training (The Guide to your Child from One to Four)*.

The first clinic dedicated to the care of children suffering from inborn errors of metabolism was set up in 1965, largely due to the efforts of Dr Sara Campbell, senior lecturer in the Department of Child Health. It had become necessary as a result of the increasing number of cases being

JOHN FREDERICK TURNBULL GLASGOW, consultant paediatrician, 1971–, gained his postgraduate experience at the Great Ormond Street Hospital, London, and the Hospital for Sick Children, Toronto. In 1971 he was appointed senior tutor/senior registrar in the Department of Child Health, QUB and RBHSC. His elevation to senior lecturer/consultant paediatrician came in the same year, and in 1984–5 he acted as head of the Department of Child Health, following the retirement of Professor Ivo Carré. He became reader in child health in 1987, and in 1988 assumed administrative and clinical control of the Accident & Emergency Department of the RBHSC, a department which sees twenty-five thousand new patients annually.

diagnosed by the screening tests pioneered by Dr Nina Carson. The gap in the department left by the departure of Christopher Green was filled by Dennis John Carson, one of the first paediatricians to pursue a subspeciality interest. Prior to taking up his appointment, he had worked in North America, as a clinical fellow in endocrinology at the Johns Hopkins Hospital, Baltimore, where he had 'little authority and minimum responsibility'. On returning to Belfast he took charge of the Diabetic and Metabolic Clinics, and when screening for hypothyroidism became available this also became part of his remit. With Nina Carson's post remaining unfilled on her retirement in 1984, it fell to Dennis Carson to assume clinical responsibility for the large numbers of patients suffering from phenylketonuria (PKU) and other diseases of metabolism. Treated from birth, these children are able to undertake normal schooling, rather than being the victims of severe mental handicap. This workload has continued to grow, with up to 160 patients attending the clinic; in 1996 eight newly diagnosed cases were added. Forty patients having reached adulthood are now under the care of endocrinologists in the Royal Victoria Hospital.

In October 1996, Carson handed over the clinical care of these patients to Professor Elizabeth R. Trimble. With training in both clinical endocrinology/metabolism and chemical pathology, she can bridge the divide between the clinical and laboratory aspects of the diseases seen at the Metabolic Clinic, which include the usual range of inborn errors of amino acid, fatty acid, carbohydrate metabolism and so on. This regional clinic is run jointly with a member of Staff from the Department of Medical Genetics, emphasizing that a multidisciplinary approach is essential for the provision of the best possible care to this group of patients.

Michael David Shields, a graduate of Bristol University, was appointed senior lecturer/consultant in 1991, with a special interest in respiratory disease of children. His appointment coincided with major changes in the teaching of medical students and the organization of the clinical examinations, and Shields was associated with several innovations. He was involved in running the Child Health Lecture Course and the Faculty Personal Tutorial Scheme, and carried out an assessment of the so-called Objective Structured Examination. Under this new format, which is reckoned to be a fairer assessment of a student's ability, the examination is set up in ten stations covering a wide range of subjects, such as history, communication with patients and a clinical examination involving an actual patient. Four out of the ten stations deal with laboratory data or objects for identification and some practical procedures. The aim is to eliminate

IVO JOHN CARRÉ, Nuffield Chair of Child Health at Queen's University Belfast, 1963–84, was a polite, urbane man, whose image stood in vivid contrast to that of his predecessor. His approach to a problem was non-confrontational and his views were put firmly but without rancour. He strove to redress 'the discouraging and unfortunate misconception that many people had of the Children's Hospital'. Carré was a good diagnostician and teacher and a wise director of careers. He published many important research papers, either singly or jointly, and made professional visits to twenty different countries. In addition, he was external examiner at fifty universities at home and abroad. He retired to his beloved Guernsey in 1984.

examiner bias.

John Ashton Dodge, a Welshman, educated at the Welsh National School of Medicine, first came to Belfast in 1964 as a lecturer, later senior lecturer, in child health. In 1971 he returned to his native heath, where he was elevated to reader in child health at the University of Wales College of Medicine. On 19 October 1985 he succeeded Carré as Professor of Child Health in Queen's University Belfast and was appointed consultant paediatrician at the Royal Belfast Hospital for Sick Children. On his arrival, Dodge was asked by the chief medical officer of the Department of Health & Social Services, Dr Robert Weir, for his personal impressions of the Hospital as an academic centre. In response, he praised the evident expertise of his colleagues and the extensive range of paediatric services provided but he was highly critical of the problems of accommodation which these advances had highlighted. His particular concern was for improved outpatient and academic facilities, goals which were not immediately attainable.

Nevertheless, since 1985, the Department of Child Health has continued to develop and has been academically and clinically enhanced in such areas as accident and emergency, nephrology and neonatology. The interests of members of the department cover virtually the whole spectrum of paediatric medicine and an active research and teaching programme has been maintained. (A list of members of the Department of Child Health in 1997 appears in Appendix 5.)

JOHN ASHTON DODGE, Nuffield Chair of Child Health at Queen's University Belfast, 1985–97, will be remembered as a courteous man of able intellect, whose quiet voice and air of gravitas belied a firm sense of purpose. Well known both nationally and internationally, he has held prominent positions in various spheres of paediatric medicine, including director of the United Kingdom Cystic Fibrosis Society and adviser in human genetics to the World Health Organization. A prolific writer, he has produced 5 books, 120 WHO reports, 140 papers, 20 book chapters and a video film. In 1996 he was prominent in the establishment of the new Royal College of Paediatrics and Child Health, London. The call of Wales has remained strong and John Dodge will enjoy retirement in the principality.

THE CHANGING PATTERNS OF PAEDIATRIC MEDICINE

The development of the National Health Service coincided with marked changes in the pattern of childhood disease. Vaccinations, antibiotics and other new drugs, together with better social conditions, all contributed to the improved health and welfare of the children of Northern Ireland. Diphtheria, poliomyelitis, tuberculosis, and nephritis were brought under control. A clinical event of widespread significance had occurred during World War II, with the discovery by doctors in Holland that gluten in wheat was the cause of coeliac disease. In a tragic paradox, starving children deprived of the staff of life were recovering from the disease. Pink disease was eradicated when it was recognized that the disorder was due to mercury in teething powders liberally administered at home; the discovery of cortisone brought new hope to sufferers of childhood leukaemia. With

SARA LAVERTY CAMPBELL, consultant paediatrician, 1971–89: before joining the RBHSC, she worked in the Infectious Diseases Hospital in Purdysburn and between 1955 and 1970 as, successively, tutor, registrar and senior registrar in the Department of Child Health. She had a great interest in the teaching of medical students, aiming 'to impart to them some knowledge, some common sense and not least the idea that kindness and consideration are necessary in the handling of patients and their parents'. She advocated 'training in teaching' to balance the current vogue of courses in medical administration. Campbell is remembered for a successful campaign to abolish what she called the 'barbarous' procedure of stomach washout in children suspected of having swallowed a poisonous substance; instead she induced vomiting by the use of Ipecacuanha syrup. This method avoided unnecessary washouts and removed the potential hazard of the inhalation of stomach contents into the lungs during the passage of the stomach tube.

the advances in laboratory medicine, diseases such as hypothyroidism became diagnosable and a wider range of drugs made epilepsy more treatable. Rheumatic fever disappeared from the clinical map.[4]

In the 1970s parents were becoming better informed, more inquisitive and more demanding. No longer were the statements of doctors being taken at their face value. These attitudes began to influence the Hospital's policy on visiting times. At first, visiting was confined to Wednesday and Saturday, 2.00–4.30 p.m. All the families arrived at the same time, thereby bringing routine nursing to a virtual standstill. To establish some semblance of order and to control the traffic flow, a table was set across the door of the ward, presided over by a nurse who extracted bags of buns, chocolate and lemonade, from parents, to be rationed out to the children at a later time. However, there was no guarantee that a particular child would eventually get the sweetmeat originally intended by the parent. When the parents left, not to return for another three days, there were often distressing scenes. Some children were extremely upset while others remained quiet. As Sara Campbell records, the latter were thought to be well-settled, 'good' children, but later observation revealed that they were stressed and withdrawn, deeply affected by the lack of family contact. In 1975 daily visiting was allowed from 11.00 a.m. to 5.00 p.m., to be followed eventually by open visiting, the only restriction being 'the contingencies of the service'. Aside from relieving the former congestion, this arrangement gave more opportunities for parents to talk to clinicians and the children benefited greatly from more frequent parental contact.[5]

CARDIOLOGY

The closing years of the 1940s and the beginning of the 1950s saw the dawn of the age of technology, which was to revolutionize clinical medicine and surgery. Nowhere were the advances in technology so rapid, far-reaching and potentially beneficial to patients as in the field of medical cardiology. Prior to the National Health Service, the care of cardiac patients was in the hands of general physicians. Diagnostic tools consisted of little more than a stethoscope and, where available, a single-channel electrocardiograph, coupled with the individual doctor's clinical acumen. (The Children's Hospital had acquired its first electrocardiograph in June

1946.) Treatment revolved around bed rest and oxygen – augmented by a limited range of drugs, such as morphine and digitalis.

The physician taking the major interest in cardiac disease in children at that time was T. Howard Crozier. He was an imposing figure, soft-spoken but with an acerbic wit, which he could use to great effect. Stories abound – some true and some of doubtful authenticity – of his devastating ripostes. It is said that on one occasion he came upon a temporary obstruction in the roadway, marked by an indistinct halt sign. Crozier pulled out to pass, only to be peremptorily brought to a standstill by the upraised hand of a junior member of the constabulary. 'Can you not read?' asked the officer. Requesting identification, he scrutinized the proffered driving licence, then looked up in some surprise: 'Are you Dr T.H. Crozier?' Crozier's response was typical: 'Can you not read either?'

A further milestone on the technological road was passed with the appointment, in February 1949, of Dr Violet St G. Breakey. Dr Breakey had trained in cardiology, under the tutelage of Alfred Blalock and Helen Taussig, at the Johns Hopkins Hospital in Baltimore, a centre reckoned to be foremost in cardiological investigation and treatment. In some respects, Dr Breakey's appointment was premature, in the sense that the Hospital was not yet geared to embrace the demands of the new technology. Her main interest was in the radiological screening of 'blue babies', which procedure she carried out in cramped, unsuitable surroundings with the technical help made available to her – willing, but thin on the ground. Moreover, her arrival did not diminish the influence of Crozier on all cardiological matters. He remained in control of the ordering of equipment, negotiations with regard to extra accommodation, even decisions on the number and size of filing cabinets.

Crozier severed his connection with the Hospital in November 1951, after some twenty-two years' service, to take charge of wards 3 and 4 in the RVH. Dr Breakey benefited by the acquisition of another outpatient session, although three years were to pass before she was allocated four beds and a further one on loan from Dr Muriel Frazer. In the same year, 1954, the Hospital Management Committee showed its lack of appreciation of the importance of the emerging speciality by asking the Medical Staff to investigate the accommodation occupied by the Cardiac Unit, as it was felt that these rooms were being underused. Predictably, Breakey strongly objected and demanded that the use of the clinic should be expanded. A further suggestion that physiotherapy classes should be held in the Cardiac Unit was firmly rejected by Kathleen Yarr, chief physiotherapist, thereby reinforcing Breakey's position. (In May 1951 the Cardiac Unit was designated the Department of Electrocardiography, a label which reflected the embryonic status of the new speciality.)

In the midst of these difficulties, Violet Breakey found a friend in the person of Douglas Boyd, the consultant radiologist, who demonstrated the gift of prescience as to the future of radiology and cardiology, and the drive and skill to surmount the inevitable obstacles.

Breakey's interest in the investigation and treatment of children with Fallot's Tetralogy (blue babies) had been hindered by the limited radiological techniques available at that time, which made the diagnosis of structural abnormalities within the heart a very inexact science. Radiological diagnosis focused on cardiac shape rather than function; multiple measurements were taken and studied on complex charts describing the outline of the normal heart and major blood vessels, thus indicating the changes which would be evidence of disease. There was as yet no radiological way to record cardiac movement or the manner in which blood flowed through the heart – all that could be done was to take X-ray pictures in rapid succession and display them in sequence for later study.

Dr Boyd reasoned that the best and, possibly, the only indication of the presence and size of an intra-cardiac shunt (an abnormal flow between two heart chambers due to a 'hole in the heart') would appear in the first few radiographic records taken after the intravenous injection of an opaque substance. He used his considerable engineering skill to sketch out an X-ray couch incorporating a rapid-action cassette changer, and took the initial drawing to his friend William Rickerby, who was in charge of the large and well-equipped garage and joinery works of Melville & Company, the Belfast undertakers. (The idea of a piece of medical equipment being designed in a workshop attached to a funeral parlour has its own irony.)

The first trial of the prototype took place in the spring of 1950, with Dr Boyd turning the appropriate wheels by hand. The carriage of the cassette worked perfectly and it was deposited at exactly the right place. There was delight all round when ten exposure sequences were successful. However, when a week later the apparatus was 'motorized', the cassettes were landing up to six inches away from the point where they should have been delivered and there was no uniformity. Boyd and Rickerby retired to contemplate this setback and devise a solution. Happily, the redesigned apparatus worked smoothly and accurately, delivering ten cassettes in under forty seconds.

The next problem to be tackled was the type of opaque medium to be used, the quantity to be administered and the optimum speed of the injection. Boyd knew it would be essential to inject the medium quickly in a large bolus, which would fill a long length of vein, completely displacing the blood. This would require the use of some sort of spring-loaded syringe. Bayer Pharmaceuticals of Germany supplied the medium, and for the syringe Boyd enlisted the help of the Genito-Surgical Manufacturing Company in London, with whom he had already collaborated in the manufacture of a number of different gadgets to his own design, including what were perhaps the first inflatable self-retaining catheters.

With everything now in order, the machine was transported to the

X-ray Department and a few dry runs were carried out. The interested bystanders may not have understood fully what was going on but they were certainly startled by the sudden explosive torrent of noise, like a machine gun fired in a confined space, as the metal cassettes tumbled into the cassette bin. Deirdre Capper, the senior radiographer, testified to 'being frightened to bits by the rapid fire apparatus'. Boyd described the procedure on the first patient as follows:

> Our first patient was a very 'blue baby' and on the way from the wards there had been a visit to the operating theatre to have an intravenous cannula inserted and ligatured in position so that it would not be disturbed by the pressure of the injection. When all was ready, I released the safety catch on the charged syringe, in its holster, and then the catch on the charged syringe compression. All the rest was automatic and in less than a minute, ten X-ray exposures had been made and there was silence. Thankfully, the anaesthetized child was breathing normally and seemed undisturbed. Within a few minutes the restraining straps were released, the injection gear removed and the baby returned to the ward, apparently unharmed.[6]

The child was not the only one in the room breathing more easily.

Further progress was soon made, in the form of two significant advances which dramatically changed the whole technique of cardiological examination. The first was image intensification, which made it possible to screen with a minor reduction in room lighting: previous to this, the radiologist carried out the procedure in almost complete darkness – a situation which terrified most children. Boyd's home-made cassette angiocardiograph had cost a mere £150, while the new Phillips 4-inch Field Image Intensifier was purchased for approximately £3,000. The second breakthrough was the development of intravenous catheterization of the heart and great vessels.

Dr Breakey's problems were not diminished with the coming of cardiac catheterization techniques. The necessary equipment and skills were not yet available to her and she petitioned for the services of a physiologist to carry out catheterization and to assess the resultant blood gas analysis. The view of the Professor of Physiology at QUB, A.D.M. Greenfield, was sought. His advice was that cases from the Children's Hospital should be sent to the RVH, where there was already £3,000 worth of equipment. This ushered in a period of tension between the two hospitals. Rather reluctantly, Children's Hospital Staff agreed to the arrangement, on condition that the team from the Hospital would accompany patients to the RVH and assume full responsibility for their care. The atmosphere was not improved when it came to light that a meeting regarding cardiology had been held between Professor Allen, Professor John H. Biggart, Professor Greenfield and Dr Frank Pantridge of the RVH. Dr Breakey had not been invited.

On 3 May 1955 Dr Douglas Boyd tabled a letter regarding the use of the angiocardiographic equipment located in the RVH. He suggested that the

Medical Staff should approach their opposite numbers in the RVH seeking permission to use the equipment on specific occasions and with proper safeguards for the apparatus. Furthermore, he reported that Sir Frank Montgomery and Dr David C. Porter, senior radiologists at the RVH, and Ralph Leman, the chief radiographer, had declared themselves happy to co-operate in every possible way. This statement of intent was immediately blocked by the formidable figure of Dr Frank Pantridge, consultant cardiologist, RVH, who refused to allow 'any outside group to use the equipment in the angiocardiographic unit and would maintain this attitude unless directed by a higher authority'. However, Pantridge said that he would be prepared to admit children to the RVH and carry out all the investigations himself, but would require the X-ray records for filing in his own department. This ultimatum prompted a long discussion among the Medical Staff, followed by the unanimous but less than strong minute: 'It would be desirable that the cardiac team should have access to the special equipment in the RVH, thus avoiding interruption of clinical control.' In a rider, it was recommended that 'a meeting be arranged to consider the question of a physiologist for the cardiac unit', indicating a faint hope that interventional procedures would somehow continue at the RBHSC.

Eventually, it was established that the angiocardiographic equipment in the RVH was the property of the Medical Education and Research Committee of the Northern Ireland Hospitals Authority, and it was up to the Committee to decide to what purpose it should be put. Not surprisingly, the equipment remained in the Royal Victoria Hospital.

On 4 December 1956 Dr Breakey reported to the Medical Staff that she had been offered a World Health Organization fellowship for the months of April, May and June 1957. She accepted this assignment with the congratulations and blessing of the Staff, but it was a break that presaged her withdrawal from the Hospital. She resigned in April 1958, an event greeted with regret by all, but with no great surprise.

The uncertainty surrounding the future development of cardiology in the Children's Hospital was again demonstrated by a memorandum recommending that Dr Breakey should be replaced by a paediatrician for whom there would be three outpatient sessions and five beds, with duties in country clinics and the Lissue Branch Hospital. Dr Breakey and her colleagues had been stranded on the somewhat rickety bridge between old-style clinical cardiology and the new age of technology, unable to advance or retreat. Other evidence of this appeared in the discovery of the files of some two thousand cases screened by Dr Breakey on whom no subsequent diagnostic or operative procedure had been carried out.[7]

One must not be too hard on the Medical Staff of those days regarding their lack of foresight. Dr Helen Taussig of Baltimore, the mother of paediatric cardiology and mentor of Dr Breakey, wrote to a colleague in the mid-1950s: 'I am sure you will agree with me that the new technique of cardiac catheterization has very little to add to our diagnostic armamentarium' – a grossly inaccurate prognosis.

On 1 October 1957 Medical Staff had reaffirmed their decision of May 1955 that 'clinical control of cardiac patients should not be lost'. However, with the departure of Dr Breakey, a volte-face occurred: they were now prepared to recognize that the special cardiological investigations required for patients from the Children's Hospital could best be carried out by Dr Pantridge in the Royal Victoria Hospital. They were anxious, however, that the outpatient Cardiology Clinic should continue.

In September 1958 Dr Pantridge was welcomed as a new member of Medical Staff. His appointment signified a reawakened recognition of the importance of the development of cardiology, a process in which Frank Pantridge was to play no small part. At first he stated that he was prepared to do all the investigations of cardiac abnormalities of children in the Children's Hospital, but equipment costing several thousand pounds would be necessary. A month later he informed Staff that the Cardiac Department in the RVH was to be enlarged, and so the necessary children's investigations could be performed there. In the first month of this arrangement, Pantridge carried out twenty-five cardiac catheterization investigations from the RBHSC, a report received with general satisfaction. (Henceforth the Electrocardiographic Department at the RBHSC was to assume the title 'Cardiac Department', although its remit was confined to a half-day outpatient session per week.)

Professor James Francis Pantridge, consultant cardiologist, 1951–82

From the latter months of 1958 until the autumn of 1976, Dr Pantridge was in titular control of the outpatient clinic at the Children's Hospital and the subsequent treatment of those patients. However, with increasing demands upon his time and energy in the expanding adult department in the RVH, his children's work was largely delegated to his capable colleague, Dr George Patterson. Dr Patterson had come to the Cardiac Department of the RVH in 1956 after three years' experience in physiology. It was natural therefore that the task of cardiac catheterization, in both adults and children, should fall to him. For several years, almost single-handed, he carried on the outpatient clinic at the Children's Hospital, performed cardiac catheterization in the RVH and made himself available for calls from the wards at any time. His dedicated work in the interests of the Children's Hospital received little acknowledgement, though eventually he was invited to join the Medical Staff Committee.

The next significant appointment in 1976 was that of H.C. Mulholland, the first paediatric cardiologist of the technology school, a 'hands-on' physician. Dr Mulholland came back to his roots in Belfast, having been trained in the Mecca of paediatrics, the Hospital for Sick Children in Toronto. He found a service that had still not reaped the benefits of the massive advances in cardiological diagnosis and treatment of the previous ten years. The way ahead, to the goal of a satisfactory paediatric

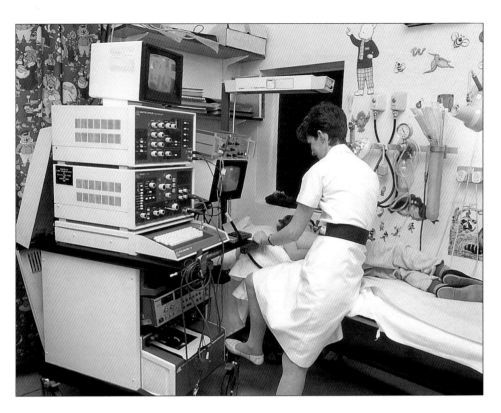

cardiological service, was strewn with various difficulties. For example, the proffered accommodation was in the original private wing of the Children's Hospital, the Clark Children's Clinic, consisting of a nine-bedded unit which cardiology was to share with ear, nose and throat, haematology, orthopaedics and any other overflow. Initially, only children in need of treatment for heart failure were admitted. Children coming in for cardiac catheterization were accommodated in wards 5 and 6 of the RVH and discharged from there following their investigations. Similarly, children requiring surgery, even those under one year of age, were admitted to the cardiac surgical ward in the RVH for their pre- and post-operative care. There was concern that these young patients were being cared for by nurses with little or no paediatric training.

Meanwhile, word was getting around the public of Northern Ireland that the service was expanding and that the message was: 'No baby is too small or too sick to receive cardiac catheterization.' As a result, patients present-ing for diagnostic catheterization multiplied tenfold, with as many as five or six children undergoing the procedure every week. This increasing workload placed on the cardiological staff, and not least on Mulholland, an almost intolerable burden, alleviated to some extent by two further advances in cardiological technology: i) the development of echocardi-ography, which reduced considerably the numbers of emergency catheteri-zations, and ii) the administration of the hormone prostaglandin, which improved blood flow through the lungs and reduced the necessity for immediate surgery.

By the mid-1980s it was apparent to all, except those holding the purse

strings, that a second paediatric cardiologist was needed. Dr Mulholland had great difficulty persuading those in authority that paediatric cardiology was a speciality within a speciality, and that practitioners working in the adult field could not substitute satisfactorily for a fully trained paediatric cardiologist. He was variously accused of empire building, scaremongering and even shroud waving, and it required a long period of strenuous lobbying in the media to convince both the Eastern Health & Social Services Board and the government that the money should be found for the post. In 1986 Dr Brian Craig, a previous registrar in the unit, joined his colleague, having spent two years in Toronto.

In 1994 Dr Mulholland described the position of the unit as follows:

> We have seen the workload expand further as clinics are held in Altnagelvin, Londonderry, the Waveney Hospital, Ballymena, and the Craigavon Hospital, in addition to the Ulster Hospital, Dundonald. The opening of the 'Heartbeat' accommodation has provided badly needed high-quality parent accommodation. [The Heartbeat movement started in the early 1980s as a support group for interaction among parents; it progressed to a fund-raising organization and eventually became a ginger group campaigning for a better paediatric cardiologist service.] The continuing refinement of non-invasive diagnostic techniques with ultrasound equipment, incidentally purchased mainly by public subscription, the development of interventional cardiac catheterization with valvuloplasty, arterioplasty, and, more recently, occlusion of the patent ductus arteriosus, has made possible the avoidance of heart surgery for thirty to forty children each year. This has been supplemented by the increasing sophistication and skills of the cardiac surgeons and

Dr Frank Casey and Dr Connor Mulholland with the televideo equipment, 1995

J.M (MARTIN) BEARE, consultant dermatologist, 1949–85, was born in Ballymoney, Co. Antrim, made a significant contribution to adult and paediatric dermatology. A lucid and elegant writer, he produced some seventy original articles and chapters in various books. Nationally and internationally known, he was the president of the British Association of Dermatologists in 1983–4, and a member of the Canadian Dermatological Association and the lyrical-sounding Academia Española de Dermatologie. In retirement he pursued his equestrian interests from his home in Comber, Co. Down.

Ivan Henry McCaw, first consultant dermatologist at the RBHSC, 1925–61

anaesthetists, whose perioperative care has made all the difference to the survival of these children. Complementing the high-tech developments has been the addition of a play specialist and a play room in the ward. A clinical psychologist has been appointed to the task of helping staff, parents and children to cope with ongoing difficult and often traumatic situations.

The unit now has a highly trained interdependent specialist team comprising nurses, physiotherapists, an echocardiographer, a social worker and the consultant Medical Staff. Each year eight hundred children are referred there for diagnosis; ten years ago the number was less than three hunded. A clinic for teenagers and adults with congenital heart disease is getting larger each year. Not the least important part of the work is the reassurance of many anxious parents that their child's heart is normal.[8]

In December 1995 a new system for identifying heart defects in newborn babies was launched in the Paediatric Cardiac Unit. The paediatric cardiologists based at the RBHSC deal with patients from all over Northern Ireland. Consequently, in the past, a child born outside Belfast showing signs of a serious cardiac defect had to be rushed to the unit by ambulance before a definitive diagnosis could be made. Now, the development of a pilot scheme, using the latest televideo equipment, allows doctors in Altnagelvin Hospital, 120 kilometres away, to beam images of the heart directly to the paediatric cardiologists in the Children's Hospital, for immediate expert consultation.

Other valuable members of the cardiological team receive, perhaps, less credit than they deserve. The present cardiographers are Jayne Rogers (a specialist in ultrasound techniques), who has been with the service since June 1978, and Lorraine Mornin, who joined in October 1996. Ann Smillie has been a member of the Hospital's clerical staff for over twenty-eight years. She is much more than a ward clerk in her role as co-ordinator of the service, dealing with waiting lists and cardiac investigations. As a long-serving member of the department she has had the pleasure of seeing many critically ill infants pass through the unit into a healthy adulthood.

A third paediatric cardiologist, Dr Frank Casey, was appointed on 1 December 1996.

DERMATOLOGY

The first specialist in diseases of the skin to be appointed to the Hospital was Ivan Henry McCaw, son of the pioneer paediatrician John McCaw.

Ivan McCaw had seen service with the Royal Irish Rifles in World War I. He was severely wounded in the shoulder and arm, injuries which no doubt influenced his choice of speciality. He studied dermatology under Sir Norman Walker in Edinburgh, gaining further experience at Guy's Hospital, London, and in Paris and Vienna. On his return to Belfast in 1925 he was appointed lecturer in dermatology and joined the Medical Staff of the Belfast Hospital for Sick Children in Queen Street.

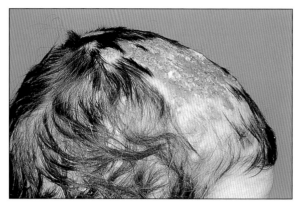

Ringworm on scalp

The speciality received new blood when John Martin Beare joined McCaw in 1949, at the age of twenty-eight. Beare was very much the junior partner; he had no office of his own and was obliged to address his senior colleague as 'Sir'. Furthermore, McCaw acquired all the dermatological titbits, leaving Beare to deal with the warts and the ringworm. Somewhat ironically, in June 1951, a letter from the Northern Ireland Hospitals Authority congratulated both gentlemen on their success in eradicating ringworm from the school population. The treatment used was depilation by X-ray, a technique superseded by the drug Griseofulvin. Martin Beare's continued work in this area was to bring worldwide recognition.

The closure of the Ringworm Unit did not decrease the workload of the dermatologists, but it was not until May 1960 that approval was granted for the use of the medical annexe which became vacant with the imminent opening of the new Allen and Knox Wards. The official opening in 1962 of the new dermatological ward, named Paul Ward, was a welcome event. For the first time, children with contagious skin disease from poor backgrounds could be adequately cared for, and facilities for the investigation of rare conditions led to fruitful research and the publication of information which received international recognition. The clinic dedicated to paediatric dermatology that McCaw and Beare set up at the Hospital was one of the first in the UK. Sadly, Ivan McCaw did not live to see this realization of his early endeavours – he died on 16 March 1961 and was succeeded by Desmond David Burrows in the same year.

Martin Beare and Desmond Burrows formed an association which lasted nearly twenty-five years, during which they jointly and separately made a considerable impact on the development of both adult and paediatric dermatology at home and abroad. In 1978 they were joined by Jocelyn Roger (Rory) Corbett as consultant lecturer in

DESMOND DAVID BURROWS, consultant dermatologist, 1961–95, although deeply committed to the investigation and treatment of contact dermatitis in adults, was good with children and his contribution to paediatric dermatology was energetic and enthusiastic. In 1990 he was appointed honorary professor in the Clinical Medical School, the first dermatologist to be so honoured. A prolific writer and a popular speaker at scientific meetings at home and abroad, he was made an honorary member of associations in North America, Spain, Finland, Sweden and Norway. He was at various times president of the British Association of Dermatologists, the Irish Association and the European Society of Contact Dermatologists. Desmond Burrows retired in 1995, and doubtless the enthusiasm he brought to his work will be equally manifest in his leisure activities – his garden, his grandchildren, golf at his beloved Royal County Down. He is on the Council of Reference of the Christian Medical Fellowship and his involvement with the Baptist missions overseas has led to visits as far afield as Peru.

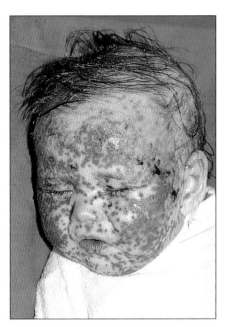

Eczema herpeticum continues
to afflict 10 per cent of the
childhood population

dermatology, an appointment which further expanded the formal teaching of dermatology to undergraduate students.

Social developments and therapeutic advances have led to a changing pattern of dermatological disease. In the 1950s and 1960s cases of severe psoriasis, eczema and scabies and children with head lice were admitted to the ward, as were children suffering from the widespread seborrhoeic dermatitis (nappy rash), a distressing condition which disappeared with the advent of disposable nappies. New housing with bathrooms resulted in improvement in hygiene. Family attitudes changed: the deeply ingrained belief that a child suffering from a skin disease was somehow unclean gave way to a realization that these children could be treated at home. The increasing array of medicaments came to be accepted and used by parents to good effect, so that the only valid reason for admitting a child with a skin lesion to hospital was where the case required the availability of a nurse trained in paediatric dermatology. One such was Sister Winifred Simpson, a person with special insight and expertise in this field.

Ann Elizabeth Bingham was appointed consultant dermatologist to the RBHSC in 1985, in a period of further change in the orientation of the paediatric dermatological service. In 1995 she was appointed chairperson of the British Society for Paediatric Dermatology, one of the first sub-specialities within the British Association of Dermatologists.

While many of the skin diseases occurring in children have disappeared, eczema remains – afflicting 10 per cent of the childhood population. Recently, increasing attention is being paid to the investigation and treatment of genetically inherited diseases of the skin. A joint project is ongoing, involving the molecular biopsy facilities available in the Department of Medical Genetics at the Belfast City Hospital. As a result of this research, several people have produced work meriting a higher medical degree.

MEDICAL GENETICS

The Hospital became involved in medical genetics when in November 1953 Staff received a letter from Professor A.C. Stevenson, Professor of Social and Preventive Medicine at Queen's University, asking for their co-operation in establishing a Genetic Clinic. He offered to liaise with colleagues on a flexible basis to see children with diseases in which there might be a genetic element. This ad hoc arrangement got off to a slow start and ceased altogether after Stevenson resigned in March 1958. The subject was resurrected in 1961 when John Pemberton, Stevenson's successor, requested a monthly session in the Hospital for Dr Peter Froggatt (later Sir Peter Froggatt, vice-chancellor of QUB) to run a special clinic where cases of genetic interest could be seen and investigated. This proposal was received by the Staff with enthusiasm and became the base from which the modern Department of Medical Genetics emerged.

Norman Cummings Nevin joined the Medical Staff in 1969, having been appointed lecturer, then senior lecturer, in human genetics at QUB. In March 1972 he established a weekly Human Genetics Clinic at the Children's Hospital. He became Professor of Medical Genetics in 1976. Instinctively an individualist, Norman Nevin built up a genetic counselling and laboratory service for Northern Ireland virtually single-handed. For over a quarter of a century no additional medical consultant appointment was made, until Dr Fiona Stewart joined the department in 1995. The clinical component of medical genetics is now called the Northern Ireland Regional Genetic Service, and the original QUB Department of Medical Genetics is now part of the university's Division of Molecular Medicine.

The genetic service continues to provide a weekly clinic at the Hospital and, where required, in-patients are seen, particularly when urgent surgery is being contemplated for a child with multiple congenital abnormalities. Information and advice on inherited disorders are given to couples where there is a greater than normal risk of foetal abnormality occurring or to individuals carrying a gene which could give rise to a genetic disorder. The aim of family genetic counselling is to try to ascertain 'at risk' individuals and to advise parents of children with genetic disorders of the probability of having another similarly affected child. The service also offers chromosome testing and an increasingly large number of DNA tests for many of the new conditions that are being identified. The clinical role is not neglected; children are seen who are of unusual appearance whose evaluation is purely clinical, as many of these conditions carry unidentified genes and cannot be diagnosed by a blood sample.

JEAN NEVIN has charge of the amniocentesis prenatal diagnostic laboratory which takes in samples from all hospitals in Northern Ireland and checks the baby's chromosomes for the abnormality indicating Down's Syndrome. Amniocentesis is the removal of a sample of the fluid surrounding the baby in the womb. A substance called alphafetoprotein found in the amniotic fluid is higher in cases of spina bifida, and lower in Down's Syndrome.

Public perception has been that Down's Syndrome is prevalent in Northern Ireland but analysis of the figures has shown that the incidence of this condition is no higher than anywhere else in the UK. However, the region does lead the world in the incidence of spina bifida. Although the numbers have dropped dramatically over the past thirty years, recent reports suggest that one in every four hundred pregnancies here is affected with a neural tube defect, less than a third being detected antenatally. Fiona Stewart is a member of a European Working Party on Spina Bifida called the Integer Project, which is carrying out research to find the genetic defect that causes the condition.[9]

NEONATOLOGY

Mark McClean Reid's interest in paediatrics began in 1962 when, as a house officer in the Belfast City Hospital, his duties in the Jubilee Maternity Hospital and the Ava Children's Hospital brought him under the stimulating influence of Muriel Frazer. Following a two-year period as a senior house officer and registrar in the RBHSC, he expressed a desire to make a career in neonatology, an aspiration running contrary to the received paediatric wisdom of the day, according to which little could be done for critically ill newborn babies. Mark Reid believed that the low survival rates must be capable of improvement, a view reinforced by his observation that his anaesthetist colleagues in the Children's Hospital, Gerald Black and Harold Love, were achieving results in older babies and children suffering from a wide variety of life-threatening conditions. He thought it probable that this approach could be adapted to the treatment of newborn babies, and in 1968 he travelled to the Hospital for Sick Children, Toronto, on a Sam Haslett Brown Scholarship, encouraged by the anaesthetists and at least one paediatrician, W.A.B. Campbell. In Toronto at that time Dr Paul Swyer was developing a technique of respiratory support called intermittent positive pressure ventilation for babies with severe breathing difficulties. When Reid returned to Belfast there were no suitable posts immediately available, so he continued his career in general paediatrics from 1971 to 1977, in the Craigavon Area Hospital. Fortunately, he was permitted to retain a session at the Intensive Care Unit in the Children's Hospital, where he sent all seriously ill children from his base at Craigavon. This arrangement had at least two benefits. Firstly, Mark Reid was able to carry out follow-up examination of individual patients and undertake detailed analysis of results. Secondly, it emphasized to him and others the vital importance of caring for very sick children in a specialist centre.

In 1977 Mark Reid was appointed to a tripartite position at the Royal Maternity Hospital, the Jubilee Maternity Hospital and the Ava Children's Hospital. At the RMH he joined B.G. (Garth) McClure, who had been in post since 1973, an association which was to lead to far-reaching developments in neonatology. At that time, the required skills of intubation of the trachea (windpipe), mechanical ventilation of the lungs and other remedial measures used in the treatment of newborn babies were in the hands of the anaesthetists at the Children's Hospital, into whose care babies from the RMH were transferred. However, in 1978 McClure and Reid began to develop resuscitative and supportive techniques themselves on the premise that it was logical and beneficial to care for the sick newborn baby in close proximity to the Maternity Unit. At first, this change caused a frisson of anxiety throughout the anaesthetic establishment but good sense and mutual esteem prevailed, with both institutions coming to fulfil complementary roles. The newborn babies with a surgical problem were treated in the RBHSC, while those with respiratory and other difficulties remained in the care of the neonatologists at the RMH.

Such was the increasing burden that McClure and Reid presented the Department of Health with an ultimatum, declaring that, if more help was not forthcoming, they would be forced to close down the service.

WILFRED AYRE BOYD CAMPBELL, consultant paediatrician, 1948–83, son of Samuel Burnside Boyd Campbell, well-known physician at the RVH, was one of the first post-war appointees. An extremely loyal member of Staff, he was alert to any measures – from whatever source – which he judged likely to be detrimental to the RBHSC. He was the first to advocate an appointment system for outpatients and was a pioneer in the exchange blood transfusion of rhesus babies. A particular interest was the care of children in Lissue Branch Hospital. Campbell was a kindly man, a stalwart colleague, devoted to the good of his patients and the prestige of his Hospital. He retired in 1983 to North Berwick in Scotland.

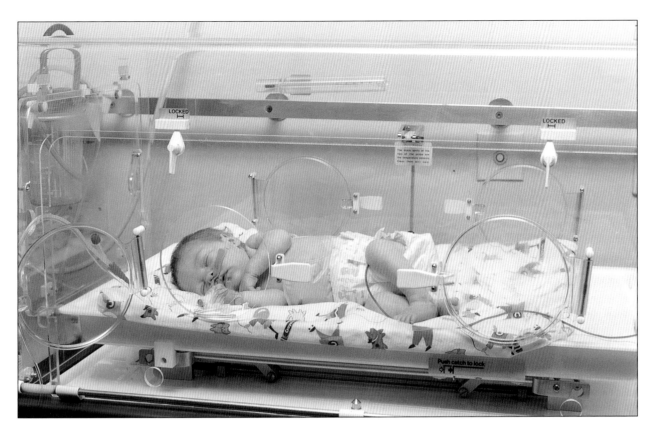

A baby in an incubator, 1994. The care of both medical and surgical infants forms an important part of the Hospital's work.

However, with the good offices of Dr R.J. (Bob) Weir, chief medical officer of the Department of Health & Social Services, the crisis passed with the appointment of Dr Henry Halliday to a post encompassing the Royal Maternity Hospital, the Royal Belfast Hospital for Sick Children, the Belfast City Hospital and the Mater Hospital. Currently, all three neonatologists contribute to the clinical life of the Children's Hospital in advisory and supportive roles. Mark Reid has maintained his interest in general paediatrics at the Hospital and was chairman of the Medical Staff in 1996–7.

The status of neonatology was finally confirmed when in 1990 Garth McClure was granted a personal professorship and in 1992 Henry Halliday became an honorary professor in the Department of Child Health.

CYSTIC FIBROSIS

The changing face of paediatric medicine has been exemplified by the striking progress in the diagnosis and treatment of the distressing condition of cystic fibrosis (CF). It is the commonest genetically determined disease in Europe and North America, affecting one person in two thousand. The incidence in Ireland is higher than elsewhere and may be as high as one in sixteen hundred. In Northern Ireland approximately fifteen affected babies are born each year and one person in twenty is a carrier of the defective gene. The condition was first recognized as a disease entity in 1936. With

WILLIAM IAN FORSYTHE, consultant paediatrician, 1957–76. A valued member of Staff, he left to take up a post of consultant paediatrician in Leeds General Infirmary and St James's Hospital, Leeds. He considered the troubled Northern Ireland of the day an unsuitable environment in which to bring up his children. Before his appointment to the RBHSC he was a travelling scholar at the Barnkliniken Queen Caroline Hospital, Stockholm, and research fellow at the Children's Medical Center, Boston, USA.

This Christmas card by Rowel Friers was sold in aid of the Cystic Fibrosis Research Trust, for which he is an ardent fundraiser.

both lungs and bowels affected, the unfortunate children presented a pitiable sight. Knowledge of the aetiology of the disease was scarce and an early demise inevitable, often before the child had reached the age of three. Mothers had noticed that the children tasted salty when kissed and it was found that the sweat in affected children contained four times the normal amount of salt due to a biochemical failure to reabsorb salt from the sweat in the sweat ducts. In 1955, a diagnostic sweat test for high salt content was developed.

In Belfast the first moves towards definitive diagnosis and intensive treatment were made by Ivo Carré and his junior colleague, John Dodge, in the 1960s. With the arrival of Aileen Redmond on the Staff in 1971, a further impetus was given to the control of this condition. In 1960, as a house officer in the RBHSC, she had seen the well-nigh hopeless outlook for children with CF, an impression strengthened while she was an associate chief resident in the Hospital for Sick Children in Toronto. In 1967 she obtained a fellowship from Harvard University, providing one year with Dr H. Schwachman at the Children's Medical Center in Boston. Under the care of this 'father' of cystic fibrosis, the life expectancy of patients was significantly extended. Despair at the outcome of the disease had given place to modest expectations of success. However, with no immediate prospect of an appointment in Belfast, Aileen Redmond went off to South Africa to study malnutrition at the Red Cross Hospital in Cape Town. However, her return to Belfast was hastened by W.I. Forsythe's premature resignation.

The small clinic introduced by Carré and Dodge has grown year by year, under Aileen Redmond's charge, to the present complement of 280 patients, one of the largest in the UK. Specially trained nurses and physiotherapists developed their interests and are now working exclusively in this field, together with dieticians and social workers. The jewel in the crown has undoubtedly been the provision of a special unit for adolescents suffering from CF, opened in 1986. (See Chapter 18.) Recently the caring team has been augmented by a psychiatrist and an artist.

NEPHROLOGY

The career of Joseph Maurice Savage has striking similarities to that of his colleague Aileen Redmond. Early in his training he identified a need that was not being met and focused on redressing that deficiency. As a medical registrar in the Ulster Hospital in 1974, he had seen a number of children with severe kidney disease, all very ill and gradually deteriorating. At that time little could be done for them except the administration of steroids, with a disappointing response. Savage made his way to the Great Ormond

Aileen Redmond, consultant paediatrician, 1971–, with special interest in cystic fibrosis

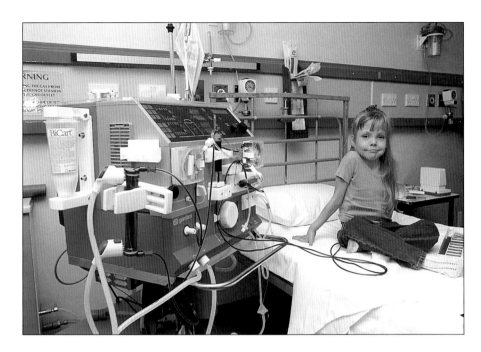

Child receiving haemodialysis in
Musgrave Ward

Street Hospital, London, where he found a unit headed by Professor
Martin Barrett, who had the ambitious vision of setting up specialized
paediatric nephrology units throughout the country. Inspired by his experience, on his appointment to the Children's Hospital in 1980 Savage
began the task of establishing a comprehensive nephrology service in
Belfast.

The path of the pioneer is often difficult. In the first place, the confidence of parents had to be gained. It was not easy to persuade those whose
children were suffering from what appeared to be a simple urinary infection to agree to a further investigation, with the chance of finding an
underlying renal abnormality. (In fact, an ultrasound scan of 650 normal
babies at two days old showed 14 of them to have an identifiable renal
defect.) Furthermore, new discoveries and new treatments are not neces-
sarily followed by new money with which to fund them, and the nephrology service was no exception. The battle to obtain adequate funding was
long and arduous.

The two cornerstones of treatment in severe kidney disease are dialysis
and transplantation, both intensive users of manpower and equipment. At
first, in the absence of a dialysis machine in the Children's Hospital, equipment had to be borrowed from the Regional Renal Unit at the Belfast
City Hospital. The training of nurses in the intricacies of haemodialysis and
peritoneal dialysis took time, and again the facilities of the City Hospital
were put at Savage's disposal. The kidney transplantations were carried out
in the City Hospital, but with the increasing identification of severe renal
disease in younger children it became obvious that surgical facilities would
have to be provided in the Children's Hospital. By 1993 renal transplantation had been successfully accomplished in fifty-three children. The bigger
children are transplanted in the City Hospital and those under twenty

Maurice Savage, consultant
paediatrician, 1980–, with
special interest in nephrology

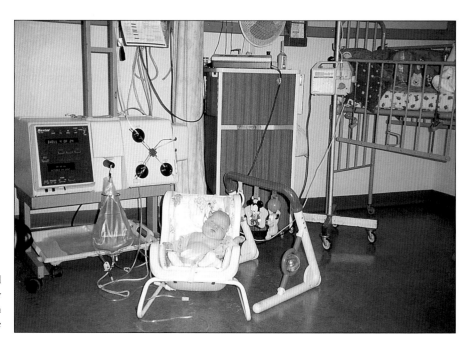

Baby receiving peritoneal dialysis, 1997; a facility now available to children at home

kilograms – that is less than five years of age – in the Children's Hospital.

A final difficulty is the shortage of child organ donors in the UK and in Europe. Savage and his colleagues made a plea for a greater awareness of the problem, especially to the staff of Intensive Care Units (ICUs). They argued that vastly more children die in IUCs following road traffic accidents than the maximum demand for donor organs. When faced with the hopeless situation of a brain-dead child on a ventilator, it is important for staff to be conscious of the potential for organ transplantation and to be prepared to ask parents about possible donation. The only hope for the child with end-stage organ failure is organ grafting, and it can be of some comfort to parents of a dying child to know that they are providing an appropriate donor organ for a fellow human being.

The RBHSC now offers a regional paediatric nephrology service involving a multidisciplinary team. This service includes the provision of patient and parent training, the management of peritoneal dialysis and haemodialysis, and the treatment of acute and chronic renal failure. Between ten and sixteen patients are constantly on chronic peritoneal dialysis, the majority of whom are cared for at home. Four to five children will be on haemodialysis and each year a similar number receive a donor kidney. Additionally, ten patients each year require acute dialysis or haemofiltration following cardiac surgery or prolonged intensive care.

In November 1992 the first paediatric renal nurse was appointed – Joanne Clingen. The nursing role includes assessment of children prior to dialysis, and their subsequent care during dialysis or transplantation; other vital aspects are the education of children and their families about dialysis and the provision of support in the community.

The department now has three consultants. J.M. Savage leads the team, assisted by Dr Moira Stewart, general paediatrician, and Dr Mary

O'Connor, appointed in 1995.

Savage's work has not been entirely devoted to nephrology. In association with Dr Colin Boreham, of the Department of Physical and Health Education, Queen's University Belfast, and Professor Sean Strain of the Nutrition Research Unit at the University of Ulster, he has carried out a study of coronary risk factors in schoolchildren aged twelve and fifteen years. A history of low birth weight was found to be associated with an increased risk of coronary artery disease in adulthood. Breastfed babies were less likely to be threatened in later life. The disturbing fact emerged that of risk factors such as high blood cholesterol, high blood pressure and obesity, smoking and lack of exercise, three or more were identifiable in 20 per cent of the children at twelve years of age. The plea was made for preventative measures, some economic, others involving changes in lifestyle and diet, in an effort to reduce the tendency to coronary disease in an increasingly sedentary childhood population. Only 4 per cent of children cycle to school and less than 10 per cent walk, figures that may reflect the reluctance of parents to expose their children to the dangers of a violent society.

This study was sponsored by the Northern Ireland Chest, Heart and Stroke Association and in 1997–8 by the British Heart Foundation.

AUTO-IMMUNE DISEASE

The upsurge in the investigation and treatment of auto-immune disease led, in 1984, to the appointment of David Rolande McCluskey as honorary consultant clinical immunologist, covering allergic diseases and immuno-deficiency, when the body is unable to defend itself effectively against infection. His clinic liaises with other relevant departments, such as respiratory medicine.

COT DEATH

The phenomenon of sudden death in an apparently healthy infant in its cot is not new, but only comparatively recently has there been a concerted effort to understand the condition and make progress in its prevention. Between 1966 and 1968 Dr Peter Froggatt and his colleagues carried out a study of sudden unexpected death in infants, based on 162 cases. Their conclusion was that cot death victims were essentially healthy throughout life; they died because, during the developmental stage of physiological vulnerability, mainly between one and six months, some combination of intrinsic and extrinsic factors proved fatal. They noted that often the only clinical sign was an upper respiratory tract infection which might interfere with breathing in the sleeping baby, a finding supported by the fact that the condition was commoner in the winter months.[10]

In 1978 a group of health visitors from Carnmoney Health Centre approached Dr J.F.T. Glasgow on behalf of several parents who were complaining about the lack of support and of official information on the subject. At that time the only source of such information was the London-based Foundation for the Study of Infant Death, established in 1971. As a direct result of the representations from Carnmoney, a local professional group was set up to study the problem of cot death. (The generic term cot death is reserved for infant death due to a conglomeration of conditions, while Sudden Infant Death syndrome is used for cases where a thorough autopsy fails to establish a specific cause of death.)

Two early measures were taken: the state pathologist was requested to inform the Children's Hospital when cases of so-called cot death came to his notice at autopsy, and a booklet was issued through general practitioners to concerned parents, with the object of imparting information and allaying fears.[11]

In the late 1980s an important change occurred, when it was observed that a cot death was more liable to occur in overheated babies who were placed on their tummies or sides to sleep. The simple act of laying the baby on his or her back to sleep could dramatically reduce the incidence of the syndrome. This measure was succinctly stated in slogan form: 'Back to sleep, feet to foot' – in other words, place the baby on its back and put the feet against the foot of the cot (to prevent the baby slipping down under the clothes and becoming overheated). The ensuing widespread publicity focused on television presenter Anne Diamond, who had lost her infant son, Sebastian, through cot death. While in the space of two years in the 1960s Froggatt had reported on 162 cases, now not more than twenty cot death infants are encountered every year.

One other significant factor detrimental to infant health remains and is a massive problem in Northern Ireland – smoking within the household. Far too many parents still smoke near their children in homes or motor cars. On 31 May 1993 the Ulster Cancer Foundation presented its Smoke-free Award to the RBHSC in recognition of the provision of a totally smoke-free hospital.

SUFFER THE CHILDREN

Child abuse and neglect is a major clinical challenge for the paediatrician. Thousands of children from Northern Ireland call the counselling service Childline, many complaining of physical or sexual abuse. Approximately thirty-five suspected cases are seen in the Accident & Emergency Department or the wards of the Hospital annually.

In 1962 Dr Henry C. Kempe coined the now famous phrase 'battered child syndrome'. At a time when professionals, particularly doctors, held a narrow view of child abuse and neglect, Kempe characterized the syndrome as an often undiagnosed clinical condition in which young children, generally under three years of age, had received serious physical abuse from a caregiver, usually a parent. He urged his fellow professionals to consider the possibility of the syndrome if the history given by parents was out of keeping with the clinical findings, especially if these were confirmed by X-ray examination.[12] Since then, the abuse and neglect of children has become a focus of worldwide attention. Its recognition and treatment involves multidisciplinary teams of accident and emergency paediatricians, psychiatrists, social workers, surgeons and nurses, among others. Specifically, social workers have a statutory obligation in the prevention of child abuse, the investigation of alleged cases and presentation of evidence in court, and the provision of services, treatment and rehabilitation of victims and their families.

In 1979 Dr Alice Swann took up a clinical medical officer post with duties in schools in north Belfast. She was given a mandate to study the problem of child abuse and neglect and to establish a medical role in what was a cause of growing concern. Subsequently, she set up a clinic at the Royal Belfast Hospital for Sick Children, at which cases of physical abuse and neglect were investigated and followed up, an arrangement which served as a link between the Hospital, the community and social workers in the community.

Child abuse and neglect is an area of extreme sensitivity requiring both gentle handling and a high level of suspicion in circumstances where the clinician's personal emotions are liable to get in the way of an objective assessment. Staff of all grades are being educated to be alert to any case showing incongruity between what parents allege happened and what is seen when the patient is examined. Exaggerated signs, such as fractures or extensive bruising, said by the parents to be merely the result of the child's clumsiness, are not taken at face value. The recognition of and intervention in child abuse and neglect have come a long way since Henry Kempe's plea to doctors to identify the battered child. Much more sophisticated levels of analysis, assessment and intervention are now needed, an approach in which the Staff of the RBHSC have played a significant role.

Staff at the RBHSC remain alert to the problem of child abuse and neglect

RETURN TO THE COMMUNITY

The appointment of Heather Jean Steen as a consultant paediatrician, in 1995, was in keeping with the current philosophy of care in the community rather than in hospital. Simply stated, Dr Steen's task is to prevent unnecessary admission to hospital or, in today's jargon, to deal with issues associated with ambulatory paediatrics. An important component of her brief is the education of colleagues, doctors, nurses and other professionals towards the possibility of treating more and more children in the home environment. The message appears to be that the Hospital, with all its specialities, high technology and expertise, has still a vital role in child health but, ultimately, there is no place like home.[13]

This philosophy was examined in Dr Moira Stewart's thesis, 'An Examination of the Factors Associated with the Presentation of Children at the RBHSC and of the Hospital Resources used in their Management (1984/1986)'. Among her key conclusions were i) that the majority of children who attended the A & E Department were referred from one of two sources: direct parent referral accounted for 68.58 per cent and referrals from family doctors 21.34 per cent; and ii) that almost half the attendances were neither accident nor emergency cases, more than half of the children did not need a specific hospital facility and 11.61 per cent were found to have no physical abnormality. Only 17 per cent of children required admission to hospital.

This analysis revealed that a number of children who presented at the Hospital during a twelve-month period were found not to require the unique facilities of a paediatric hospital. This is not a denial of the appropriateness of parents seeking and receiving hospital care for their children when this is felt to be necessary. It may, however, indicate differences in the perception of the role of the Hospital by those outside, lack of established lines of communication between all levels of the childcare services, and the problems involved in determining which children require referral and admission to hospital.[14]

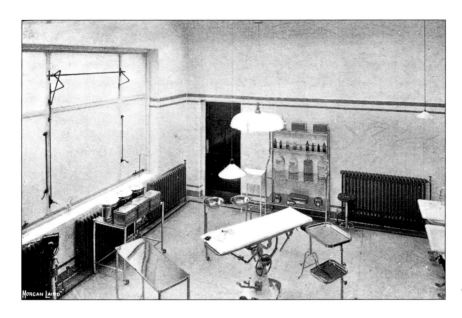

An operating theatre in 1932

4
SURGERY

IN THE EARLY DAYS OF the Belfast Hospital for Sick Children senior surgical appointments were for life, with no mandatory retirement age. There was a somewhat perfunctory review of the appointment every three years as a precaution against incapacitating illness, alcoholism or some unacceptable misdeed. (The NHS abolished the 'tenure for life' option, introducing a mandatory retirement age of sixty-five for hospital appointees.)

Sir Ian Fraser has clear recall of his own appointment, which was to initiate forty years of service to the Hospital, interrupted only by World War II. One day in the autumn of 1927 he was preparing to assist Professor Andrew Fullerton at an operation in the Royal Victoria Hospital when Fullerton said:

I am president of the Association of Surgeons of Great Britain and Ireland, president of the Royal College of Surgeons in Ireland, Professor of Surgery at Queen's University, Belfast, and visiting surgeon to the Royal Victoria Hospital and the Hospital for Sick Children. I am going to give up something and it will be my appointment to the Children's Hospital – you must apply, but you will not get it.

There followed some three weeks of feverish activity by the candidates, involving the assembling of testimonials, the printing and circulation of these to about forty people and a hectic round of personal canvassing in the grand houses of Malone and the humbler dwellings of the Working Men's Committee. The vote of this disparate group resulted in the appointment of Ian Fraser as assistant surgeon, overcoming the competition of C.J.A. (Cocky) Woodside.

Fraser had never before visited the Hospital and was unaware even of its location in Queen Street. The building, now a police station, still stands opposite the office of the American Consul. His first impression was that the most important part of the place was the office of the chairman of the Management Committee, which was elegantly furnished and never used. By contrast, the surgical outpatient accommodation, where he did most of his work, was rather like a greenhouse tacked on to the back of the Hospital.[1]

At the time of Ian Fraser's original appointment, attainment of a Staff position at the Children's Hospital was not the pinnacle of one's surgical aspirations but rather a stepping stone to greater things. The ambitious surgeon had one goal – to become surgeon-in-charge of one of the surgical units on the long corridor of the Royal Victoria Hospital. The realization of this objective inevitably took time and more than a modicum of patience. Senior RVH Medical and Surgical Staff of that era jealously guarded their privileged status and were viewed by many as a self-perpetuating oligarchy. It took the hammer of the NHS to begin the process of chipping away at this monolith, and indeed the 1960s were well advanced before it was finally demolished. Henceforth, all persons of whatever speciality appointed to a consultant post at the RVH automatically became a member of Medical Staff.

The transfer of the Children's Hospital from voluntary to public control in 1948 coincided with the gradual process of change in training and technology which was to transform paediatric surgical practice. Heretofore, surgical progress was highly individualistic and depended largely on the motivation of the

IAN FRASER, consultant surgeon, 1927–65, was the outstanding medical student of his time and was appointed to the BHSC at the early age of twenty-six. The interruption of World War II only enhanced his growing surgical reputation; he saw distinguished service in India and Europe, particularly in the Battle of Anzio, and was awarded the DSO. Demobilized in 1946, with the rank of brigadier, he resumed work at the RVH and the RBHSC, becoming one of the most amusing and inspiring of teachers. His bedside clinics were crammed with eager students, who regarded him almost as a cult figure. Fraser's public persona was of a highly intelligent, ambitious, swashbuckling character, confidant of the great and the good, master of the throwaway line and the quick riposte. Those who knew him better saw other facets to his character, a generosity and kindness offered without fuss or display. When Bill Cochran, his junior colleague at the Children's Hospital, was seriously ill, Fraser turned up at his back door bearing wine and a hamper of food. In 1946, as a house surgeon in the RVH, I travelled with him to Londonderry to assist at an operation, and the following morning he sent a note of thanks and a crisp £10 note – a massive windfall to one whose annual salary was £75. Ian Fraser became arguably the best-known medical figure in Northern Ireland and it was no surprise when, shortly after his tenure of the presidency of the BMA in 1962, he was knighted. He retired in 1966. In his nineties he remains the same entertaining, ebullient character – the Peter Pan of surgery.

surgeon concerned. For example, when Robert Campbell joined the Staff of the Hospital in 1897, it was not the practice to treat uncomplicated hernias in young children by operation. In 1899 only eight operations for inguinal hernia were performed, all probably strangulated. The figures for subsequent years show a striking change in surgical practice.

ADMISSIONS FOR INGUINAL HERNIA

1900	11	(4 strangulated)
1902	35	(4 strangulated)
1903	47	(1 strangulated)
1904	63	(2 strangulated)
1907	108	

In 1920, 227 cases of inguinal hernia were treated in the Hospital, and 212 patients were operated on by Campbell in the Outpatient Department and carried home by their parents.[2] Thus began day case surgery in the Children's Hospital, largely due to the innovative efforts of one man. His death from Bright's disease, at the age of fifty-five, was as tragic as it was untimely.

Robert Campbell's record is a good example of progress through personal motivation and initiative, which foreshadowed the day, yet distant, of organized specialization in paediatric surgery, backed up by the burgeoning developments in the allied sciences. Following the cessation of hostilities in 1945, the first milestones on the road to specialization began to appear. Prior to 1947 academic surgery had no distinctive shape, its form being entirely dependent on the inclinations of the incumbent of the university chair. Andrew Fullerton ran the Department of Surgery from his own consulting rooms. His successor, Percival Templeton Crymble, carried on in the same vein, so that during his tenure there was no structured postgraduate teaching and no centrally organized surgical research. The change from the individualistic to the corporate, departmental approach began in 1947 with the arrival of Harold William Rodgers, from St Bartholomew's Hospital, London, the first Englishman to occupy the chair of surgery at QUB. Among his first tasks was to organize the Department of Surgery to oversee undergraduate and postgraduate teaching and research. His interest extended to the Children's Hospital, where he was one of the first to advocate the appointment of a surgeon exclusively devoted to paediatric surgery.

No senior surgical appointments were made during the war and the service was maintained by P.T. Crymble, H.P. Hall and J.S. Loughridge. Known to students and colleagues alike as 'P.T.', Crymble had been a radiologist during World War I. Halfway through that conflict he was called back to the Department of Anatomy at Queen's to fill the gap left by the sudden illness of the professor, Johnston Symington. (His colleague in the

Harold Rodgers, professor of surgery, Queen's University Belfast, 1947–73, consultant surgeon, RVH and RBHSC

department was Margaret Purce, sister of surgeon G.R.B. 'Barney' Purce.) Crymble's name will always be associated with Man 50, an anonymous cadaver, placed in a container holding water, deep-frozen and then sliced, resulting in serial anatomical specimens. The next step in P.T.'s career was part-time Professor of Surgery, later full-time at a salary of £1,500 per year. The other candidates for the chair were G.D.F. McFadden and Ian Fraser; Fraser withdrew from the contest as he could not contemplate doing animal research.

As the approach to surgical training and research grew more structured, individuals continued to press forward with their own initiatives. In 1950 J.A.W. Bingham decided to confine his work to thoracic surgery. (See p. 56.) In wishing him well in his new venture, the Staff noted that a vacancy would be created for a 'general' surgeon, and on 2 October 1951 the appointment of a consultant surgeon to the Hospital was on the agenda. Nevertheless, the subsequent minute reveals that they were still unconvinced of the need for a surgeon fully committed to paediatric surgery and were at pains to reject insinuations that involvement in adult surgery in any way diluted a commitment to the Children's Hospital:

> The Medical Staff Committee fully subscribes to the view that no children's surgeon is a better children's surgeon by depriving himself of the experience of the general surgery of adults. Medical Staff resent the suggestion that the first interest of no surgeon on the Staff lies with this hospital. It is only necessary to point out that four of the present staff of surgeons have given many more years of service to the RBHSC than to any other hospital.

A letter from the RVH surgeons, in December 1951, did much to change the conservative attitude of the Staff. They were unhappy with its suggestion that a surgeon would be 'allocated' to do a session at the Children's Hospital, believing that they should have a say in who would be appointed. Their stated preference was that the appointee should have a special inclination towards children's surgery, take a real interest in the Hospital and be prepared to continue as a specialist in this branch. No further action was taken until October 1952, when Professor H.W. Rodgers suggested a surgical registrar appointment exclusively to the RBHSC. The appointment should not be terminated for any reason without ample warning or without the approval of the Children's Hospital Medical Staff. As an interim measure, Rodgers lent, on a part-time basis, his departmental registrar, Jack McCredie, although he was not trained in paediatric surgery. His commitment ceased when he emigrated to Canada in 1954.

Throughout this period the Northern Ireland Hospitals Authority remained resistant to strong representations for the appointment of a paediatric surgeon. Even the retirement of H.P. Hall in 1956 failed to clear the log jam as the vacancy was not filled. On 12 November 1957 the NIHA was again pressed to agree to the appointment of a surgeon 'who would have beds by right, would correlate surgical activities, supervise the juniors and be a stimulus to his colleagues'. He or she would specialize in the problems encountered in the newborn baby and in paediatric urology.

At the grass roots, so to speak, the eight years 1951–8 are remembered with mixed feelings by the junior Medical Staff of that period, among them D.M. Bell, W.J. Glover, D.S. Gordon, J.S. Loughridge, B.T. Smyth and Willoughby Wilson. On occasions, they were given freedom to work unsupervised. For example, Glover, as a first appointment house officer, recalls conducting an entire outpatient clinic completely on his own, and Loughridge was sometimes permitted by his seniors to operate without immediate supervision – he was once visited in the operating theatre at the dead of night by the chairman of Medical Staff, a physician, expressing horror at the consequences of any mishap. It is fortunate that the junior Staff, while given responsibility above their status, did not find the challenge beyond their capabilities.

Willoughby Wilson's term as a registrar, 1951–2, was not one of unalloyed contentment. Soon identified by his seniors as a potential paediatric surgeon, he impressed by his acquisition of a list of some two hundred successful operations for congenital pyloric stenosis and his handling of every sort of surgical emergency. However, a rather peremptory order from the Professor of Child Health to seek further training in Toronto was refused. Wilson felt that he was being driven, rather than guided, into what he perceived as an uncertain future. Happily, he found fulfilment in adult surgery at the RVH.

On 3 February 1959 Brian Turbett Smyth joined the Medical Staff of the RBHSC and the Ulster Hospital for Women and Children, the first surgeon in Northern Ireland to devote himself exclusively to the care of children. It had taken such a long time to shift the NIHA from its original, somewhat obscurantist, position, that, as there were eight general surgeons at the RVH and four at the RBHSC, there was no case for additional surgical consultant staff at the latter hospital. The uniqueness of paediatric surgery, particularly of the newborn, was a concept only slowly appreciated by those who controlled the money supply.

Brian Smyth, when a senior house officer in the Children's Hospital during 1952, decided that he liked working with children and began to consider the possibility of specializing in paediatric surgery. Encouraged to seek further training by Norman Hughes, Ian Fraser and J.S. Loughridge, his chiefs at that time, he obtained a post as senior house officer at the Hospital for Sick Children, Great Ormond Street, London. It was there that he had his first introduction to the surgery of the newborn, particularly the correction of tracheo-oesophageal fistula (a congenital obstruction of the gullet, with a passage connecting gullet and windpipe). A further period was spent as a registrar in paediatric surgery at the Royal Liverpool Children's Hospital, where Isobel Forshall and P.P. Rickham had created a

DAVID LYNCH

Brian Turbett Smyth, consultant paediatric surgeon, 1959–86

surgical paediatric service which rivalled those in Great Ormond Street and the Royal Edinburgh Hospital for Sick Children. Between 1953 and 1956 Smyth gained experience in general surgery, culminating in a further year at the Children's Hospital. In October 1957 a research fellowship enabled him to work in Boston with Dr Orvar Swenson, a highly respected paediatric surgeon who had pioneered the operation of rectosygmoidectomy for Hirschsprung's disease (a childhood condition characterized by gross hypertrophy and dilation of the colon). During his time there Smyth gained special experience in paediatric urology, an interest he was to carry with him into his consultant appointment at the Royal Belfast Hospital for Sick Children.

Also in 1959 William Cochran, from Edinburgh, was appointed to a new post of senior registrar in paediatric surgery at the RBHSC and the Ulster Hospital. His high standards and untiring efforts were to play an important part in the development of the paediatric surgical service in Northern Ireland. With the retirement of S.A. Vincent from the staff of the Ulster Hospital, in 1962, Bill Cochran was appointed as a consultant paediatric surgeon to that hospital, with three sessions weekly. The NIHA refused to change his status at the Children's Hospital so at one and the same time he was a consultant at the Ulster Hospital and a senior registrar at the RBHSC. Five years were to elapse before the Authority redressed this injustice, although it had been patently obvious that Cochran's work deserved the recognition of consultant status.

Nevertheless, it would be unfair to assume that prior to the appointments of Smyth and Cochran no paediatric surgery of consequence took place. On the contrary, a wide range of surgical procedures were undertaken without the aid of today's specialized anaesthesia, body fluid replacement, antibiotic cover and intensive care. The commonest operations were for inguinal hernia, undescended testes, circumcision, appendicectomy, congenital pyloric stenosis and nephrectomy for tumour or hydronephrosis. On rare occasions a repair of cleft palate or harelip was performed. During World War II, J.S. Loughridge travelled throughout Northern Ireland, often operating in primitive conditions. In addition, he carried a heavy burden of emergency paediatric surgery.

GENERAL SURGERY

NEONATAL SURGERY

During the 1960s, with the gradual development of thoracic surgery, hope was brought to the parents of newborn babies suffering from such hitherto fatal conditions as tracheo-oesophageal fistula and congenital diaphragmatic hernia. At first, progress was slow and frustrating but gradually a

JAMES STEVENSON LOUGHRIDGE, known by students and colleagues as 'Jamesie', was a Ballymena man of imposing figure, with a fine leonine head. He was famous for his aphorisms, many culled from Holy Writ. When the overhead light was off target he would say, 'When there is no vision, the patient perishes' (paraphrase of Proverbs 29, Verse 18), and he would reprove a fidgety or wilting assistant with the words 'A good sentry stays put.' Loughridge was a man of wide outside interests, including geology and ancient Greek history. He often spent his summers on Hellenic cruises, in the company of such authorities as Sir Mortimer Wheeler, the well-known antiquarian. His ambitions for a long retirement were sadly cut short by illness and he died on 6 April 1980, aged seventy-nine.

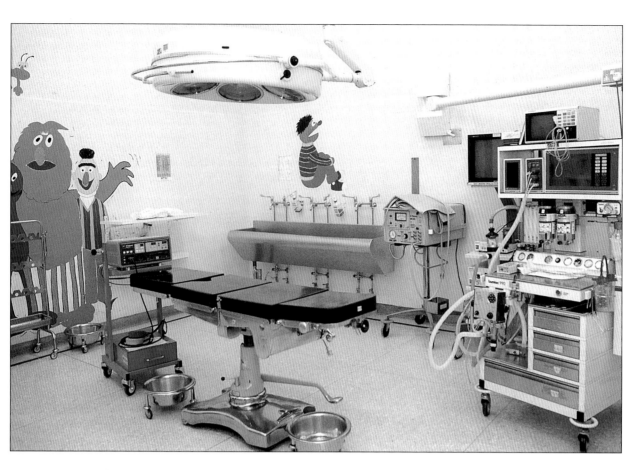

survival rate of approximately 80 per cent was achieved. The availability of intensive post-operative care, from 1967, made a significant contribution to the outcome of the surgical effort.

An RBHSC operating theatre, 1997

UROLOGICAL SURGERY

In 1956–7 Ian Forsythe introduced the technique of micturition cystography to Northern Ireland, following his experience in Sweden. In conjunction with intravenous pyelography, this enabled congenital abnormalities of the genito-urinary system to be demonstrated, such as double kidney and ureters, hydronephrosis, ectopic ureter and bladder diverticulum. The assistance of G.D.F. McFadden, at Haypark Hospital, was enlisted for the surgical removal of such lesions as posterior urethral valves, where diagnosis and result were confirmed by urethroscopy and radiology. At that time the RBHSC did not possess the necessary children's urethroscope or rectoscope. (The Haypark Hospital was the location of the Ulster Hospital, following the destruction by German firebombs of Templemore Avenue Hospital, and before the opening of the new hospital in east Belfast on 16 November 1962.) In association with the plastic surgeons (N.C. Hughes and W.R. Dickie), Smyth and Forsythe used these techniques to investigate some sixty children with hypospadias (eccentric position of the urethral opening), revealing that 25 per cent of them had an accompanying abnormality of the urinary tract. As a result they were able to add thirteen cases of bladder diverticulum to the forty-five previously reported in the world literature.

The most common emergency operation was for acute appendicitis. Even in the 1960s several children were admitted annually with severe established peritonitis and dehydration, and, on average, one child each year was lost to this disease. From 1967 onwards, children began to be referred earlier, the pre-operative management of fluid and electrolyte balance had been stabilized and wide spectrum antibiotics became available. These measures reduced the death rate to zero.

Penicillin had been available in limited quantities during World War II. The only source of supply in Northern Ireland was the American Army Medical Corps, a unit of which was based at Campbell College, Belfast. (As a resident pupil at the RVH, I can recall being sent by tramcar to obtain two ampoules of the new drug.) One of the first patients to benefit from penicillin was T.G. Gibson, surgeon at the Banbridge Hospital. He had the misfortune to damage a finger while operating on a case of highly infectious osteomyelitis, resulting in a distressing cervical spine fistula. Gibson described in colourful language not only the discomfort of the disease but the exquisite pain following the injection of the then unpurified drug.

During 1946 Smyth was penicillin 'officer' at the RVH, charged with the equable distribution of the precious substance.

TRAUMA

With the steady increase in road traffic in the post-war period, trauma continued to be the commonest cause of death in children. Notwithstanding improved methods of resuscitation and antibiotic therapy, multiple injuries involving more than two vital systems were, and are, frequently fatal.

Relatively few children were injured as a result of the civil unrest in Northern Ireland from 1969 onwards. There is no record of any child being injured as a result of the Troubles prior to 1971. These are the figures for the following years:

1971	36
1972	101
1973	33
1974	13
1975	32
1976 (1 January–20 July)	10

Most of these children attended the casualty department and were not admitted. Three suffered injuries from rubber bullets. Of the small number of children admitted with bomb blast or gunshot wounds, two stand out, one because of the extent of the injuries and the other due to the unique

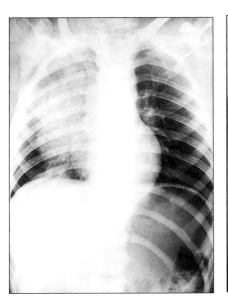 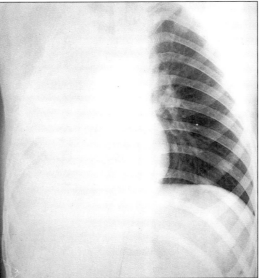 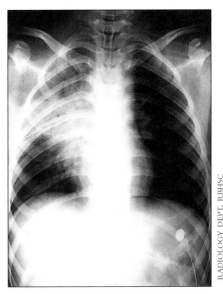

circumstances in which the injury was sustained.

On the morning of 23 April 1975 Toni Meli, aged ten, saw a blue plastic transistor radio sitting on a shelf in his father's chip shop, and with childish curiosity turned it on. The result was a devastating explosion within inches of the unfortunate boy. I arrived at the Hospital as the ambulance containing Toni drew up at the front door. The first sight was of a severely injured child with pieces of blue plastic and three-inch nails protruding from his chest and upper limbs, like some devilish collage. As well as having extensive superficial wounds to his face and upper body, Toni lost an eye and the fingers of one hand. The other arm required amputation at the elbow. Even more life-threatening was the effect of bomb blast injury to his lungs, which necessitated prolonged use of a life support machine. In spite of these horrible injuries, he left hospital some two weeks later and was soon able to return to his favourite sport of swimming. Having shown remarkable courage throughout his ordeal, Toni learned to cope successfully with his permanent disabilities, becoming particularly adept at manipulating the hook which replaced his right hand.

About 7.30 p.m. on 2 July 1976 Mary Gilmore left the Mater Hospital after visiting a friend. She was thirty-seven weeks pregnant. As she approached her home there was a burst of gunfire from a fast-moving car and Mary Gilmore was hit. She was taken back to the Mater, where an emergency Caesarean section was carried out by J.A. Versin. The baby, to be called Catherine Anne, was found to have an entry wound in the right lumbar region, and was immediately transferred to the RBHSC in the care of Bill Cochran. Exploration of the wound revealed that the bullet had traversed the tissues of the back and entered the pelvis, before lodging in the baby's rectum, whence it was later removed. This case attracted extensive media attention, not because there was anything spectacular about the surgery but because an injury to an unborn child had added a new dimension to the violence on the streets of Belfast.

X-rays showing blast damage to the lungs, 1975:
left: on admission to hospital
centre: collapsed right lung
right: resolution beginning

Some events of the Troubles had a tragicomic character. Cochran recalls the case of a three-year-old child who was with a man on a building site above Ballymurphy when they were caught in a hail of bullets, allegedly fired by a terrorist squad; one bullet hit the child in the thigh. At operation, Cochran removed it and handed it to the assistant, the assistant handed it to the scrub nurse, the scrub nurse to the theatre sister; it then passed through a succession of theatre nurses, night nursing staff, administrative staff and finally, on the following morning, to the police. Little did they know that about two years later every one of them would be called as witnesses for the Crown against one of the alleged gunmen. In court, Cochran found a throng of RBHSC Staff – about twenty in all. Each was duly sworn in, a procedure which took some time, contributing further to the already ill temper of the judge. When the case started, the senior crown counsel intervened to inform the judge that there was a problem: 'We appear to have mislaid the prisoner.' The judge demanded an immediate, straightforward explanation. Apparently, the day before, the prisoner had requested that he should be allowed to attend the funeral of his best friend. He arrived at Milltown Cemetery escorted by a number of police officers and prison guards. As the coffin was being lowered, several hooded men with rifles arose from the ground and fired a volley of shots. Startled, the escort lost concentration, whereupon the prisoner leaped over the grave and was swallowed up in the crowd. Predictably, a path did not open up for the officers. There was no further trial.

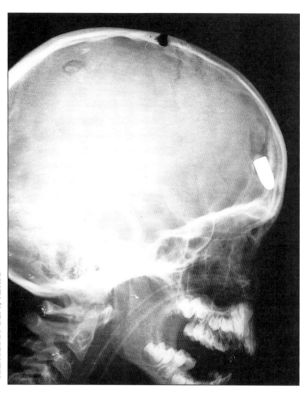

Gun shot wound to head, showing entrance wound and lodged bullet

On the evening of 20 December 1996 the sanctity of the Hospital was callously violated when gunmen opened fire in the vicinity of the Intensive Care Unit. Their intended target was Nigel Dodds, a prominent member of the Democratic Unionist Party, who was visiting his seriously ill son, Andrew. He was not hurt but a policeman suffered a slight gunshot wound to his back.

The next appointment to the consultant Surgical Staff was that of Victor E. Boston. Having obtained the diploma of FRCS in 1972, he had proceeded to Alberta with the aim of becoming a general surgeon. However, he discovered that in Canada the term 'general' had a wide application, even extending to the practice of gynaecology. He returned to Northern Ireland in order to redress this anomaly. Instead, he found himself exposed to the challenge of paediatric surgery, as a paediatric surgical registrar at the RBHSC from August 1973 to January 1974. His potential did not go unnoticed, especially by his anaesthetist colleagues, and G.W. Black advised him to consider a career in paediatric surgery, an example of the spectator

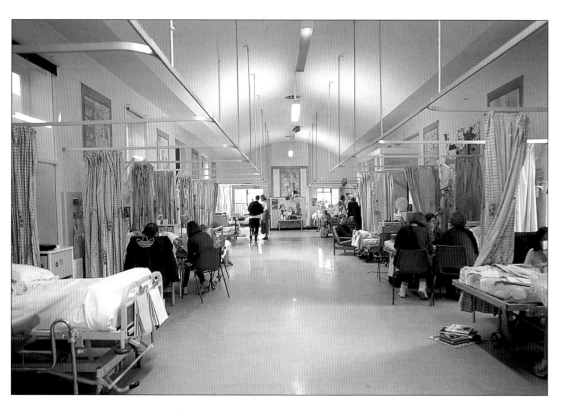

Barbour Ward (surgical), 1997

seeing the most of the game. Black's advice bore fruit for, in February 1977, after two years in Newcastle upon Tyne, at the Hospital for Sick Children, and a further year in the Red Cross Hospital in Cape Town, Boston joined Smyth and Cochran as a consultant surgeon. His work, particularly in the surgery of the newborn, contributed to the recognition of the Hospital as Northern Ireland's referral centre for neonatal surgery.

Of special concern to Boston was the pain caused to the child by needle injection, especially when frequently repeated. In 1980 he challenged Dr Dermot McCafferty and Professor David Woolfson of QUB to produce a rapid action surface anaesthetic to use on healthy skin. At first the magic cream was unstable but after refinement it was supplied to local hospitals with encouraging results. Worldwide interest was aroused and eventually the new anaesthetic was licensed to be marketed by the drug company Smith & Nephew, under the name Ametop Gel. It is applied to the injection site, left for forty-five minutes and removed; having penetrated the skin to 'freeze' layers below, it leaves the area numb for up to six hours.[3] Negotiations are under way for its sale in America, Australia, Europe and South Africa.

Soon after Boston's appointment, the Hospital lost the valuable and dedicated service of William Cochran. In 1975–6, he had been afflicted by a serious abdominal complaint which necessitated major surgery, although it is likely that this had only a minimal influence on his decision to leave Belfast. During his eighteen years in Northern Ireland Cochran never made any secret of the fact that his heart was in Scotland.

One of the traditional old wall tiles in Barbour Ward contrasts with Disney cartoon characters

His coffee table chat often centred on Scottish personalities and experiences. Nevertheless, the high tension on the streets of Belfast in the 1970s was a significant factor in his decision to accept a post in the Hospital for Sick Children, Yorkhill, Glasgow. In the same year, 1977, Stephen Brown was appointed consultant surgeon to the RBHSC and the Ulster Hospital. He was formally welcomed to the Staff in April 1978, together with Trevor Taylor, orthopaedic surgeon. Brown had received his postgraduate surgical training in the Royal Manchester Children's Hospital and Great Ormond Street, London. His special interest in medical administration was recognized when the new system of Resource Management was introduced in 1989; he was appointed the first clinical director of paediatrics. Brown, together with Boston and Smyth, carried the general surgical service forward into the 1980s, consolidating the Hospital's special place as a referral centre of excellence.

In 1982 there began an ongoing debate with the Eastern Health & Social Services Board about the reorganization of paediatric surgery. Smyth wrote to Dr J.F. McKenna, chief administrative medical officer of the Board: 'As you know it has been recognized for some time that the provision of acute paediatric surgical services in three hospitals in the greater Belfast area is wasteful and puts a severe strain on surgical personnel.' Traditionally, the paediatric surgical service had been distributed between the Children's Hospital, the Ulster Hospital, Dundonald, and the Belfast City Hospital. While recognizing and supporting the need for rationalization by the closure of Ava II, at the City Hospital, Staff were concerned that this event would take place without improvement in the facilities at the RBHSC. Smyth's letter continued:

> This hospital must take all severe accidents, children who need intensive care and newborn babies for surgery. If an adequate acute surgical service is to continue there is a very urgent need to improve the facilities at the RBHSC, so that the surgical service, currently provided in the City Hospital Ava Hospital, can be transferred to the Children's Hospital.

A TYPICAL SAMPLE OF PAEDIATRIC SURGICAL UNITS IN THE UK:
ADMISSION STATISTICS AND STAFFING, 1982

	Glasgow	Liverpool	Sheffield	Newcastle	Birmingham	Nottingham	Southampton	Belfast
Acute hospitals	2	1	1	1	1	2	3	3
Total admissions	6,000	4,708	2,205	1,255	1,940	3,552	2,975	4,481
Emergencies	3,000	2,351	1,477	N/A	960	1,632	N/A	2,957
	(50%)	(50%)	(67%)		(49%)	(46%)		(65%)
New outpatients	4,500	2,695	1,407	1,203	1,803	2,388	1,808	2,114
Review outpatients	13,500	7,104	3,994	3,689	3,717	7,428	7,107	6,076
Consultants	7	4	2	2	2½	2	2	3
SR registrars	6/7	4	4	2	3	1	3	2
Surgery SHOs	0	0	0	2	0	2	0	3

Urgently required facilities at the RBHSC were outlined by Smyth as follows:

1 four new theatres – Outpatient, Orthopaedic and General;
2 a new enlarged Intensive Care Unit;
3 a new Neonatal Surgical Unit;
4 the provision of ten to twelve beds for orthopaedic patients;
5 the Day Care Unit as already planned and an enlargement of the Outpatient Department. (See Chapter 18.)

When Brian Smyth retired in October 1986, none of these demands had been met, although the new Day Care Unit was well advanced. Another decade was to pass before new outpatient, intensive care and theatre facilities could be provided. Paradoxically, as regards bed accommodation, even leaner times were at hand for, in the 1990s, the beds available to the surgical service were drastically reduced:

General surgery: fourteen beds in Barbour Ward, three in Knox Ward;
Neonatal surgery: twelve in the Infant Surgical Unit;
Orthopaedic surgery: eight beds in Barbour Ward and three in Knox Ward.

Nevertheless, Smyth could look back with satisfaction on nearly thirty years of paediatric surgical progress, in which he himself had played no small part. Totally dedicated to the Hospital, he was in the forefront of every movement to preserve its status and enhance its reputation. He retired to Dartmouth in Devon, there to hone his skills as a yachtsman and photographer. He was succeeded on 1 April 1987 by Stephen R. Potts, sometime poet and Himalayan mountaineer, whose postgraduate experience had been gained at the Royal Manchester Children's Hospital. To Boston, Brown and Potts fell the task of guiding the paediatric surgical service into the unforeseeable future of the internal market.

THE UNIVERSITY DEPARTMENT OF SURGERY

The contribution of the university department to the RBHSC has tended to vary with the interests of the professor in post. H.W. Rodgers was a regular attender at Staff meetings and strongly initiated or supported any proposals designed to further the interests of paediatric surgery. In times of staff shortage or other crises, he matched his words with action, seconding junior members of his staff to the Children's Hospital. This ad hoc solution was not universally accepted, especially by Cochran.

However, this view was balanced by the later experience of Victor Boston, who found the association with the Department of Surgery of mutual benefit. As an honorary lecturer, he has access to laboratory and other facilities, and in return the cost of the research is met from the Endowments of the Children's Hospital.

CARDIAC SURGERY

The early development of paediatric cardiac surgery in the RBHSC is associated with the name of John Alexander Walton Bingham. F.M.B. Allen, in his review of the Hospital's status in 1954, claimed that 'Mr Bingham has done more cardiac surgery on children in this unit, than any other surgeon in the United Kingdom, apart from Guy's Hospital, London'. In 1953 the surgical operations included eighty-seven acyanotic cases, twenty-seven cyanotic (blue babies), one coarctation of the aorta and one anomalous aorta. The waiting list at that time was sixty.

Bingham joined the Staff in December 1947. He had gained his FRCS in 1938, and on the outbreak of war he joined the Indian Medical Service with the rank of major. Bingham returned from war service with materials in his briefcase for what was to prove a successful M.Ch. thesis on the subject of phantom limb pain (causalgia), based on work which he had carried out on amputees in the Far East. Less than a year after his appointment he took leave of absence in order to further his knowledge of thoracic surgery at the Brompton Hospital, London, and in November 1950 he gave up general surgery, confining himself to the surgery of the thorax. In the following years Bingham operated with great skill on many children with various lesions of the oesophagus, lungs and heart. In the latter field he tackled pulmonary valvotomy for Fallot's tetralogy, ligation of the patent ductus arteriosus and relief of coarctation of the aorta.

The next logical step forward was from closed to open heart surgery, carried out under hypothermia, in which the patient's whole body, encased in ice and submerged in a tin bath, was cooled to a temperature of 32°–30° Fahrenheit. This prevented brain damage during the short period of four to eight minutes when the heart was deliberately stopped. This rather clumsy technique had definite limitations and in the process of time gave way to a new one, in which the patient's blood was redirected through a pump oxygenator, during which the arrested heart could be operated upon in a relatively relaxed manner. Accordingly, in May 1959 Bingham made an application for the purchase of a heart/lung bypass machine, Lillihei apparatus, at a cost of approximately £1,500. In view of the expected increase in the number of cardiac operations, he requested that T.B. Smiley and H.M. Stevenson,

J.A.W. BINGHAM, consultant thoracic surgeon, 1947–76, was a shy man, not given to verbosity, though when crossed he could explode in a torrent of staccato volubility and in his leisure moments he could wax expansive on his favourite subjects of golf, cricket and the Stock Exchange. Punctuality was not his forte and his interpersonal communication with patients and colleagues did not match his surgical skill, which meant that any detailed information his patients required as to the nature of their illness and the extent of their surgery was gleaned from other sources. In the operating room often the only way his colleagues could tell how the surgery was progressing was by listening intently to the pitch of Bingham's rather tuneless whistle! He retired in September 1976 and died on 1 January 1983.

T.B. (TOM) SMILEY was the first of the new generation of thoracic/cardiac surgeons. During World War II he survived a horrendous bayonet attack by the Japanese in the operating theatre of the military hospital in Singapore by feigning death. A bluff exterior hid a sensitivity within; he thrived on encouragement and was wont to sing the songs of Zion while operating – a favourite was the 23rd Psalm. On retirement in 1971 he went to live in East Anglia. Smiley died suddenly on 2 August 1981, after reading the lesson in church.

thoracic surgeons at the RVH, both Brompton Hospital trained, should be asked to join the Medical Staff. A year later, in April 1960, Bingham's proposal that open cardiac surgery, to include both adults and children, should be carried out in the Children's Hospital was received with enthusiasm by the Staff. Child patients were to be accommodated in a six-bedded ward on the first floor of the Clark Children's Clinic and one bed would be required to house the occasional adult patient. Subsequent events were to prove the gross inaccuracy of this prediction.

The first open heart surgery operation at the RBHSC was carried out on 17 August 1960 by T.B. Smiley, with Dr Maurice Brown administering the anaesthetic. Smiley was soon to transfer his main attention to the surgery of adults at the RVH and H. Morris Stevenson took up the burden of open heart cardiac surgery at the Children's Hospital, but beds were hard to come by, Nursing Staff were scarce and theatre time was taken up by other specialities. Despite these obstacles, the next few years saw strenuous efforts to expand the service. Eventually, however, it became obvious to all, except the more fervent supporters of the Children's Hospital's case, that a comprehensive cardiac surgery unit involving both child and adult patients in close proximity to the burgeoning cardiological empire at the RVH was not a feasible option. Nevertheless, Bingham continued to press the claims of the RBHSC, supported by his anaesthetist colleagues G.W. Black and S.H.S. Love. This enthusiasm was not shared by Stevenson and it came as no surprise when in February 1965 he intimated his intention to discontinue open heart surgery at the Children's Hospital. The reason given was that these cases required prolonged assisted artificial ventilation in the post-operative period, which was available only at the recently established Respiratory Intensive Care Unit at the RVH. (The paediatric intensive care facility was still a couple of years away.) Thus open heart surgery faded from the Children's Hospital scene, never to return.

Both Smiley and Stevenson were fortunate in benefiting from the precepts and principles of the father of thoracic/cardiac surgery in Northern Ireland, G.R.B. Purce.

The early development of open heart surgery at the Children's Hospital was greatly influenced by the figure of James Francis (Frank) Pantridge, CBE, MC, appointed consultant cardiologist in 1958. He had returned from the war, a physical wreck, but with spirit unbroken, having survived the Burma Railroad of Death, cardiac beriberi and other manifold privations. In the eyes of the public an aura of near infallibility surrounded him. A quite bizarre story had wide circulation that the reason he did no surgical operations was that the Japanese had sewn his hands together during his

HOWARD MORRIS STEVENSON, son of Howard Stevenson, surgeon at RVH and Stormont MP, served in the Royal Navy during World War II. Blessed with exceptional manual dexterity, his method of tying knots deep in the thorax remained a mystery to many an assistant. He was debonair in appearance and polite in manner, as befitted a former public school boy, yet he did not suffer fools or incompetents and was a master of the telling phrase.

GEORGE RAPHAEL BUICK (BARNEY) PURCE, consultant surgeon, 1929–50, eldest son of James Purce of Ballyclare, Co. Antrim, was a general surgeon in the widest sense and ahead of his time. He was a big man, slightly stooped, with a shining bald head and prominent eyes, peering over half-moon spectacles. He had the huge hands of a heavyweight boxer, which could perform the most delicate of surgical manoeuvres. Barney Purce had honed his skills during World War I, in the Eighth Battalion of the Royal Irish Rifles, and was honoured with a Military Cross. His extramural activities were legion – he had played hockey for Ireland, was a first-class shot with rifle or shotgun, enjoyed golf, fly-fishing and the navigation of yachts. It is little wonder that he was the hero of junior Medical Staff. The whole human body was Purce's surgical field, and he dealt expertly with every challenge, without the luxury of the advanced helpmeets which the surgeon of today takes for granted, such as controlled ventilation anaesthesia, body fluid balance and intensive care. He performed the first lobectomy for bronchiectasis in Northern Ireland, in September 1939, on a female patient at the RVH. Derek Gordon, neurosurgeon, recalls that as a student in 1947 he assisted Purce in the Children's Hospital at thoracic operations, such as the repair of patent ductus arteriosus. Barney Purce was not at home lecturing to large groups but was at his best around the bedside or over a cup of coffee in the ward kitchen. Great was the loss to surgery and, more particularly, to patients when he died on 29 June 1950, at the early age of fifty-nine.

incarceration in the Far East. Nevertheless, he made his presence felt in the operating theatre, handing out unsolicited advice to surgeons, anaesthetists and nurses alike, indicating the progress and, often, the likely outcome of their combined efforts. The situation was in some ways reminiscent of the early days of surgery when the 'Mister' barbers were instructed by the 'Doctor Physicians' to do the menial tasks of washing, cutting and sewing, for which they got little or no credit or remuneration.

Colleagues deferred to Pantridge, as it was recognized that he was expert in his understanding of the new technology, particularly the monitoring of cardiac action. His confrontational style spread beyond the confines of the operating room. There were from time to time clashes over rights to beds, allegations of changed outpatient times without consultation and the occupation of extra rooms not allocated to him. This complex character, of unpredictable behaviour and obsessional drive, was disliked by some, feared by others, but respected by all as a physician–cardiologist without peer. He was awarded a personal professorial chair in 1971 and retired in 1982, a rather solitary but still politically active figure.

After the withdrawal of open cardiac surgery from the Children's Hospital in 1965, hopes were raised again in June 1968 with the appointment of New Zealander Patrick J. Molloy as the first full-time cardiac surgeon. He was given responsibility for the development of open heart surgery at the Royal Hospitals site and was joined in 1970 by Jack Cleland. When Molloy returned to the Antipodes in 1973, he was replaced by Hugh O'Kane. Subsequently, Cleland and O'Kane, with increasing success both in quality and quantity, built upon Molloy's early work.

Bingham's concept of undertaking both adult and paediatric cardiac surgery at the Children's Hospital was always greatly cherished by the Medical Staff, although no one in the early 1960s could have envisaged the expansion of cardiac surgery to its present massive proportions. Valve replacement and coronary artery bypass had yet to appear. Nevertheless, in 1976 the notion of a major role for the RBHSC was floated again, without manifest results.

By the early 1980s, however, the Eastern Health & Social Services Board had become convinced of the need for additional facilities for paediatric cardiology and surgery. The cardiac surgeons responded by requesting extra beds, either in the RBHSC or the RVH. A.E. (Fred) Wood was appointed in June 1982, and soon produced a document outlining his proposals for paediatric cardiac surgery. He estimated that two hundred operations would be carried out each year and half of these would be on children under the age of one. A further four intensive care beds would be required and an additional six beds for pre- and post-operative patients. Not unexpectedly, it was the unanimous opinion of the RBHSC Staff that these beds should be provided in the Children's Hospital but only if operating theatre and intensive care areas were upgraded and the extra beds provided. The best-laid plans of men often go awry, for on 30 September 1983 Wood intimated that he was resigning to take up a similar appointment in Dublin. As a result of Wood's departure, it was estimated that 40 per cent of paediatric cardiac surgery would have to be performed in England. However, the hope remained that if adequate facilities were available in the RBHSC, cardiac surgeons would be keen to work there. Unfortunately, the theatre time, bed space and Nursing Staff complement still fell far short of that required.

At a Medical Staff Committee meeting in January 1984, Cleland gave the views of the cardiac surgeons regarding the possibility of bringing paediatric cardiac surgery back to the RBHSC site. He suggested three options:

1 to move paediatric cardiac surgery to the RBHSC, provided that all the necessary facilities and equipment were made available; alternatively, if this was not possible, to carry out all closed paediatric cardiac surgery at the RBHSC;

2 to continue with the present arrangement that all children would be admitted to the Children's Hospital and, after surgery at the RVH, would be transferred back to the Intensive Care Unit there;

3 to set up a small satellite paediatric cardiac unit close to the main cardiac surgical unit in the RVH.

This third option was considered ideal by the cardiac surgeons.

Throughout 1984 the matter of cardiac surgery continued to be discussed but in the end financial constraints and the absence of appropriate facilities dictated the outcome. The cardiac surgeons were not in favour of moving paediatric cardiac surgery to the Children's Hospital, a decision met with deep disappointment.

With hindsight, the idea that both adult and paediatric cardiac surgery should be undertaken at the Children's Hospital was born more of sentiment than of realism. Nevertheless, with the appointment of Dennis Gladstone, in June 1988, there was hope that he might at last do some closed cardiac surgery at the Children's Hospital, but it was not to be. A point of equilibrium had finally been reached in which both the Royal Victoria and the Royal Belfast Hospital for Sick Children have assumed complementary roles – diagnosis and post-operative care in the RBHSC and surgery in the RVH. Rivalry has given way to a fairly comfortable symbiosis.

In May 1948 a letter was received from the Council for Orthopaedic Development asking whether it would be possible for the Hospital to have a fully staffed and equipped orthopaedic department. Staff would include a 'pure' orthopaedic surgeon, orthopaedic sisters and nurses, and physiotherapists, together with ancillary service. While cordially supporting this proposal, the Medical Staff felt bound to point out that the extreme congestion of the hospital beds would delay its realization.

The Northern Ireland Council for Orthopaedic Development was established in 1940 under the chairmanship of Sir David Lindsay Keir, then vice-chancellor of Queen's University. The sum of £26,000 was donated by the Nuffield Fund for Cripples. Coincidentally, H.P. Hall had been developing his interest in orthopaedic surgery. Hall, while having a major commitment to the Belfast City Hospital, was also on the Staff of the RBHSC, so it was fitting that he should be the first to set up orthopaedic and fracture clinics there. His early difficulties are well illustrated in the correspondence he had with the Management Committee in 1952–3. He complained bitterly about lack of experienced Surgical Staff, pointing out the risk of fractures being missed or inadequately treated. However, lack of trained Nursing Staff was his greatest worry. His frustration is evident in the following extract:

> The climax was reached today. I was told that sister had gone on holiday and the only replacement was a newly arrived nurse who did not even know her way around the hospital. If the Board of Management will take the responsibility for such a nurse doing this work, with the risk of cutting off fingers or toes or applying a too tight plaster, which has cost other hospitals up to £7,000, I, for my part, am unwilling to accept responsibility. The part-time surgical registrar, or myself, can certainly apply or take off plasters, but we could be more profitably occupied in seeing cases. There simply is not time or necessity for us doing this work, which is done everywhere else by a trained nurse. As a result of this, I was compelled to bring an appreciable number of cases back to the City Hospital the same afternoon, for change of plaster, and have now transferred them to my clinic there. It is disturbing that this hospital should have to depend on the work and goodwill of another hospital whose very existence would be ignored except that I am on the Staff of both, and can transfer cases needing more specialized treatment and still keep them under my supervision.

The situation improved somewhat in 1953 with the appointment of George Baker, who had trained at the Princess Margaret Rose Hospital in Edinburgh. Hall retired in September 1956, and in 1957 B.T. (Barry) Crymble, son of P.T., was appointed consultant to the Northern Ireland Orthopaedic Service, with sessions at the RBHSC. Baker

HENRY PORTER HALL, M.Ch., consultant orthopaedic surgeon, 1920–56, deserves credit for his pioneering work at the RBHSC, carried out in the face of a reluctant administration, slow to be convinced of the importance of orthopaedic and fracture care in children. He was a family man, elegant in dress and urbane in manner, and was politely persistent in furthering the interests of his speciality.

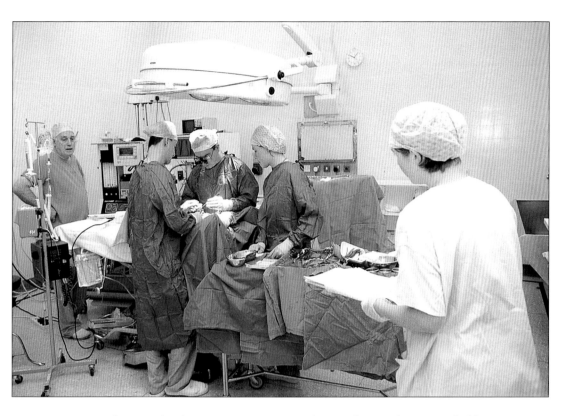

returned to Scotland in 1961, to a post in the Borders, to be succeeded by James Piggot, who had extensive orthopaedic training under Norman Capener in Exeter, Devon. He shared four outpatient clinics with Crymble.

At that time there was no operative orthopaedic surgery being performed in the RBHSC, as the NIHA had decided to concentrate children's orthopaedic beds in Musgrave Park Hospital. However, with the increase in consultant appointments at the Musgrave Park Hospital, operating time and space for paediatric orthopaedics became hard to come by. The problem was not resolved until the spring of 1965 when cardiac surgery moved from the RBHSC to the RVH. This provided a niche for orthopaedic surgery.

Trevor Taylor, who had worked in the Hospital for Sick Children, Toronto, was appointed in 1977, and this further increased the operative throughput. Following the retirement of Crymble in 1982, Piggot became the first full-time paediatric orthopaedic surgeon in Northern Ireland, working in both the RBHSC and the Ulster Hospital.

The period since the establishment of orthopaedics as a separate speciality in the Children's Hospital has seen profound changes in the nature of the work. Initially, large numbers of patients with bone and joint tuberculosis made up the bulk of the workload. The introduction of BCG inoculation and anti-tuberculosis drugs greatly diminished the number of children suffering from TB. When James Piggot retired in 1988 he had not come across a new case in the previous twenty years. Children who had suffered from poliomyelitis in the 1940s had to be admitted for long periods, averaging two years. The facilities for long-stay patients at Lissue Hospital and at the Orthopaedic Hospital, Greenisland, were invaluable for this purpose. The Salk vaccine, developed in the 1950s, led to a rapid decrease in poliomyelitis. Perthe's disease, the victims of which were often hospitalized for up to five years, became the subject of more rational treatment. Piggot thought it wrong that this non-infectious disease should require such a protracted stay in hospital while patients with tuberculosis were now going home in three to six months. A new regime whereby an initial period of rest with traction was followed by surgery, where indicated, resulted in the patient being fit to return home in about eight weeks. The advances in the treatment of tuberculosis, poliomyelitis and Perthe's disease reduced the need for beds at Lissue and Greenisland, leading to change in the function of these hospitals. (See Chapter 9.)

JAMES PIGGOT (consultant orthopaedic surgeon, 1961–88), from a well-known Londonderry family, was educated at Foyle College and QUB. He played rugby for the university and for Ulster, and in 1984 contributed a paper to the *Journal of Bone and Joint Surgery* on 'Injuries of the Cervical Spine in School Boy Rugby Football'. Piggot was a skilled and caring surgeon, with a gentle manner towards both children and parents. He had a knack of involving medical and nursing colleagues in the work of his department, making use of their developing skills and encouraging their interest in the children's problems. Sister Eileen Bell, who was his orthopaedic sister from 1980 to 1997, has expressed her sense of privilege of working under his leadership.

In spite of these developments, the orthopaedic workload did not decrease. One problem solved was replaced by another requiring a solution: for example, the treatment of patients suffering from such afflictions as cerebral palsy. The increase in cerebral palsy was due to the survival of premature babies of low birth weight, 90 per cent of whom were affected. Surgery had some value in certain children, with operations designed to release muscles at the hip, knee and heel, with the aim of improving posture and gait. Often the decision to operate was a difficult one and involved a multidisciplinary team of surgeons, physiotherapists, an occupational therapist, a schoolteacher (to give IQ assessment), a post-operative nursing sister and an orthotist. This special clinic, originally held in the RBHSC, was later transferred to the Fleming Fulton School, for the greater convenience of patients and staff.

In the 1960s three children with spina bifida were born each week in Northern Ireland. The problem was how to deal with the original surgical condition of spina bifida and myelomeningocele. In 1963 Sharrard, Zachary et al. in Sheffield reported a 'Controlled Clinical Trial of Immediate versus Delayed Closure of Spina Bifida Cystica' and concluded that closure should be regarded as a surgical emergency. They were invited to Belfast the following year to present their findings. Subsequently, it was decided to set up a similar trial in Belfast as it was felt that the Sheffield workers had not proved their case conclusively. The Belfast trial continued until 1973, when the number of patients exceeded one hundred. The conclusions drawn from the study were that early closure of the spinal defect had no effect whatsoever on the muscle power in the lower limbs and did nothing to improve the figures for morbidity or mortality. However, a fortuitous finding was that the muscle power in the lower limbs was a very helpful prognosticator of both survival and probable mobility in these children.

In 1965 a Spina Bifida Clinic was established in the RBHSC, to bring together all the various disciplines with a bearing on this distressing condition. The team included Brian Smyth, James Piggot, Ian Forsythe and Claude Field. This approach greatly assisted the parents and reduced their visits to the Hospital. On the nursing side Sister Marie Bogues (whose term of office covered some twenty-six years) and her successor Sister Eileen Bell organized plaster treatment and splintage while an orthotist was present to measure or repair splints. Sister Bell's adaptation of Permagum (a material used mainly by dentists) to the moulding of splints has gained widespread recognition throughout the UK and beyond. In 1992, in a UK-wide competition run by the Nursing Standard and BUPA, Eileen Bell MBE won the Paediatric Nursing category for her work in paediatric orthopaedics, receiving her award from HRH Princess Margaret. A stomatologist, Sister May Thomson, advised the parents about sphincter problems. Survival rate significantly increased with the use of broad spectrum antibiotic therapy to prevent meningitis and recurrent renal infection. Hydrocephalus was controlled by the use of the Holter Valve to bypass the obstruction to cerebrospinal fluid flow. The incidence of this condition has fallen from 150 to between 20 and 30 per annum, largely due to the excellent preventative work of Professor N.C. Nevin's genetic counselling service.

The treatment of osteogenesis imperfecta has also changed dramatically. Previously, children with severe degrees of the condition were bedridden and remained in hospital throughout growth. As the condition undergoes a spontaneous remission at puberty, many of them were then able to go home in wheelchairs. However, the introduction of intramedullary rodding in the 1990s meant that these severely affected children, following operation, were not only able to bear weight but were discharged from hospital to attend one of the special schools. By the time they had reached puberty they had enjoyed a more normal life and had received a full education. The early intramedullary rods had to be replaced every two to three years because of bone growth, but nowadays extensile rods are available which stretch gradually with the bone.[4]

In the 1960s the orthopaedic service was suddenly confronted by forty to fifty cases of dysmelia (limb deficiency), the children having been deformed as a result of the treatment of their mothers' morning sickness in pregnancy by the drug Thalidomide. So serious was the problem that the NIHA set up a clinic in the Ava Hospital, under Dr Muriel Frazer. On Dr Frazer's retirement in 1976 the clinic was transferred to the RBHSC, where the patients were seen jointly by James Piggot and John Colville, who advised on the treatment, particularly of the upper limbs.

The development of children's orthopaedics is a good example of the trend of specialization within a speciality. Specialist clinics appeared for such conditions as congenital hip abnormality and congenital foot problems and for leg equalization. As far back as the 1960s, Piggot established a Scoliosis Clinic, a task later handed over to John Halliday, who undertook the major surgery for this condition. With an increasing workload, Ian Adair now shares the outpatient and operating sessions.

The days are long gone when a general surgeon was expected to treat everything, including adult and children's orthopaedics and fractures. Now, even an orthopaedic surgeon cannot treat children without further specialist training. It is a credit to all concerned that this degree of progress was achieved during twenty-five years of the Troubles in Northern Ireland, which increased further the workload in trauma. All this was sustained by the equanimity and good humour of James Piggot and his colleagues. Piggot recalls coming to the Hospital at midnight on one occasion to see a young boy who had been shot in the heel. The father explained that he had been carrying the child in his arms when the shot was fired. Piggot suggested to the man that somebody did not like him but he was insistent that it was a stray ricochet bullet rather than one aimed deliberately at him. The next morning he rang Piggot asking how his son was, and was invited to come in to discuss the boy's progress. 'I can't,' he said, 'I am phoning from London!'[5]

Norman Hughes operating on a patient with a cleft palate, *c.* 1960s

James Piggot retired in 1988, to be succeeded by Kerr Graham, appointed with a full-time commitment to paediatric orthopaedics. He had trained in Great Ormond Street, London, and the Hospital for Sick Children, Toronto. The Surgical Staff was further augmented in 1992 by Harold G.H. Cowie, who had trained in the Scottish Rite Children's Hospital, Atlanta, Georgia. In 1994 Kerr Graham emigrated to the Melbourne Children's Hospital, Victoria, to assume the chair of paediatric orthopaedic surgery, leaving with what the media described as a devastating attack on the state of Northern Ireland's health provision.[6] He was quoted as saying that 'the effort to maintain district and area hospitals is simply gobbling up resources in a way that means we cannot provide the excellence in central areas that we need, i.e. in the RBHSC'. He maintained that he had experience of children being referred to his care in Belfast with equipment attached to them in terms of external fixators, or other apparatus used to stabilize fractures, that he could not afford to use. 'With this kind of maldistribution we had all the complex work and the majority of patients, yet resources were on the periphery . . . this was a nonsense.' Trevor Taylor took over the sessions vacated by Graham.

PLASTIC SURGERY

The first name that springs to mind in the context of plastic surgery in Northern Ireland is that of Norman Campbell Hughes. He came back to the North in 1946, as a surgical registrar, after a distinguished and often dangerous war service attached to Number 12 Commando Unit, operating in the Norwegian area, where his role was more that of soldier than of doctor. In order to pursue his interest in plastic surgery, he proceeded to East Grinstead, the temporary home of the so-called guinea pigs, badly burned airmen who needed prolonged plastic surgery. The director of this high-profile unit, Sir Archibald McIndoo, went on record to state that Norman Hughes was the best trainee plastic surgeon he had ever come across.

Hughes returned to Belfast on 1 June 1950, and was given the task of initiating a comprehensive plastic surgery service for Northern Ireland. At the Children's Hospital a start was made with the establishment of an outpatient clinic every Thursday morning, and operating sessions on Friday morning and afternoon, which frequently extended into the evening. The treatment of burns and scalds soon became a priority, as severe burns in children had previously often been fatal, the need to replace lost fluid not being fully appreciated. Hughes enlisted the help of Dr Joan Logan in the supervision and acute treatment of severe burns, with greatly improved results. Accurate assessment of fluid and electrolyte loss with adequate and rapid replacement was the key to success, followed by early skin grafting.

In the 1950s burns and scalds in the home were a major problem, and Hughes launched a campaign to educate parents in measures to prevent such disfiguring and frequently fatal tragedies. Parents' Associations, the Women's Institute and other interested groups throughout Northern Ireland were addressed with almost evangelical zeal. The danger of the mirror above the unprotected fire was pointed out, as was the paramount necessity of a secure fireguard at all times. One tragic case involved a family about to emigrate to Australia; the furniture had been removed, including the fireguard, and as the infant daughter, Assumpta, was trundling around in her 'walkie' pen, a wheel struck the edge of the tiled hearth, tipping the child head first into the fire. Hughes and his colleagues extended their campaign to the

NORMAN CAMPBELL HUGHES, first consultant plastic surgeon in Northern Ireland, 1950–79, was an ideal colleague. In the clinical field he was a natural surgeon. His approach to the problem of cleft lip/palate was typical: first, a measured look, then deft outline of the surgical area with pen and ink, followed by sure, unhurried exposure and impeccable repair. A skilled medical politician, he came to committee prepared to speak only if necessary. Without fuss or raised voice, his carefully reasoned argument nearly always won the day. He is remembered for his surgical expertise, administrative ability, strength in the face of physical adversity and for his sterling work in the interests of the RBHSC. In 1974 he received national recognition with his election as president of the British Association of Plastic Surgeons, and in 1979 he was awarded the OBE. On retirement he pursued his many extra-curricular activities. He delighted in his garden, his horses, and deep-sea sailing. He was a noted collector of objets d'art, fine paintings and books. Together with his wife, Rosemary (née Fullerton), also a doctor, he was a welcoming and generous host. Norman Hughes died on 1 June 1995.

clothing and furniture industry, resulting in the gradual emergence in Northern Ireland of fireproof clothes and furniture fabric.[7]

During the Vietnam War many children suffered severe burns from the extensive use of napalm, an incendiary substance used in flame-throwers and firebombs – the former being particularly lethal because of their accuracy. The Hospital was among several in the UK which received children from the war zone. They were admitted under the care of the plastic surgeons for prolonged surgery and nursing care.

In 1950 Hughes had been joined by Wilbert R. Dickie, appointed as a senior registrar, his post being upgraded to consultant status in 1954. Dickie was a quiet, unassuming man, yet with a wry sense of humour. His approach to surgery can be described in one word – meticulous. The slightest deviation in the alignment of a surgical repair resulted in the immediate removal of all the offending sutures and a restitching until his eagle eye was satisfied. This became known to the theatre staff as 'doing a Dickie', subdivided into a major or minor 'Dickie' according to the number of stitches requiring replacement! He had a special interest in the repair of hypospadias, and indeed made the repositioning of the outlet of the male urethra something of an art form. When Dickie retired, his pioneering work on hypospadias was carried on by other members of the consultant surgical staff.

An important feature of the paediatric plastic surgery service was the setting up of outpatient clinics to cover the whole of Northern Ireland, in Londonderry, Newry, Ballymena and Omagh. However, the in-patient treatment of the children seen at these outposts continued to be carried out at the Children's Hospital, thus maintaining its importance as the referral centre of excellence. In a contribution to the universality of scientific knowledge, the unit has, from time to time, hosted aspiring Australian plastic surgeons, who come to increase their expertise, an arrangement which has been mutually beneficial.

Concomitantly with the expanding service, the consultant team grew in numbers. Hughes and Dickie were joined by John Colville in 1968 and Ronald M. Slater in 1971. Colville's major interest was in the repair of the injured or congenitally deformed hand, the latter work particularly vital after the Thalidomide tragedy of the 1960s. He joined with his orthopaedic colleagues in setting up the Dysmelia Clinic at the Children's Hospital (see p. 63). The two foundation members of the plastic surgery service, Hughes and Dickie, retired in 1979 and 1981 respectively, to be succeeded by Michael Brennan and Alan Leonard. When Colville retired in July 1990, the responsibility for hand surgery fell on his successor, James Small, together with Brennan. Slater, whose training had included a period in Sweden, concentrated on the surgery of the cleft lip and palate, a burden shared with Leonard from 1979.

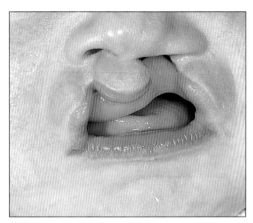

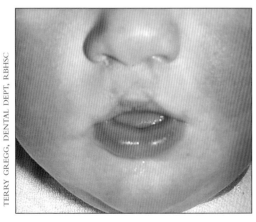

TERRY GREGG, DENTAL DEPT, RBHSC

Top: bilateral hare lip and cleft palate. The appliance (obturator) designed to help feeding before repair of the palate can be seen. *bottom*: the successful repair

Slater retired in 1989 and his successor, Geoffrey Ashall, associated himself with Leonard in the surgery of the palate. This association was short-lived as, tragically, Ashall died in March 1995, at the age of thirty-nine.

Certain changes in the care of patients with cleft lip and/or palate have occurred in recent years. More comprehensive surgery is carried out in the initial stages. Pre- and post-operatively, the patients have benefited from the establishment of a Joint Cleft Palate Clinic, staffed by the plastic surgeons, a speech therapist, audiologist and orthodontist who, consequently, are able to contribute to the patients' care at a single visit. Operating surgeons no longer depend entirely on the naked eye. Imaging glasses are worn to enlarge and illuminate the operative area. Another advance has been the development of the technique of tissue expansion where there is massive skin loss, for example in scalp wounds. A plastic bag is inserted under normal scalp which is progressively filled with fluid from a reservoir, resulting in gradual skin expansion. This facilitates the repositioning of normal scalp over the affected area. While more sophisticated techniques are being developed, the bread and butter of plastic surgery continues to mount, consisting of such operations as the repair of 'bat' ears and the removal of pigmented naevi. The reduction in open fires has resulted in a downturn in the numbers of major burns but the classic scalds from soup and tea still occupy the Surgical and Nursing Staff.

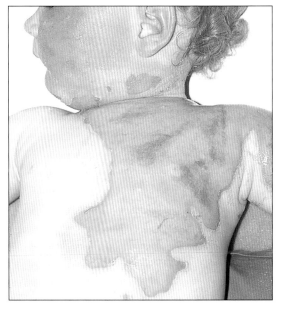

Scalds caused by hot tea emphasize the warning – 'keep out of reach of children'.

When Roy Miller was appointed consultant paediatric surgeon to the Royal Group and the Ulster Hospital in 1978, one of his tasks was to be the establishment of a burns unit for adult patients in the RVH. From the perspective of the plastic surgeons this would have been the initial phase in the realization of Norman Hughes's dream of a comprehensive plastic surgery service on the Grosvenor Road site. This hope is still deferred: only adult outpatients and paediatric plastic surgery are currently sited within the Royal Group of Hospitals; the main body of adult patients continues to reside in its 'temporary' home at the Ulster Hospital. Miller's main responsibility in the RBHSC is the care of patients with burns. Under his supervision, children with burns are cared for in the Knox Ward annexe. Nowadays, patients with severe burns are treated even more aggressively than in the past. After early initial attention to their fluid balance they are operated on within the first week for excision and restorative grafting of the affected areas. This approach results in a shorter hospitalization but, conversely, more frequent visits to the operating theatre are required, placing greater pressure on theatre staff.

NEUROSURGERY

The late Cecil Calvert, consultant neurosurgeon at the RVH, was invited to join the Staff on the same day as N.C. Hughes, in June 1950, and was offered similar facilities as those granted to the plastic surgeons. The neurosurgeons never took up this offer of a permanent home at the Children's Hospital, preferring to concentrate their elective work in Quin House, at the RVH. Nevertheless, they have rendered sterling service to the Children's Hospital, with Alan Crockard, Thomas Fannin, Ian Bailey, John Gray, Derek Gordon and the late Colin Gleadhill and A.R. Taylor all making significant contributions. It is proposed that with the provision of new operating theatres and other facilities in 1998, paediatric neurosurgery will be carried out at the RBHSC.

EYE, EAR, NOSE AND THROAT SURGERY

The surgery of the eye, ear, nose and throat (EENT) for the children of Northern Ireland commenced in 1885 with the appointment of Joseph 'Garibaldi' Nelson as oculist to the Belfast Hospital for Sick Children, a post which he held until 1910. The sobriquet 'Garibaldi' was acquired as a result of Nelson's exploits with Giuseppe Garibaldi's Reggimento Inglese. He fought in the Battle of Volturno against the Neapolitans, and for his deeds on behalf of Italy, its newly proclaimed king, Victor Emmanuel II, presented him with a Sword of Honour and two medals. Nelson was succeeded by Wyclif McCready, who in turn was followed by Fred Jefferson in 1924. Ten years later F.A. McLaughlin became clinical assistant in the EENT department of the RVH and his duties included sessions at the BHSC. On his elevation to full EENT surgeon, in February 1938, he resigned his appointment as ophthalmic surgeon to the Children's Hospital, suggesting to the Medical Staff that D.H. Craig, who had been carrying out duties in the children's Ophthalmic Department for the past four months, would be very suitable as his successor. Craig was formally welcomed to the Staff on 6 June 1938. His department was situated in that part of the outpatients' first floor now occupied by the Medical Records Department.[8]

With the introduction of the NHS in 1948 the speciality was divided into two sections, ophthalmology and otorhinolaryngology. It was left to the individual surgeon which option to choose, and it is said that McLaughlin and J.R. Wheeler (ophthalmic surgeon at the RVH) tossed a coin to decide which part of the speciality each would follow. However, for several years David Craig continued to cover all elements of eye, ear, nose and throat surgery in children. In February 1950 Craig personally saw 896 patients at his clinic, and in March a total of 957.[9] Such was the upsurge in work that by April the burden was becoming intolerable. As an interim measure he demanded that the NIHA be asked to appoint V.A.F. Martin on a temporary basis as

DAVID CRAIG (consultant ENT surgeon, 1938–74). His association with the Children's Hospital lasted thirty-six years, interrupted only by service in World War II. Small of stature, of ruddy complexion, he bore a striking resemblance to Captain Mainwaring of television's *Dad's Army* fame. An overseas postgraduate visitor actually congratulated him on his performance in that role. He had a wicked sense of humour and could be teasingly sarcastic on occasions. Much in demand as an after-dinner speaker, he made good use of a slight speech impediment to enhance the impact of his many amusing stories. Craig had a strong loyalty to the Hospital, equalled only by his enthusiastic and persistent support for the upgrading of his colleague, Noreen Simpson, over many years. He died in 1994.

ophthalmic surgeon. However, it was not until April 1956 that the Authority approved a substantive post, and Victor Martin commenced duty on 5 June of that year. The ophthalmic component of the service was further strengthened in January 1974, when S.S. Johnston joined the Staff.

The appointment of Dr Noreen Simpson in October 1950, albeit in a junior capacity, did much to alleviate Craig's burden of audiology work. The Audiology Department was situated in the Hospital basement between the laboratory and the dermatology ward. In 1966 a move was made to 185 Mulholland Terrace on the Falls Road, where conditions were primitive. The newly appointed audiology technician, W.D. Martin, tested the children in the kitchen, which housed a makeshift soundproof booth. Dr Simpson had an office/consulting room in the back bedroom and the teacher of the deaf occupied the attic. The department returned to the main Hospital basement in 1970, and the following year, with the opening of the new lecture theatre, accommodation was provided in its vicinity, with better facilities than heretofore.[10]

Noreen Simpson made a significant contribution to the welfare of the deaf children of Northern Ireland. She was instrumental in the establishment of Audiology Clinics throughout Northern Ireland: in Ballymena, Larne, Downpatrick, Omagh, Dungannon, Enniskillen and Londonderry. In addition, she organized the training of health visitors to recognize the early signs of deafness in newborn children. This selection procedure ensured that the neediest children received prior and prompt attention. To Simpson must go the credit for the introduction of evoked potential audiometry in the assessment of children who were difficult to evaluate by more conventional means. In 1971 she visited two major centres for the electrophysiological investigation of young children with hearing problems, one in Bordeaux and the other at the Nuffield Centre for Hearing and Speech, Oxford. Subsequently, she laid the groundwork for the establishment of evoked response audiometry services in Northern Ireland.

The first equipment for carrying out evoked potential audiometry arrived in 1975, the year of Noreen Simpson's premature death. Her loss to the Hospital necessitated the temporary recall of David Craig, who had retired in 1974.

Noreen Simpson's successor was R.S. (Bob) McCrea, already a consultant in the RVH. McCrea had no paediatric experience so he took a year's crash course prior to joining the Staff in September 1976. He became the driving force in the upgrading of the Audiology Department and was among the first to suggest the formation of an assessment centre for handicapped children which would involve audiology, speech therapy and so on. He had a vision of a purpose-built combined adult and children's audiology department located at the interface between the RVH and a 'new' Children's Hospital. McCrea's first aim was to develop a service for 'difficult to assess cases' and extend the use of the new evoked potential audiometry in audiological assessment. In this he collaborated with Dr R.J. McClelland, later Professor of Mental Health. Together they were instrumental in setting up the evoked response audiometry service in Northern Ireland, the evolution of which resulted directly from the work of the clinical and research team under their joint supervision. The first electrocochleography was recorded in 1977, by which the research group was able to demonstrate a clear gender difference in the evoked response – the first group ever to do so.[11]

Bob McCrea died in harness in 1983 and a Memorial Lecture was established in his honour. The first lecture, entitled 'The Rehabilitation of the Hearing Impaired', took place on 15 October 1986. In the same year Victor Martin died suddenly while on a skiing holiday in Switzerland. In 1983 David Alexander Adams joined the Staff as consultant and lecturer in the university Department of Otolaryngology.

In 1976 Michael J. Cinnamond, trained in the Hospital for Sick Children, Toronto, and later based at the Belfast City Hospital, was invited to join the Medical Staff in view of his special interest in paediatrics. His particular forte was in the area of bronchoscopy and tracheostomy, especially in trauma and infective cases such as epiglottitis, and he built upon the work of Roy Gibson and John Byrne in intensive care situations. In 1989 Cinnamond assumed the chair of otorhinolaryngology at QUB, a post he resigned in 1995. His main commitment is to the Belfast City Hospital, though he continues to advise on cases of compromised airway at the Children's Hospital.

Throughout the 1950s and the early 1960s the Medical Staff were concerned at the probable loss to the Hospital of the EENT service. In 1945, in an article in the *Ulster Medical Journal*, J.R. Wheeler had suggested that the Belfast Ophthalmic Hospital, the Benn and Ulster Hospitals and the EENT Department of the RVH should amalgamate in a purpose-built unit.[12] By 1953 this proposal was gathering support. The suggested transfer of the Children's Hospital facilities to a new EENT hospital was received by the Staff with dismay. They adopted a 'no surrender' attitude, in spite of warnings from Hughes and Bingham that there would be difficulty in maintaining such an entrenched position, in view of the likely backing for the idea from the Group as a whole. Concessions proffered by the Group Management Committee, such as a separate section of the new building to be staffed by the RBHSC Staff, were brushed aside. The Staff simply re-affirmed their original view that, far from closing, the EENT Department should be not only maintained but expanded. Nevertheless, they were forced to concede that bed accommodation had been a persistent problem. In 1957 there were eight hundred children waiting for tonsillectomy, with only eleven effective beds available. Various internal rearrangements were discussed to alleviate this situation but agreement was never reached, an impasse which brought nearer the day of dissolution.

In September 1958 Brigadier Thomas Davidson, the medical superintendent of the Royal Victoria Hospital, invited Staff to discuss children's beds in the proposed new EENT hospital, in which there was not yet special provision for children. Predictably, the Staff reiterated their position, namely that, i) the Eye and ENT units should not be removed from the Children's Hospital, and ii) a new EENT block with an adequate number of beds should be erected on the Children's Hospital site, administered by the Children's Hospital and staffed by the EENT consultants within the Royal Group, including staff members of the Benn and Ophthalmic Hospitals.

This rearguard action continued and on 7 March 1961 Dr W.A.B. Campbell submitted a memo to the Medical Staff on the subject of the new EENT hospital. They unanimously agreed that 'steps to remove the Eye, Ear, Nose and Throat department from this hospital would have a disastrous effect, both on the efficiency and on the general character of the hospital and on the proper treatment of children who were ill from any cause, not only referable to the upper respiratory tract'. It was resolved that all possible support should be given to the Hospital Committee in its resistance to this proposal. This determination was reiterated in September 1963, with the statement that 'the nursing of adults and children together was not in the best interests of our patients'.

In 1965 the Staff were forced to bow to the inevitable when the new Eye and Ear Clinic of 154 beds, facing the Falls Road, between the Outpatient Centre and Bostock House Nurses' Home, opened for the admission of patients. The formal opening was performed on 19 February by Her Royal Highness Princess Alexandra. The clinic included, on its fifth floor, thirty-four beds for the exclusive use of children, and henceforth all paediatric eye and ear, nose and throat cases were admitted directly there.

Nevertheless, the Children's Hospital was not stripped of all ear, nose and throat surgical activity. The outpatient clinics were preserved until 1974. Electrocochleography and aural venting are still carried out; difficult children and those with cardiac defects are treated; tonsil and adenoid surgery takes places; and night emergencies are handled. Much of the work consists of day surgery; if beds are required they are borrowed from Knox Ward. Four consultants are involved: David Adams, David Brooker (successor to the late Gordon Smyth), Joseph Turner and Peter Walby. All eye surgery is performed in the EENT clinic at the Royal Victoria Hospital and John Bryars and Gerald McGinnity hold paediatric clinics there. The Audiology Clinic remained in the Children's Hospital until 1993, but with the demolition of the lecture theatre and its environs, it joined its fellow specialities on level 7B (ward 30) of the EENT clinic, Royal Victoria Hospital.

DENTISTRY

Prior to 1929, there was no formal dental service at the Children's Hospital. In that year Ian Fraser, concerned at the great number of children coming to his surgical clinic with extensive dental disease, invited Joseph Cuthbert McNeill (a cousin of his wife, Eleanor) to join him as a clinical assistant. Two years later, McNeill's work was recognized with his appointment as an honorary attending dental surgeon. An operating theatre was allocated to him and he was supplied with an anaesthetist and a nurse. The parents were charged 6d for each extraction.

By 1934 there was a growing awareness of the necessity for conservation of teeth, and the Board of Management was asked to equip a room for conservative dental treatment, at a cost not exceeding £100. In the event, £85 15s 3d covered the cost of a dental chair, an engine to drive the drill and the necessary instruments. With this expansion of work, McNeill had to enlist further help, which came in the person of R.H. (Bob) Elliott, a general dental practitioner from east Belfast. Their association was unbroken for nearly forty years. Cuthbert McNeill was the quieter of the two, soft-spoken, correct in dress and manner, naturally polite, but persistent in pursuit of the interests of dentistry within the Children's Hospital. A consultant member of the Medical Staff Committee since the inception of the NHS, he pressed successfully for his colleague's upgrading from general practitioner to clinical assistant, and then to senior hospital dental officer. To his disappointment, Elliott did not make the final step to consultant status until McNeill retired in 1967. Bob Elliott was more expansive than his colleague, with a ready smile and a transparent sense of humour. Self-effacing, he sought no other privilege than that of serving his patients. His idea of an earthly heaven was a summer's day in Portaferry, by Strangford Lough. McNeill and Elliott never relinquished their general practices, yet they are recognized as having laid the foundations of the comprehensive dental care which the children of Northern Ireland now enjoy.

The NHS was hardly a year old when rumours began to circulate that a children's dental department was to be established at the Royal Victoria Hospital. Confirmation was received in the form of a letter on 1 February 1949, from the honorary secretary of the dental staff at the RVH, stating that the establishment of a children's department, in connection with the Dental School (then on the top floor of the King

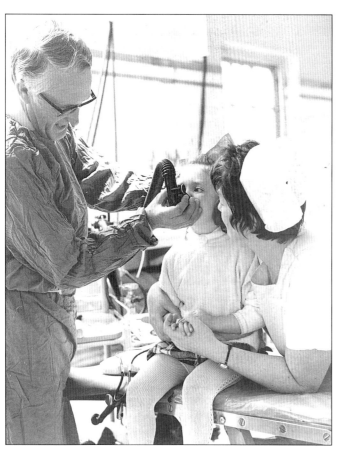

In the 1950s induction of anaesthesia for dental extractions in the Outpatient Department was by nasal mask.

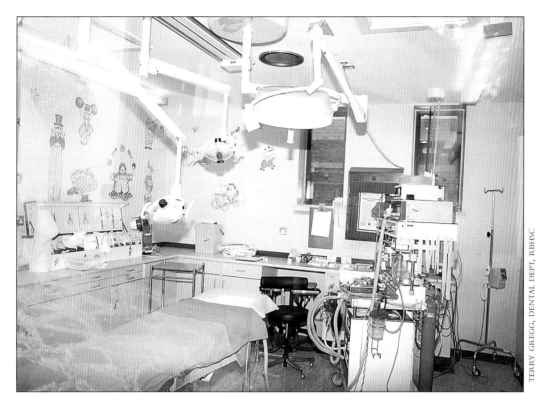

Dental operating theatre in
the new Day Care Unit, 1994

Edward Building), was under consideration and requesting that a subcommittee from the RBHSC should meet with a similar subcommittee from the
RVH. Professors Fred Allen and Harold Rodgers were appointed. Those
were the days when only physicians and surgeons were considered capable
of representing their colleagues in matters political. The idea that members
of all specialities were able and willing to conduct their own affairs was
slow in taking root.

McNeill was deeply concerned at the idea of a children's department at
the RVH in competition with his clinic at the RBHSC, and in July 1949 took
matters into his own hands by arranging a meeting with the new Professor
of Dentistry, Professor P.J. Stoy (the first full-time member of the dental
staff at the RVH). Stoy's rather stark message was that he would support the
Children's Hospital Dental Department if the training of six students was
undertaken but not otherwise. Furthermore, he pointed out the inadequa-
cies of the accommodation and the lack of a regular anaesthetic service.
Unless these difficulties were overcome, the possibility was that the RBHSC
Dental Department would collapse. Undeterred, McNeill and Elliott continued their efforts to improve the dental service at the Children's Hospital
and accommodation was found in the ENT Department on the first floor,
providing an operating theatre for extractions and another room for conservation. Growth was slow but in December 1951 an additional extraction
session was required to deal with the increasing number of children
referred from the Department of Cardiology. This was the seedbed of the
dental service for the sick and handicapped child. McNeill's oft-repeated
demand for a consultant anaesthetist with regular sessions in the Dental

Department was not met for a further two years, when S.H.S. Love was appointed on 1 February 1953.

In February 1951 the NIHA set up a subcommittee, consisting of the vice-chancellor, Lord Ashby, Professor J.H. Biggart, A.T. Boyd, M. McAuley and Professor Allen, to discuss dental and physiotherapy departmental development. This subcommittee, which did not include a dentist or a physiotherapist, recommended that the NIHA proceed at an early date with the building of dental and physiotherapy departments, with contributions being made from the private funds of the Children's Hospital and the Royal Victoria Hospital and supplemented by a grant from the Authority. The site of such a building was not specified. The following year, on 4 November 1952, Professor Stoy put forward a scheme to provide accommodation for a Department of Child Dentistry, including orthodontics. Further provision would be made to accommodate physiotherapy and speech therapy, together with lecture rooms. However, further study of the original plans revealed errors of omission and commission; too much room had been allocated to student accommodation and an X-ray facility had been omitted altogether. With hindsight, it is hardly surprising that this somewhat unrealistic plan never materialized. It was not until November 1958 that plans for the new Dental Hospital and School began to take shape, although the uncertainty as to the site was indicated by Stoy's statement that it would probably be built alongside the Institute of Clinical Science and would include a Department of Child Preventive Dentistry which, it was hoped, would be mainly a teaching and research department.

In December 1958 the chairman of the Medical Staff reported the result of a meeting of a subcommittee, comprising Professor Stoy, H.T.A. (Theo) McKeag and Phillip Adams of the RVH Dental Hospital. In view of Stoy's previous statements, its conclusions were surprising: all children's dental treatment, including orthodontics and teaching, should be centred at the RBHSC. This, it estimated, would require a floor space of some 6,600 square feet. The cost would be met partly by the university and partly by the NIHA and, possibly, by a grant from the Free Funds of the RVH and the RBHSC. McNeill felt that the magnitude of the problem had been underestimated and that 10,000 square feet would probably be required for adequate accommodation. However, the proposal was welcomed cautiously by the Medical Staff with the proviso that any new department had to be an integral part of the RBHSC. Its administration, day-to-day running and the treatment of the children should be the responsibility of the Hospital Committee through the Medical Staff Committee.

This proposal came to nothing and in 1962 the Dental School opened at the north side of the Hospital Road, next door to the university building housing microbiology. Included was a paediatric dental department with teaching, service and research functions but no provision for the type of dental work that was being carried out in the RBHSC. McNeill took the opportunity to redefine the function of the Dental Department of the Children's Hospital. Its activities could be divided into three categories:

1 casualty department where most of the treatment is extraction of carious teeth under general anaesthesia;

2 conservative treatment and some orthodontic treatment for outpatients by appointment;

3 treatment of in-patients referred from medical and surgical consultants, including Lissue Hospital. The numbers of children seen with spastic disease, haemophilia and cardiac problems were steadily increasing.

In 1957 a new clinic to deal with fractured incisor teeth was set up. In the same year W.D. (Des) Pielou, then a general dental practitioner in Newtownards, Co. Down, was invited by Ralph Smyth, dental consultant in charge of the Conservation Department in the old Dental School (RVH), to undertake sessions at the RBHSC. Coinciding with his first days in the Hospital, Norman Hughes was asked to see a grossly abnormal child in the Royal Maternity Hospital. The child had a bilateral harelip and cleft palate, making suckling almost impossible. Hughes sought help from Pielou, who devised an obturator (a bridging device) to fill the palatal gap, thus enabling the child to assimilate nourishment. This measure made the child more presentable to the mother and reduced the risk of post-operative tissue breakdown, a danger always present in an undernourished infant. Thus Des Pielou began a career which was to contribute much to the development of paediatric dentistry in Northern Ireland.

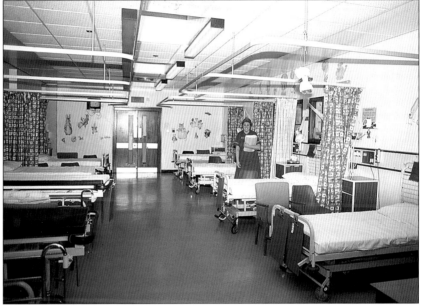

Recovery area in
Day Care Unit, 1994

Another significant step was taken when David J. Stewart was appointed lecturer in child dentistry in January 1960. He had been trained at the Eastman Dental Clinic, in London, location of the only paediatric dental department in the UK at that time. Stewart's 'hands-on' approach combined successfully with his extensive research. He studied trauma to the young dentition and became an authority on the deleterious effect of tetracycline drugs on teeth. It was largely through his efforts that tetracyclines were the subject of a hazard warning in the *British National Formulary* in 1969. Another interest was the effect of trace elements, lead in particular. The old lead piping of west Belfast came under his scrutiny, as did the lead content of the exhaust emissions from motor cars. The dental care of patients with blood dyscrasias was another sphere of his work. He was involved with

Donald Davies, then chief dental officer in Northern Ireland, in establishing a pilot study of water fluoridation. His colleagues David Kernahan and Des Pielou carried out the examination of children in two areas, Holywood and Banbridge, to obtain a base level of decay prior to the fluoridation of the Holywood water supply. The data were submitted to the Department of Health & Social Services but no further action was taken. In January 1979 Stewart was awarded a personal professorial chair in recognition of his sterling contribution to children's dentistry.

Over the years, perhaps the greatest challenge facing the department has been combating the destructive effect on the early dentition of sweetened drinks. The comfort bottle enriched with sugar has now been supplemented by the availability of a wide range of fizzy drinks, equally responsible for the high incidence of dental caries in young children. The palatal surfaces of the upper teeth are most affected and it matters little whether the drinks come in ordinary or diet form.[13]

DAVID KERNAHAN was singled out early in his career as a person with interest and ability in the field of child dentistry. Having reached the status of lecturer and consultant, he was appointed deputy to David Stewart in 1978. His main aim was to provide dental care throughout childhood into adolescence, but adolescents could not be accommodated in the mixed wards of younger children. Kernahan diverted into adult dentistry in the Department of Primary Care in the School of Dentistry (RVH).

Retiring in 1967, Cuthbert McNeill left his colleagues with this plea: 'We should be doing still more for the handicapped child.' Six months later, a memorandum on the dental care of the sick and handicapped child was presented. This document, largely the work of Stewart, Pielou and Kernahan, formed the basis of future dental practice at the RBHSC and the Department of Child Preventive Dentistry at the School of Dentistry in the RVH.

The categories of patients to be treated were comprehensive:

1 referred patients;

2 patients with behavioural problems;

3 sick children;

4 children with cleft lip/palate and other developmental abnormalities;

5 a casualty service for infants and children of pre-school age; and

6 children requiring oral surgery.

(Formerly, oral surgeons, such as R.I.H. Whitlock and John Gorman, based at the School of Dentistry, operated in the Children's Hospital on an ad hoc basis. With the development of the service, RBHSC dental surgeons I.D.F. Saunders and Terence Gregg took over the task of dealing with cases of trauma and oral pathology.)

Bob Elliott retired in 1974 and was succeeded by I.D.F. Saunders, whose knowledge of paediatric dentistry during the Final Examination so impressed his examiner, David Stewart, that he encouraged him to apply for a post at the Children's Hospital. Ian Saunders brought to the department a wide range of interests, particularly in the areas of oral surgery and the dental care of the 'sick' child. He promoted the use of computers in dental surgery and his administrative ability was acknowledged when he became the first dentist to be honorary secretary of the Medical Staff of the RBHSC. Under the new system of Directorates, set up in 1990, he was appointed director of dentistry.

Pielou retired in 1987, to be followed by Terence Gregg, well known outside dentistry as an Irish international hockey player and coach. He built upon Saunders's work in computerization, which has had widespread recognition throughout the UK. His database for audit within the speciality has been adopted by several dental centres and has attracted interest from other medical specialities.

The work of Dr Martin Kinirons, senior lecturer/consultant since the early 1980s, related to the dental status of children with cystic fibrosis, later extended to sufferers from leukaemia and heart disease. He took on the task of dealing with paediatric dental problems throughout Northern Ireland from the perspective of the epidemiologist.

Another lecturer/consultant, A.D. Valentine, appointed in 1979, assumed the chair of paediatric dentistry when David Stewart retired in 1983. His approach was more academic in nature and orientated towards the community rather than the Hospital. Since his retirement in the early 1990s there has been no professorial appointment in paediatric dentistry.

For more than sixty years the Department of Dentistry at the RBHSC has cared for the dental needs of children, first in the local district and then in the greater population of Northern Ireland as the Regional Paediatric Dental Centre. Throughout much of this period its staff have coped with inadequate resources and often poor accommodation. It was not until 1989 when the Day Care Unit opened that the department had a home of its own. Pielou, together with J.M. Bridges, then consultant haematologist, was a driving force in the conception and establishment of the unit. He first raised the matter at a Paediatric Division/Staff meeting on 6 November 1978, requesting a 'day stay unit convenient to the outpatients departments. It should consist of a small three-bed ward, an operating/treatment room and a four-couch recovery area.' This facility was used to accommodate the two specialities of dentistry and haematology/oncology, but now accommodates an increasing number of medical and surgical disciplines. Having retired two years prior to its opening, Des Pielou, like Moses, was denied the opportunity to savour the fruits of his labours in the long-promised land of the new Day Care Unit.

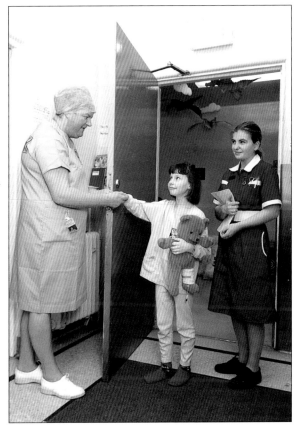

Staff nurse Frances McMahon (*left*) allays fears and builds confidence during a pre-operative visit to the theatre, *c*. 1996

PAEDIATRIC OPERATING THEATRES

The operating theatres within the Hospital deal with up to five thousand cases each year. These include elective operations as well as patients

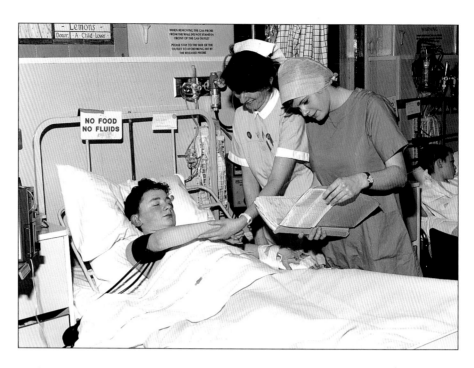

Staff nurses Ray Bloomer (*left*) and
Paula McAuley (*right*) check final
details before the patient goes to
the operating theatre, *c.* 1997

admitted through Accident & Emergency or referred from hospitals
throughout Northern Ireland.

The operating theatre nurses in 1991–2 carried out research into the perception of patients and parents regarding surgical procedures. Thirty-six
surgical patients between the ages of three and thirteen were interviewed.
Even allowing for the stage of cognitive development of the younger ones,
it was disturbing to find that half of the children did not know the reason
for their operation; of these, further questioning revealed little or no
understanding of why they were in hospital at all. Parents were largely
ignorant of the need for operative preparation, the constitution of the surgical caring team and the sequence of events within the theatre.

As a result of this research, a system of pre-operative visits to the theatre
was instituted, giving an opportunity for patients and parents to ask questions about the impending surgery and for the theatre nurse to gain information which would help staff to reassure families. Children readily
perceive and often mirror their parents' anxiety; if parental concern is alleviated, their own stress can be reduced.

This research, part of a joint operating department course, led to Sister
Jacky Devine winning the Marie Wilson Award in 1992. (Marie Wilson, a
staff nurse at the RVH, was killed by a terrorist bomb at the Cenotaph
in Enniskillen while attending a Remembrance Day service on Sunday,
8 November 1987.)

Lily Craig on duty at the
old reception desk, *c.* 1970

5

THE ACCIDENT & EMERGENCY
DEPARTMENT

UNTIL THE EARLY 1970S the arrangements for the
reception of patients in casualty were, on the surface
at least, uncomplicated. A semicircular desk situated
inside the front door was occupied by a clerk who
was responsible for taking details and giving the
patient a casualty card. The hall porter sat opposite,
alert to any untoward incident (a duty carried out
with cheerful efficiency by Harold Whitten and then John Gibson, until
the latter's retirement in 1995). The receptionist performed an unofficial
'triage' function, channelling patients to the area appropriate to their need.

The outpatient waiting area of the RBHSC from the 1930s to the 1960s was drab and dismal and often overcrowded.

Patients waiting for attention sat on wooden bench seats, all facing the same way, towards a large tropical fish tank, the only gesture towards the relief of a rather bleak institutional atmosphere. Later, some nursery rhyme murals by Rowel Friers were added, though one psychiatrist condemned these as likely to be harmful to children because such illustrations as Jack and Jill depicted accidents for which they were to blame! On certain days, teas were served by members of the Ladies' League, and two or three times a week the 'Toy Ladies' attended.

When called, patients gave their casualty cards to a nurse who assessed them and recorded the relevant details in a large ledger. They were seen and examined by the house officer in a room containing a desk for the doctor and two chairs for the walking wounded and parent. Couches with surrounding curtains were provided for the more serious cases. Patients next in line sat on a long bench with a good view of what to expect when their turn came. After the consultation, the doctor wrote his or her observations on the casualty card and the patient was directed to the appropriate area for treatment.[1]

In the 1970s a room was provided for resuscitation and minor operations and the original desk was replaced by two offices, one for casualty, the other for admissions, at a cost of some £25,000. A separate entrance to casualty helped to ease the flow of patient traffic. Among the worthy ladies who ran the desk were Lily Craig, Isobel Bell, Doreen Hamilton and Joan Lawther.

For nearly fifty years the Accident & Emergency Department has dealt with the whole range of children's medical and surgical conditions, some trivial, some serious, injuries sustained in the home, on the streets and – peculiar to Northern Ireland – as a result of terrorism or public disorder. There have been lacerations and burns, fractures and poisonings, injuries – accidental and non-accidental – caused by foreign bodies from beans to bottles pushed into every available body orifice (the more spectacular specimens were preserved in a display cabinet as a reminder and a warning), together with acute medical conditions such as asthma, croup or meningitis, requiring immediate action to save a life. This demanding work has been carried out in the face of two major handicaps: i) the shortage of both junior and senior Medical Staff, and ii) inadequate accommodation. The architectural arrangements of the 1930s were not designed to cope with the increasing patient and parental traffic of later years.

In November 1962 Elizabeth Gray was appointed departmental sister in overall charge of the Outpatient and Accident & Emergency Departments. She was struck by the bleak appearance of the waiting area. On a visit to the Department in 1964 Brigadier Thomas Davidson, the Group medical superintendent, described conditions as 'distressing and primitive. The waiting areas and side rooms were packed with patients, some waiting long periods for attention; nursing staff was taken up with clerical work or

John Gibson, the last hall porter, retired in 1995. The Hospital's head porter is now Michael O'Neill.

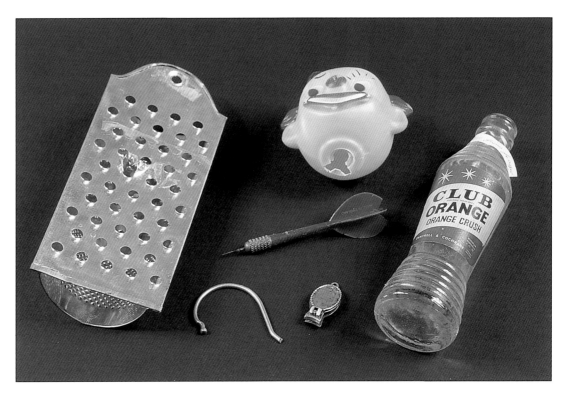

dealing with the complaints of parents.' Staff took the occasion of these strictures to press for the appointment of a medical officer with a full commitment to the Accident & Emergency Department, a demand that would go unanswered for more than twenty-five years. A counter-proposal that the casualty department be closed and all emergencies diverted to the Royal Victoria Hospital was rejected.

The wheels of progress grind extremely slowly, especially without the lubrication of an adequate money supply, so repeated requests to the Board for a consultant post were turned down and, as late as 1983, the RBHSC was the only hospital in Belfast with a major Accident & Emergency Department without a consultant in full-time charge. (B.T. Smyth had acted as a 'caretaker' consultant, to a degree dictated by other onerous duties.)

ATTENDANCES AT A & E DEPARTMENTS IN BELFAST HOSPITALS, 1982

	New	Total (including new)	Staff
Royal Victoria Hospital	54,441	78,870	2 A/E consultants
Mater Hospital	32,997	52,846	1 A/E consultant
Belfast City Hospital (1981)	28,500	51,064	2 A/E consultants
Ulster Hospital	35,235	50,760	1 A/E consultant
RBHSC	19,746	33,989	No registrar or consultant

Until 1985–6 overall medical cover was provided by one house officer, 8 a.m. to 4 p.m.; general practitioners covered the period 4 p.m.–10 p.m.

in two three-hour sessions. Throughout the night a house officer, allocated to the wards, could be called when required. By 1984 moves were afoot to replace the general practitioners with up to three full-time senior house officers but a submission along these lines elicited the reply that the Board was not in a position to fund the necessary £45,000 per annum. This rebuff was coupled with the suggestion that consultant medical cover could be improved by redeployment from elsewhere in the Hospital, an idea which Staff felt was impractical. The case was resubmitted and legal advice sought as to the implications of junior Staff working unsupervised. An official document was unearthed (CMAC 5/84) which stated that every accident and emergency department must be under direct consultant control; in units without a full-time consultant, direction must be achieved by other means.[2] The Board was unmoved and made it clear that casualty staffing was not high on the agenda. The help of the Group Medical Executive Committee was enlisted, and its chairman, Desmond Burrows, wrote to the Board supporting the Staff's case for an A & E consultant. A crisp reply was received: 'Consultant staff of the Hospital carry the ultimate clinical responsibility for patients within the casualty department and if they are not prepared to take this responsibility, the department will have to close.'[3] There was no alternative but to accept this ruling.

In June 1985 Dr James McKenna, chief administrative officer of the Board, visited the Hospital at the request of the Staff. He explained that, with the severe cutbacks in the money supply, funds were not available to create new posts, and Accident & Emergency would have to compete with thirty-three similar applications at present under consideration by the Board. He did offer a morsel of hope by saying that, as a shortage speciality, it might have an advantage over some of the other submissions. A further year elapsed and on 12 May 1986 a small committee of Staff met to discuss how to provide consultant cover in the A & E Department pending a permanent solution. It was agreed that one consultant would accept nominal responsibility for administration and another would visit the department daily for two hours, in order to review cases or deal with clinical problems that may have arisen during out-of-hours work. However, it was to be another two years before a satisfactory rota system was established.

Running in parallel with these staffing difficulties was the continuing problem of the inadequate accommodation throughout the outpatient area. Various internal structural rearrangements and the reshuffling of clinics had failed to keep pace with the increasing patient numbers.

In 1988 A & E attendances had risen to 42,309, compared with 35,000 in 1974, a 20 per cent increase.

Meanwhile approval had been gained for two senior house officer posts, restricted to a tenure of two years because of the inadequate level of supervision. This proviso galvanized Staff into further action and in early

Speciality	Number of clinic sessions held during year	New outpatients during year	Total attendances new and old outpatients during year
1980			
General medicine including genetic counselling clinic	444	2,122	6,628
Dermatology and wart clinic	193	1,244	3,238
Neurology	23	33	96
Cardiology	68	174	925
General surgery, ISU and spina bifida	240	1,028	4,220
ENT and audiology	290	1,197	4,303
Trauma and orthopaedic surgery	289	1,302	5,322
Plastic surgery and burns	108	510	2,391
Dentistry	209	850	2,712
Child guidance (psychiatrists)	250	393	1,740
Accident & Emergency	–	18,991	38,412
TOTAL	2,114	27,844	69,987
1985			
Neurology	89	116	550
Dermatology	196	1,294	3,042
Cardiology	49	182	932
Nephrology	48	107	786
General surgery	263	1,392	5,435
Plastic surgery	114	511	1,985
Cardiac surgery	19	2	205
Trauma & orthopaedic surgery	302	2,014	8,020
ENT	98	905	3,593
Dentistry	303	968	4,300
Paediatric medicine	439	1,592	6,246
Child psychiatry	436	1,024	3,742
Accident & Emergency	–	22,617	38,394
Audiology	134	770	3,010
Genetic counselling	69	227	376
Immunology	16	21	36
TOTAL	2,575	33,742	80,652

1987 a strong submission for a consultant post in A & E medicine was made yet again, with emphasis on the continuing heavy workload and the ruling of the Royal College that 'recognition for the training of SHOs is

Royal Belfast Hospital

WILFRED GREEN

conditional upon adequate arrangements for their training and supervision'.[4] These efforts bore fruit, for in the following November the consultant post reached top priority and on 1 June 1988 Dr J.F.T. Glasgow assumed administrative charge of the Accident & Emergency Department, on the basis of five sessions per week. The appointment was received by the Nursing Staff with expectation, hope and a tinge of apprehension. The following humorous contribution, by an unknown author, neatly summed up the mixed emotions.

Eilish Smith (*left*) with John Glasgow and Roberta Burton launching the Deadly Deception campaign, which highlighted the difficulty of distinguishing potentially deadly pills from sweets

THE WINDS OF CHANGE

'Did you hear the rumour – is it really true?
We're to have our own consultant very soon.'
It echoed down the corridors from Knox to ICU,
Dr Glasgow's coming – first of June!
Well, our cardiac capacity was rather overstrained
as we wondered what this vital change would bring.
We had horrific visions of an ENDLESS round of tests,
blood and urines done for EVERYTHING!
'Nurse, this simple laceration masks a so much deeper ill –
order LFTs,★ blood pictures and the lot,
and although he has a crayon up his nostril, think again.
Do I detect a strange purpuric spot?'

Whatever lies before us, of THIS we can be sure,
the wind of change is blowing in this place.
But we can work together as a TEAM in A & E

(that is ... if all the 'oldies' stick the pace!).
So we welcome you amongst us, Dr Glasgow, yes we do,
we'll introduce you to our clientele.
And we hope that all the hassle will not weaken your defence,
as you seek to make the 'Travelling' people well!

Just treat us gently, kindly, with diplomacy and tact,
and like a fine-tuned harp we will respond.
Then whether it be measles, hepatitis or the croup
the child will sense in us a special bond.
TOGETHER may we face the tonsillitis, septic toes,
appendicitis, constipation, mumps.
The marriage of true minds cannot admit impediment.
We'll stick to you like viruses – in clumps!

Now we have our own 'Big Doctor' (in importance not in height)
our status with the militants must grow.
Like gastro-enteritis, we will run so smooth and fast,
we must order more Diasolyte – I know!
So welcome, Dr Glasgow, to our happy A & E,
to the yelling and the screaming, the complaints.
Take your orb and sceptre and your kingdom as it is
and give our worn defences some new paint!

* LFTs: Liver Function Tests

The refurbished outpatient waiting area presents a brighter face, *c.* 1995

At a more serious level Glasgow was not long in presenting a comprehensive document outlining the present and future requirements of the department. Not surprisingly, his first plea was for more junior Staff and better accommodation facilities. He made a case for five full-time senior house officers and requested immediate additional patient accommodation to allow those patients suffering from conditions such as asthma to be treated on an outpatient basis. Four full-time SHOs now staff the department.

Since 1988 there have been several striking innovations. Written clinical protocols for medical and surgical disorders and trauma were established. A biannual postgraduate teaching symposium on accident and emergency paediatrics was inaugurated in 1989, with up to a hundred trainees in paediatrics, accident and emergency medicine and general practice attending each year. In 1990 clinical records were computerized and a computer link with the National Poisons Bureau of Edinburgh was set up, work supported by a £20,000 grant from the Hospital's Trust Funds. In 1992 a Paediatric Life Support Course was produced, aimed at consultants and registrars in paediatrics, anaesthetics and A & E medicine, with thirty-two candidates each year, and since 1994 an Advanced Paediatric Life Support Certificate (APLS) has been issued to successful participants. A Disaster Plan for the RBHSC was published in 1983 and regular rehearsals initiated. Co-operating in these important advances were Michael Cinnamond (ENT), Brian Craig (cardiology), Michael Shields (respiratory medicine) and Robert Taylor (anaesthetics).

The new buildings due to open in 1998 are evidence that better days lie ahead for Accident & Emergency and Outpatient Departments. The prospect of operating in an environment conducive to efficient work and congenial for Staff and patients alike must be contemplated by John Glasgow and his colleagues with joy unconfined. This department, throughout its existence, has managed to maintain a cheerful atmosphere, in spite of the perils and pressures of life on the front line.

A well-known and well-liked face, often seen in the vicinity of the A & E and Outpatient Departments, is that of John Gibson, ambulance officer. He joined the ambulance service in 1974, and two years later was given charge of an ambulance dedicated to the needs of the Children's Hospital. This service was subsequently extended to cover all special care baby units in the Belfast area. He has raised money for such worthy causes as paediatric cardiology and cystic fibrosis by running in half and full marathon races. In 1990 he received the MBE and was awarded UK Ambulance Person of the Year, the gift of the Chief Ambulance Officers' Association of Great Britain.

The story of the Accident & Emergency Department would not be complete without mention of the part played by the general practitioners. Their experience and maturity had a stabilizing influence on a department endeavouring to cope with a multitude of human problems, compounded by the pressures imposed by a troubled city. Among the GPs who gave sterling service during difficult days were Doctors Norah (Nonie) Bryars, John Farrell, Meuros Fitch, Mary Fetherstone, Joseph Hendron (MP for West Belfast 1992–7), John Irvine, Robert Irvine and William Jackson.

John Gibson MBE, ambulance officer, 1974–

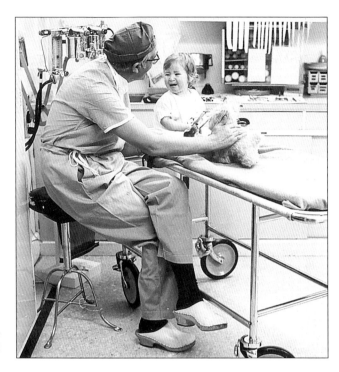

Confidence building in the anaesthetic room, *c.* 1972

6

ANAESTHESIA AND INTENSIVE CARE

Until 1878 there is no record of the anaesthetic agents which were used in children's surgery or who administered them. In 1880 it was laid down that one of the duties of the junior attending physician and the junior attending surgeon was to give anaesthetics. By the turn of the century a significant increase in the number of operations led the Staff to ask the Board of Management for permission to appoint an honorary anaesthetist. The appointments would be for six months in the first instance but renewable at the discretion of the Staff; the person appointed would attend the Hospital twice weekly. In 1901 Isaac Davidson became the Hospital's first anaesthetist.[1] The unsuccessful applicant was Miss Sproull, one of the first women to apply for a hospital appointment in Northern Ireland. Dr Davidson's administrations were obviously giving satisfaction for in 1903 he was told he could remain as long as he liked. However, his inferior status to that of his medical and

surgical colleagues was emphasized in a minute stating that he should receive a share of the students' fees as if 'a member of Staff'. Davidson resigned in 1904 and was succeeded by Dr J. McIlwaine. Henceforth, the anaesthetic service to the Hospital was a rather haphazard affair, largely undertaken for short periods by general practitioners or physicians and surgeons on their way to higher things.

In February 1910 the Staff received a letter from the Management Committee suggesting the appointment of another anaesthetist to assist McIlwaine's successor, Dr Burnside. The honorary secretary was asked to point out that there was great difficulty in finding persons to do this work and, furthermore, that in most hospitals it had been found necessary to pay the anaesthetist! At a Staff meeting on 20 August the accounts were presented and a cheque to the value of £1 8s 0d was made out to each member of the Staff and to Dr Burnside. It was noted in the minutes that 'as there were now three anaesthetists, it was decided not to allow them a share of the fees as had been done when Dr Burnside did all that work'.

In 1911 P.T. Crymble moved that 'instruction in the administration of anaesthetics be given to students of this Hospital and that certificates should be granted to those students who satisfy the requirements of the anaesthetists'. Nothing further came of this proposal.

In 1923 the Hospital made two decisions which contributed further to the advancement of anaesthesia. The appointment of a second house surgeon was requested, whose duties would include the administration of anaesthetics. At the same time, Annie Knox, the matron,

Some members of the Medical Staff, *c.* 1930; standing *left to right*: Doctors G. Hamilton, J.W. Browne, J. Boyd, Ian Fraser, A.J.P. Alexander and J.W. Nicholl; *sitting*: Matron Annie Knox and Dr Rowland Hill

GEORGE HAMILTON, anaesthetist , *c.* 1930–52, was an ordained minister of the Church of Ireland. A respected GP, he was factory doctor at John Mackie's Engineering Works on the Springfield Road, Belfast, and served in the same capacity at the Great Northern Railway. He was a classical and biblical scholar and rejoiced in elucidating for students the origins of medical terms. When an operation was situated in the male groin area, he would ask if any of them knew the meaning of the term epididymis. Invariably meeting a negative response, he would go on: 'Did you never read in the Bible of Thomas Didymus, doubting Thomas? Didymus is a twin and epi means above, so that the epididymis is the structure which sits above the twin, one on each side.' George Hamilton was one of those family doctors with an interest in anaesthesia who bridged the gap between the so-called 'rag and bottle' era and the new science. While readily acknowledging the limitations of his training, he nevertheless helped in the advancement of the speciality of anaesthesia with good humour and old-world charm. He died on 7 December 1967, aged eighty.

WILFRED MAURICE BROWN, consultant anaesthetist
RVH/RBHSC, 1946–76, was a dominant and
progressive figure in the development of
cardiothoracic anaesthesia at the RVH. His association
with the Chidren's Hospital was on an ad hoc basis
but such was his contribution that he was invited to
join the Medical Staff in 1957. Maurice Brown was a
highly intelligent man who, when the occasion
demanded, could make his presence felt. Junior
colleagues held him in awe. On better acquaintance
he was a firm friend and a gracious host. Above all,
he was a brave man who carried the scars of war
with dignity. As a wartime surgeon in the Royal
Navy he was on a convoy in the Mediterranean
when his ship was dive-bombed by German Stuka
aircraft. Brown was in his cabin when the ship was
hit, the door jammed and as he watched the water
rise, his first thought was for his revolver. A second
hit caused the cabin door to fly open and as the
vessel sank under him he went over the side into a
cauldron of burning oil. He was taken to a mortuary
but an alert attendant noticed flickering signs of life
and Brown was taken from among the dead. Later he
was transferred to the Westminster Hospital, London,
where, in intervals between multiple plastic surgical
operations, he was taught the science and art of
anaesthesia by another famous Ulsterman, Sir Ivan
Magill. In 1985 Brown was awarded a Pask
Certificate of Honour by the Association of
Anaesthetists of Great Britain and Ireland. He retired
in 1976 and died on 14 September 1993.

was relieved of the responsibility of giving anaesthetics as this activity was interfering with her other duties. Staff were at pains to emphasize that the appointment of a house surgeon/anaesthetist was in no way a reflection on Knox's abilities.

In 1928 John Boyd was appointed extern house surgeon to the Hospital. He must have demonstrated his potential as an anaesthetist for in the Hospital Report a year later he is designated honorary anaesthetist – apparently appointed by his colleagues without any reference to management. One of his first requests was for permission to order a nitrous oxide and oxygen anaesthetic apparatus: another small step towards the age of scientific anaesthesia and its acceptance as a legitimate speciality.

During the war little further progress was made and many anaesthetics continued to be given by inexperienced and untrained Staff. The task of anaesthetizing a patient was often given to the most junior member of Staff in the operating room who, at that moment, appeared to have nothing better to do. Experience was gained the hard way and sometimes rather jocular instructions were given to new colleagues: 'You see one, you do one and you teach one.'

In September 1945 the Board of Management was asked to consider the creation of the post of honorary visiting anaesthetist on the condition that the person appointed should be exclusively engaged in the practice of anaesthesia. This stipulation was in itself an acknowledgement of how far the speciality had advanced. The candidature of John Boyd was unanimously approved, and he gave up his general practice on the Ormeau Road, Belfast, to devote his time to the practice of anaesthesia of both children and adults. George Hamilton, who had worked with Boyd in the Queen Street Hospital, became clinical assistant in anaesthesia.

At the outset of the NHS the only specialist qualification available to the aspiring anaesthetist was the diploma in anaesthetics of the Royal Colleges of Physicians and Surgeons of England and of similar bodies in Ireland. Unlike the rest of the UK, in Northern Ireland this qualification was not recognized as meriting consultant status. Anaesthetists were relegated to the inferior grade of senior hospital medical officer. Fortunately, a way to consultant status was made possible through the acquisition of a higher degree in medicine in addition to the diploma. As a result, in the first years of the NHS, Northern Ireland produced the UK's largest crop of anaesthetists with MD degrees. In 1948 a Faculty of Anaesthetists was established in the Royal

College of Surgeons of England; John Boyd was a foundation fellow. This body became responsible for the setting of educational standards, with the fellowship of the Faculty by examination becoming the new requirement for consultant recognition. The Faculty of Anaesthetists of the Royal College of Surgeons in Ireland was set up in 1960. The Faculty of the Royal College of Surgeons of England became an independent College of Anaesthetists in 1988, and the Royal College of Anaesthetists in 1992.

George Hamilton retired in September 1952 and there was some irritation that a successor was not immediately sought to meet increasing demands on the anaesthetic service. Hamilton had indicated his willingness to continue his work at the Hospital until a replacement was appointed but instead he was directed to undertake sessions in hospitals in districts outside Belfast.

With John Bingham's decision in 1950 to specialize in thoracic surgery, the need for an anaesthetist in this area became urgent. Wilfred Maurice Brown, the first of a new breed of anaesthetists trained in the complexities of anaesthesia for surgery within the open chest, made a valuable contribution to the initiation of such work at the Children's Hospital, but eventually his commitments to adult anaesthesia became paramount.

The appointment of Samuel Harold Swan Love in February 1953 coincided with a major expansion in the paediatric surgical service. Anaesthesia was required for surgery in the newborn baby, in the repair of cleft lips and palates in infants and for the care of patients with severe burns. Cardiac and pulmonary surgery was developing, with more complex surgical and anaesthetic procedures being introduced. A less sophisticated but no less demanding area was anaesthesia for dental outpatients, where Harold Love by precept and practice sought to set better standards of safe patient care. In 1960 he was joined by Gerald Wilson Black, a happy association which was to last for a quarter of a century.

Gerald Black not only made a major contribution to the development of clinical practice but introduced a new dimension to the anaesthetist's perspectives through clinical investigation of new potent anaesthetic agents administered by inhalation, which had been appearing on the pharmaceutical menu since 1956. In 1958, as a research fellow at the prestigious Department of Anaesthesiology of the University of Pennsylvania, he carried out important work on the effects of Halothane

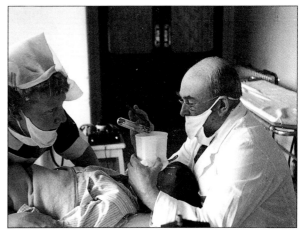
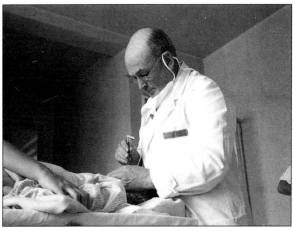
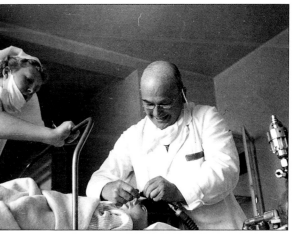

John Boyd demonstrating his unique technique of blind intubation of the trachea (windpipe) under ethyl chloride: *top*: ethyl chloride applied to an open mask; *centre*: breathing tube passed blindly through the nose into the trachea; *bottom*: tube connected to an anaesthetic apparatus

on the heart and the peripheral circulation.

On 18 April 1966 an event occurred which was to have far-reaching significance. Gail Platt, a newborn baby, was admitted with the signs and symptoms of diaphragmatic hernia, under the care of John Bingham, who operated to correct the condition that same day. Post-operatively, the baby's breathing became very rapid and she grew obviously distressed. Chemical analysis of the blood revealed gross respiratory insufficiency. At 5 a.m. on 21 April Dr Gerald Black took the decision to ventilate the lungs mechanically by means of a respirator. Curare was used to settle the little patient in synchronization with the machine. (A substance derived from a wood vine, *Strychnos toxifera*, curare was used as an arrow poison by certain South American Indians. The first useful synthetic form was developed by Daniel Bovet after World War II and used as a muscle relaxant in anaesthesia.) This regime was continued with intermittent periods of spontaneous breathing until 27 April, when the tube in the windpipe was removed and the baby allowed to breathe entirely on her own. She was discharged one month later. Gail Platt was the first patient to have prolonged respiratory ventilation following major surgery in the Children's Hospital.

JOHN BOYD, consultant anaesthetist, retired in 1968 after forty years' service to the Hospital. He was raised in east Belfast and paid his own way through the Royal Belfast Academical Institution and Queen's University Medical School by dint of hard work and business enterprise. It is said that he augmented his schoolboy's pocket money by such methods as selling the well-known Ulster soda bread. Small of stature and of somewhat cherubic appearance, he was always immaculately dressed with a rose in his lapel. To crown his sartorial elegance, he wore a large trilby hat which was often the only part of him visible above the steering wheel of his massive black Lanchester limousine. In the operating theatre he wore white cotton gloves to protect his skin from contact dermatitis caused by some of the local anaesthetic ointments then in use. He is remembered for his pioneering work with Avertin, a pre-anaesthetic agent given rectally, and for his technique of the blind intubation of the windpipe under the inhalation agent ethyl chloride, at which his skill was unparalleled. In retirement John Boyd continued to pursue his other interest: he was a dedicated Bible student and was at his happiest when teaching Holy Writ to a group of young men or to a mixed audience in a small gospel hall in Crossgar, Co. Down. He died in November 1981. Boyd's place in history is assured in that with courage and foresight he gave up a lucrative general practice to join a speciality still in its formative years, a step which without doubt contributed to the emerging art and science of anaesthesia.

Engström ventilator, 1966

What followed was largely due to the foresight and initiative of Gerald Black, supported by Harold Love and Brian Smyth. On 3 May 1966 Black drew the attention of the Staff to the deficiency of facilities in the Hospital for the post-operative care of newborn infants. He emphasized the need for a special unit for these cases with incubator facilities and safeguards against infection, provided with oxygen, suction and power points. Above all, he stressed the urgent requirement that such patients should have a nurse in sole attendance. His colleagues responded with alacrity. Sketch plans for a separate intensive care unit were drawn up and Gerald Black, Ian Forsythe, Harold Love, Brian Smyth and the matron, Molly Hudson, were dispatched to Liverpool and Birmingham to see newly established units. Their subsequent report was received with enthusiasm and ensured that intensive care facilities would have top priority. The *raison d'être* of the intensive care unit was outlined as follows:

The seriously ill patient would receive constant attention from a small number of specially trained nursing staff. Medical Staff skill in resuscitation would provide for more continuous attention than if patients were distributed throughout the Hospital. Duplication of resuscitation and monitoring equipment would be minimised. Children suffering from many different surgical and medical life-threatening complaints would be admitted to such a unit and dealt with more efficiently because of the centralisation of

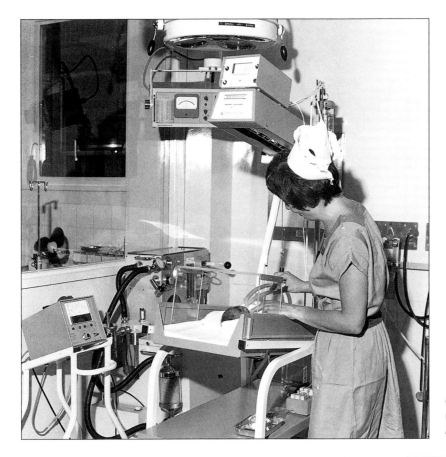

Carol Crawford, one of the first nurses trained in paediatric intensive care, *c.* 1968

both staff and equipment. In addition, the presence of an intensive care unit would raise the overall standard of nursing care.

In September 1967 a temporary Intensive Care Unit was opened on the ground floor of the Clark Clinic and the administration was placed in the hands of a subcommittee consisting of a physician, a surgeon and an anaesthetist, with the anaesthetist responsible for the day-to-day running of the unit. The medical or surgical treatment of the child continued to be in the charge of the consultant who looked after the patient prior to admission to the unit and patients were returned to the general ward when it was considered that the special amenities of intensive care were no longer required. In January 1970 a report was issued by the intensive care subcommittee detailing the work of the unit during the previous two years: 145 children had been admitted, 70 per cent of whom were under three months of age; 48 per cent required mechanical ventilation of the lungs; the operation of tracheostomy to assist in breathing was performed on 26 per cent of the patients. The chairman praised Gerald Black and Harold Love for their work in establishing the unit and also paid tribute to the work of the Nursing Staff, junior Medical Staff, the laboratory and the X-ray and Physiotherapy Departments. This was an early example of comprehensive, multidisciplinary patient care. In 1970 a new five-bed unit was opened adjacent to the operating theatres.

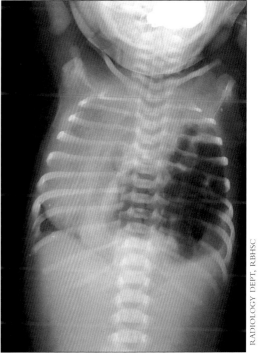

X-ray of congenital diaphragmatic hernia, a surgical and intensive care emergency. The intestine can be seen in the left chest.

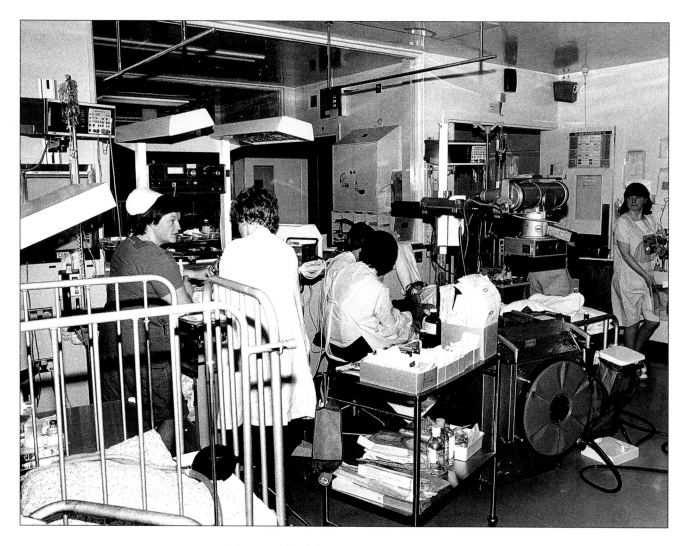

The Intensive Care Unit in the 1980s

The growth of this new area of anaesthetic practice was enhanced by the appointment, in 1970, of Samuel Robinson Keilty. He was the first consultant on the Staff formerly trained in paediatric anaesthesia and intensive care, having acquired his experience in two transatlantic centres, the Hospital for Sick Children, Toronto, and the Children's Memorial Hospital in Chicago. In 1975 Sam Keilty initiated the introduction of total parenteral nutrition (TPN) with the help of Suzanne Rosbotham and her staff in the Pharmacy Department of the Royal Victoria Hospital. This is a method of intravenous feeding, used whenever patients are unable to take food by mouth. The demand for parenteral nutrition increased throughout all departments of the Hospital, and in 1976 Dr Eleanor Magill was appointed as a research fellow and thereafter as an associate specialist. Subsequently, a TPN team was formed, in which Dr Magill was joined by a surgeon and an anaesthetist, probably the first such team in the United Kingdom. All patients in the Hospital who required TPN came under its care.

The technique of parenteral nutrition posed two problems. Firstly, infection consequent on the prolonged use of an intravenous catheter was

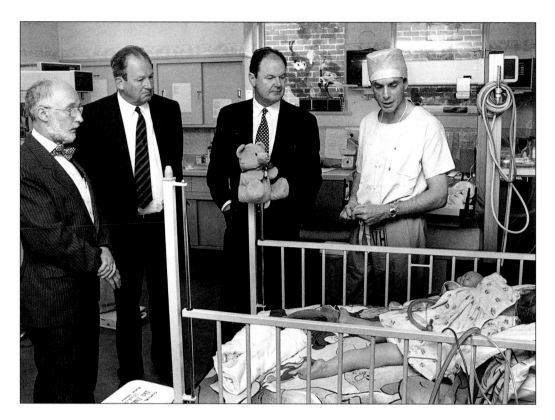

a serious and sometimes life-threatening complication, but due to the commitment and enthusiasm of the Nursing Staff, the Hospital gained an enviable record of a very low incidence of this. Secondly, in the 1970s TPN was an elaborate process involving three different solutions (protein, dextrose with electrolytes, and fat) administered by a pump in sequential order. In 1983 a total nutritional mixture was introduced, premixed in the pharmacy under strictly controlled conditions and administered from one bag, the so-called paediatric 'big bag'. This innovation was another first for the Hospital in the UK.

In 1988 the first patient was sent home to Omagh, Co. Tyrone, on parenteral nutrition. The patient was a baby of eight months with short bowel syndrome and the second youngest patient in the UK to benefit from TPN at home (Birmingham Children's Hospital had the first). Jason is now a thriving boy leading a normal active life without special nutritional support and his case is an example of the modern policy of integrating hospital and community paediatric practice.

On reflection, it is strange that the metabolic demands of children in the immediate post-operative period were disregarded until the early 1970s. It would seem self-evident that a patient receiving no nourishment, apart from that provided by clear fluids and lacking in essential nutritional ingredients, must be at risk from starvation. It was in this group of patients that TPN was first used. Now it extends to a wider spectrum of patients, including premature babies, children with intestinal malabsorption and those suffering from cancer or severe burns.

Peter Michael Crean became interested in anaesthetics as a career when

Visitors to the Intensive Care Unit, 1996; *left to right*: Connor Mulholland (consultant cardiologist), Paul McWilliams (chairman of Royal Hospitals Trust), Malcolm Moss MP, and Peter Crean (consultant anaesthetist)

HAROLD LOVE, consultant paediatric anaesthetist, 1953–84, was arguably the first anaesthetist in Ireland with a major commitment to paediatric anaesthesia. He gave devoted and unstinting service to the RBHSC for forty years, playing an important role not only in the development of anaesthesia there but in the reputation which the Hospital was to gain as the leading centre for the care of children in Northern Ireland. He was a foundation fellow of the Faculty of Anaesthetists of the RCSI, and was appointed dean in 1976. Over the years he gained a national reputation and in 1980 was elected president of the Association of Paediatric Anaesthetists of Great Britain and Ireland, being made an honorary member in 1988. He was also a founder member of the European Academy of Anaesthesia. Harold Love had a natural aptitude for administration and his skilled chairmanship of the Hospital Medical Staff, Anaesthetic Division and Group Medical Executive Committee was recognized throughout the Royal Group of Hospitals and culminated in his appointment as Group medical administrator in 1984. In this capacity he had to deal with many contentious issues, including several outbreaks of industrial action. In 1991 he became honorary archivist to the RBHSC. Endowed with a quick turn of phrase and a subtle sense of humour, Love is an accomplished raconteur and after-dinner speaker. He is a committed Christian, and as a trustee of *Medical Missionary News* was concerned with the supply of drugs and medical and surgical equipment to impoverished countries. In retirement he has been able to devote time to his grandchildren and to more rural pursuits on the golf links of the Royal County Down or assisting his wife, Nora, in their beautiful garden in Ballynahinch. A highly respected 'father' figure, we were indeed fortunate to have him as a senior colleague; his personality contributed greatly to the close personal and professional relationship we enjoyed over many years.

THIS NOTE WAS CONTRIBUTED BY G.W. BLACK AND S.R. KIELTY

a houseman in the Belfast City Hospital. On night duty junior Medical Staff had to deal with a variety of problems and he was impressed by how his anaesthetic colleagues could be relied upon to deal effectively with emergency situations. In 1980 Dr Al Conn of Toronto visited Belfast, and an introduction led to Crean treading the now well-beaten path to the Hospital for Sick Children, where he held fellowships in the Departments of Anaesthesia, Neonatal Intensive Care and Paediatric Intensive Care between 1982 and 1984. He was then appointed consultant anaesthetist to the RBHSC. Also in 1984 Harold Love retired from clinical practice.

Another appointment of the 1980s was that of Therese Marion (Tess) Gallagher, who joined the Staff in August 1988. She had previously held a senior registrar appointment at the Hospital and, by holding an RBHSC fellowship, had worked in research with Gerald Black. After the customary eighteen months in Toronto, she came back first as a locum and then gaining a substantive appointment. Having made a significant contribution to both paediatric anaesthesia and research, Dr Gallagher decided on a career break. She resigned and spent three months in the Melbourne Children's Hospital. On her return to Ireland her desire for a general change was met by her appointment to the Royal Surrey Hospital in Guildford.

PAIN CONTROL

In the 1980s Peter Crean and Victor Boston reviewed the management of post-operative pain control, the mainstay of which since time immemorial had been the intermittent injection of a narcotic, a method liable to produce an uneven pattern of pain relief. This research led to the technique of morphine infusion into a peripheral vein. At first the Nursing Staff expressed fears as to the side effects of morphine, such as nausea or depression of breathing, but this initial reluctance soon gave place to enthusiasm. Such was the success of the method that an acute pain team, consisting of a consultant anaesthetist and a pain control nurse, was established in the Hospital in January 1993.

The RBHSC has the only paediatric pain control nurse in Northern Ireland. Her role is to co-ordinate the acute pain service, a team effort which includes Medical Staff, ward nurses, clinical psychologists and pharmacists. She assesses, evaluates and documents individual care for each child and establishes sensitive communications with parents and families. With the introduction of new methods of pain relief, the role of the acute pain nurse extends to teaching and support of Nursing and Medical Staff. The first pain control nurse was Denise Floyd, followed by Pat Coulter, who is currently in post.

Canadian-born, and Toronto-trained Robert Henry (Bob) Taylor joined the consultant staff in February 1991. His appointment brought a new expertise which resulted in the introduction of a patient-controlled analgesic system. PCA, as it is called, has become increasingly popular with the children. It gives the patient control over post-operative pain relief and allows for a greater variability in the perception of pain. The system is safe and effective for children as young as five years of age. For those who are too young to receive PCA, and who have had major abdominal or thoracic surgery, epidural analgesia is a satisfactory method provided strict guidelines and protocols are followed. All patients throughout the Hospital receiving these methods of pain control are visited daily by the pain control team.

During the 1990s the Department of Anaesthetics has been under severe strain to provide a comprehensive service in the operating theatres and the Intensive Care Unit. It is not possible to attribute these problems to any one factor. The work of the anaesthetist has increased in volume and complexity, a trend not matched by comparable increase in resources. The Calman Report of 1993, with its recommendation for a reduction in the hours of junior doctors and mandatory rest periods, has profoundly affected a service which relied heavily on the participation of trainees. In recent years there has been a greater public expectation of success. Children with complex disorders and handicaps are being subjected to palliative procedures not hitherto contemplated, and those whose continuing treatment was once regarded as a futile exercise are now undergoing corrective surgery. The philosophy of care has changed from the idea that enough is enough to the feeling that nothing is impossible and that no child should die. It is within these difficult confines that the anaesthesia and intensive care service continues to operate.

In addition to caring for surgical cases and the victims of injury or acute respiratory disease, the Hospital's Intensive Care Unit has dealt with diseases which, from time to time, have been the subject of public concern. One such is the so-called Reye's syndrome. This potentially lethal disease with a mortality of 40 per cent was first described by Douglas Reye in 1963, in Australia. Symptoms include a high fever, vomiting and

GERALD WILSON BLACK, consultant paediatric anaesthetist, 1960–90, continued to pursue his interest in volatile anaesthetics throughout his Hospital career, and significant clinical investigations on other drugs such as methoxiflurane, ethrane and isoflurane soon followed. His numerous publications and presentations in this field of research established him internationally as a leading authority. Junior Staff who worked with him testified to his meticulous, almost obsessive preparation of his subject matter and illustrative slides. In addition to his research interests, he quickly recognized the need for more intensive nursing and medical care of seriously ill children. With the support of his colleagues, Harold Love and Brian Smyth, he established paediatric intensive care in Northern Ireland. Gerald Black was chairman of the Hospital Medical Staff and of the Paediatric and Anaesthetic Divisions. In a wider sphere he was a respected dean of the Faculty of Anaesthetists of the RCSI and president of the Association of Paediatric Anaesthetists of Great Britain and Ireland, becoming an honorary member of the latter in 1995. He retired from the Hospital in 1990. On a personal note, Gerry Black was a delightful colleague, co-operative and generous, totally dedicated to his work and his Hospital. He was a private man, yet gregarious, and possessed of a sense of humour all his own. Many a tense moment in the operating theatre was transformed by an amusing comment from the head of the table, delivered with perfect timing.

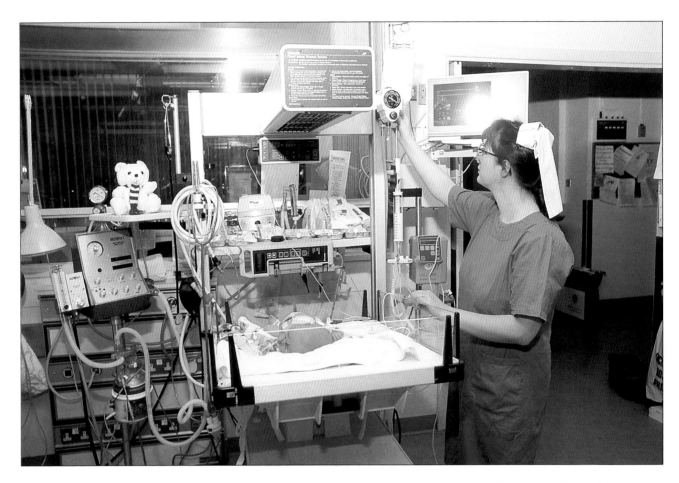

Paediatric intensive care combines high technology skills with the personal touch

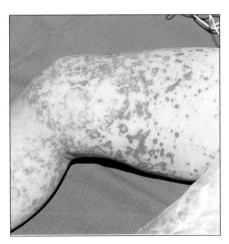

The typical rash of meningococcal septicaemia – unlike other rashes, it does not disappear when pressure is applied to the skin by, for example, a glass tumbler

mental disorientation, liver function is damaged and there is swelling of the brain. If untreated, it leads to gross brain damage or to death. The first case in Northern Ireland was diagnosed in the RBHSC in 1967, and between 1979 and 1986 fifty-six children were treated, with emphasis on measures designed to relieve the pressure of the swollen brain. The survival rate was 73 per cent, twice the national average. In 1986 the National Committee on the Safety of Medicines issued its famous 'Dear Doctor' letter advising GPs that aspirin or other salicylates should not be given to children suffering from viral infections, such as influenza or chickenpox, except on the advice of a physician. As a result of this simple instruction, the disease has declined dramatically.[2]

Meningococcal sepsis is a devastating disease occurring in previously well infants and children. It is often heralded by fever, lethargy, headache, vomiting, diarrhoea and a purple rash; neck stiffness or aversion to light may be present. It presents a massive disciplinary challenge to epidemiologists, clinicians and, crucially, the accident and emergency doctor. Surgeons may be called up to amputate parts of digits which have become gangrenous, as a result of severe impairment of circulation in the limbs. Between 1989 and 1995 forty-nine infants and children were admitted to the ICU suffering from meningococcal sepsis. Of these, nine died (18 per cent mortality) and two survivors required amputation.[3]

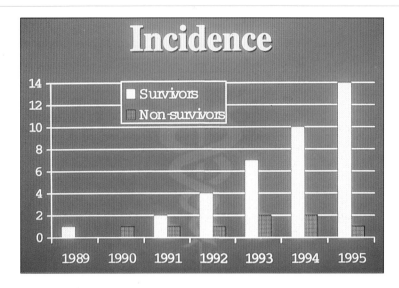

In the RBHSC Intensive Care Unit, between 1989 and 1995, mortality from meningococcal sepsis had significantly decreased.

In 1996 mortality from meningococcal sepsis had decreased in children with a similar severity of illness from previous years. This encouraging trend has resulted from media publicity, heightened parent awareness, early diagnosis and aggressive intensive treatment.

The Department of Anaesthetics and Intensive Care will soon relocate to the new buildings. Its work will not diminish – indeed, the reverse is likely, with the imminent arrival in the RBHSC of elective paediatric neurosurgery. New clinical challenges will be met and overcome. It is to be hoped that resources to support the task will not be found wanting.

7

THE NURSES

The nursing service at both Queen Street and the Falls Road is forever linked with the name of Annie P. Knox MBE. She was appointed matron of the Belfast Hospital for Sick Children in 1912. According to H.G. Calwell, she was twenty-six years of age and her commencing salary was £60 per annum.[1] This is at variance with the rules governing the age of appointment of a matron, which stated that 'the matron shall be a fully trained nurse over 30 years of age at the date of her appointment, unmarried or a widow without encumbrance'. She spent thirty-six years at the Hospital, twenty years in Queen Street and sixteen on the Falls Road, and resigned in 1948 before the introduction of the NHS, having led the nursing service through the difficulties and trauma of two World Wars. It was entirely appropriate that in her terminal days she was cared for there. In her memory, an anonymous

Matron Annie Knox and Wallace Harland, Hospital secretary, with nurses and resident Medical Staff, *c.* 1930s

Miss Annie Knox, matron, 1912–48

donor contributed £100 to establish a memorial prize for the best senior nurse, and a ward in the Hospital bears her name.

Kathleen Robb OBE was a student nurse at the Belfast Hospital for Sick Children from 1941 to 1945. She remembers days of frantic activity. Student nurses were assigned a wide range of tasks, some pleasant, some less so, and not all directly concerned with nursing patients. The philosophy was that cleanliness was next to godliness: a nurse who cleaned well was judged to be a good nurse. The cleaning tasks were not confined to floors and fixtures; head lice was rampant in the patient population and the hospital laundry would take only a small proportion of the soiled nappies (the disposables were still to appear). The regime was authoritarian and no student nurse would have dared to question the actions of the ward sister, not to speak of the matron. Miss Knox's somewhat forbidding presence was never far away. She appeared in rounds of the Hospital, at 6.30 a.m., 11.00 p.m. and indeterminate times in between. She was even known to visit the wards unannounced at such an unearthly hour as 3.00 a.m. Ladylike behaviour was expected and adherence to the permitted off-duty hours was rigidly enforced. The matron's sitting room was situated opposite the stairs to the nurses' quarters, from which sentinel post she could detect any unauthorized or irregular comings and goings. She presided at all the main meals, when a strict protocol was observed – the most junior nurses being served last, having had the chore of slicing the bread for their seniors. If a nurse fell sick and had had the foresight to take out insurance cover, the money paid in settlement had to be passed on to the Hospital, with the explanation that she was well looked after in the sick bay. From the nurse's point of view, this arrangement was far from satisfactory, as the insurance payment was usually more than that in the pay packet, a not inconsiderable loss to a student nurse earning £12 per annum.

There was no formal School of Nursing; day-to-day tuition was given by the ward sisters and lectures were delivered in medicine and surgery by Muriel Frazer and J.S. Loughridge. The highlight of the year was the annual nurses' ball. Wallace Harland, the Hospital secretary and a well-known rugby referee, rounded up some of his young playing friends to partner the nurses for the evening. The dancing was followed by supper in the kitchen but even on this occasion the guard of authority did not drop, the ever-present Miss Knox ensuring that the farewells at the end of the evening were restricted to eye contact only.

The first chinks in the authoritarian armour began to appear when a visit to the Hospital by Mona Grey in the mid-1940s led to the establishment of a branch of the Student Nurses' Association. (Mona Grey OBE was the first officer of the Student Nurses' Association in Northern Ireland, later

chief nursing officer, DHSS, Northern Ireland.) For the first time, a student nurse could go to the hierarchy with requests or complaints, emboldened by the newfound power of numbers.[2]

In 1948 M.H. (Molly) Hudson, assistant matron at the Royal Edinburgh Hospital for Sick Children, was appointed matron at the Royal Belfast Hospital for Sick Children. She controlled a Nursing Staff of twenty-five. Hudson made nurse recruitment her first priority and introduced ward assistants for other essential duties. With the aim of encouraging nurses to remain in the profession following marriage, she was instrumental in setting up a crèche in a separate building on the Hospital Road. It was controlled and staffed from the Children's Hospital with Louise McKeown, a nursing sister, as supervisor. The crèche moved to Iveagh Special Care School on Broadway when the present large boilerhouse was erected on its original site. In the 1980s it moved yet again to its current position on the car park road at the rear of the Geriatric Units. It is now run by a Parents' Committee, with all users contributing to the cost. There is space for around thirty-six children (nine babies, with the remainder made up of toddlers and pre-school children). Barbara McNeill is the present supervisor.

In 1954 Molly Hudson prepared a memorandum setting out the requirements of Nursing Staff for a hospital of 182 beds. Instead of the necessary 145, there were only 132 nurses in post. This figure was reduced by four

Group of nurses, *c.* 1941; Kathleen Robb OBE, later appointed matron at the RVH, is the nurse seated second from the left.

nurses who were seconded to the Northern Ireland Fever Hospital, and the preliminary school of twelve nurses could not be included in the establishment. The memorandum was published against the background of a demand from the Group Management Committee that the nursing establishment should be lowered to 120, a reduction that the matron and her medical colleagues deemed unacceptable.

In December 1971 Molly Hudson attended her first meeting as the Nursing Staff representative on the Division of Paediatrics/Medical Staff, an event which formalized the already good relationship existing between senior Medical and Nursing Staff.

The reorganization of the National Health Service in 1973, and the recommendations contained in the Salmon Report of 1966, had a dramatic effect on the structure and management of the nursing service at the Children's Hospital. Molly Hudson's new title of 'Senior Nursing Officer Grade 1' involved much more than a change of name. Catering, domestic and portering services were removed from her control and she no longer had responsibility for the teaching staff of the School of Nursing, who henceforth were employed and funded by the Northern Ireland Council for Nurses & Midwives. This reduced status was reflected in the level of salary, determined as it was by the number of beds under one's control, rather than by the complexities and responsibilities of the job. The assistant matrons were replaced by nursing officers, a change designed to strengthen the middle management by appointing people with special expertise and knowledge of the disciplines to which they were assigned. Logical and reasonable as this may have appeared to the planners, the new structure was received by the Nursing and Medical Staff with resignation rather than enthusiasm. Medical Staff were most vocal in expressing their deep concern at the replacement of 'matron' – a word denoting care and compassion – with 'senior nursing officer' – a title more redolent of the desk than of the bedside. In their view, the matron, a caring figure who controlled her staff, knew her patients and carried ultimate responsibility, had been removed from the scene at the stroke of a pen. Stripped of her original status, Hudson, with other colleagues similarly affected, became answerable to a higher authority, in this case, the district administrative nursing officer (Kathleen Robb, a former student of the Hospital).

Molly Hudson retired in 1975. Before the appointment

MOLLY HUDSON (matron, 1948–75). A Lancashire lass, she is remembered with affection by her many friends and colleagues. Often described as one of Ulster nursing's great characters, she was tireless in her efforts to promote the RBHSC and paediatric nursing. She did not suffer fools or incompetents gladly but administered the necessary punishment to miscreants without rancour. Fiercely loyal to the Hospital, she steered her staff through the worst days of the Troubles unruffled by the added pressures of those times. Her ready wit was seen in her remark to a senior army officer who was remonstrating with her about the dangerous practice of moving infants between the Children's Hospital and the RVH at night: surveying his large armoured vehicle, she said with a straight face, 'All right, you can take the next one in your tank.' Off duty, Molly Hudson was socially adept and could present as a prima donna hostess, when young and old enjoyed – and sometimes suffered from – her generous contribution to the conviviality. She was awarded the MBE in 1960 and OBE in 1973. On her retirement it was her intention to buy a house in the English Lake District, but in the end she could not drag herself away from Northern Ireland. Her last years were spent in a cottage in the grounds of Lady Somerset's garden on Belfast's Malone Road, where she was attended by her faithful companion, Maureen Houston. Having long been plagued by asthma and bronchitis, Molly Hudson died in 1984.

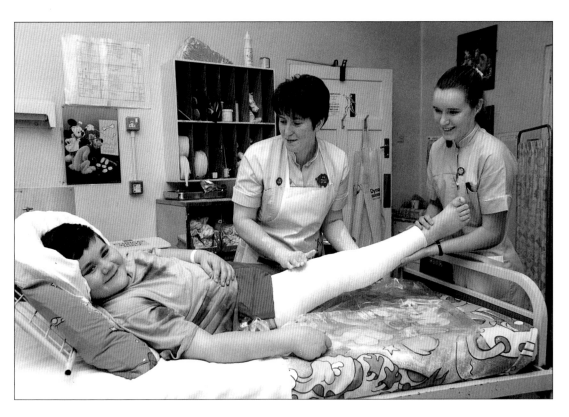

Rita McAuley (*left*) and Lyn Leech (*right*), orthopaedic nurses with a satisfied customer, *c.* 1995

of her successor, the control of the Nursing Staff fell to nursing officer S.R. Yuille, who faced a staff situation which remained difficult. Recent legislation extending annual leave and statutory holidays had imposed further stress on the delivery of the service, already under strain from a high level of sickness.

In the streets outside the Hospital, unrest and uncertainty continued, an atmosphere not conducive to nurse recruitment. The number of student nurses in training was very low. Normally, twelve to fourteen candidates would have been expected to take the Final Examination but in that academic year (1975–6) there was none, a deficit which was largely responsible for the lengthening waiting list for surgery. Junior nurses were being placed in positions of responsibility for which they had not been adequately trained. Energetic representations made to schools, various career exhibitions and advertisements in the newspapers received only minimal response.

In the autumn of 1975 Rose Isabel (Rosabel) McKay, matron at the Sir Thomas and Lady Edith Dixon Hospital, Larne, was appointed senior nursing officer 1, having formerly worked at the Hospital as theatre sister and assistant matron. During her short term of office she gave the Hospital faithful and valuable service. When she took early retirement in January 1978, Elizabeth Gray, sister in charge of the Outpatient and Accident & Emergency Departments, was asked to fill the post in an acting capacity. Eight months later she was appointed senior nursing officer 1, and held the position until her retirement in March 1990.

Elizabeth Gray's term of office coincided with significant increases in the

Elizabeth Gray, senior nursing
officer (matron), 1978–90

demands on the nursing service against a background of decreasing financial resources. She inherited responsibility for a nursing budget of approximately £2,500,000 per annum but it became more and more difficult to live within the boundaries of that resource. The extent of the problem was outlined in a letter she wrote to the Medical Staff in March 1983:

> It is important to draw to your attention that I have been notified by Miss E.N.I. Lamb, Chief Administrative Nursing Officer (EHSSB) that our [RBHSC nursing] budget is overspent by approximately £150,000 and that no additional funds will be available in 1983/84. In order to level the budget expenditure, I am therefore obliged to reduce the number of nursing staff in the hospital. This reduction will fall particularly upon trained staff, of staff nurse grade, which will have to be reduced by 25%, i.e. 20 full-time staff nurses. In effect this will mean the reduction of 2/3 staff nurses on each ward or unit. This will inevitably have serious implications for patient care. Whilst I would hope to continue to give the highest standard of nursing care at all times, you will appreciate that this will only be possible to a smaller number of patients. I consider it my duty to apprise you of these strictures, of the effect which they will have upon your work and to enlist your help in doing our utmost to avoid this situation. My hope is that with a concerted approach to the Area Board for the additional necessary finance, some way of avoiding this catastrophe can be found.

The Medical Staff responded by stating that under no circumstances would they agree to this swingeing reduction in the Nursing Staff.

Another shot in the battle came in a letter from the chief administrative nursing officer of the Board to the district administrative nursing officer, pointing out that in respect of the Royal Belfast Hospital for Sick Children, there was a total of 2.02 Nursing Staff in post in excess of the required establishment: 'It will be recognised that funds have not yet been made available for the employment of staff additional to the required nursing establishment and I need to know, as a matter of urgency, the solution which you propose to overcome this problem, as of now.' The 1981 Telford Report on staffing levels in nursing had identified the required establishment at the Children's Hospital as 306 nurses of all grades, whereas the total staff actually in post was 308.02. The demand by the Board to get rid of 2.02 nurses demonstrates the weight of pressure to which the nursing budget was subjected.

In view of the complexities of her post, Elizabeth Gray's medical colleagues felt strongly that her grading as senior nursing officer 1 was inconsistent with her responsibilities. The RBHSC was the principal children's hospital in Northern Ireland, providing most of the regional services, and an important teaching centre for undergraduate and postgraduate medical training. In the Staff's view, the head of the nursing service should have been regraded as a divisional nursing officer, a recommendation which was never fulfilled. This period of battle between insatiable demand and limited resources was a foretaste of difficult days yet to come, involving yearly demands for efficiency savings. It is a tribute to Gray and her colleagues that in such straitened circumstances the Nursing Staff continued to deliver a service of the highest standard.

Elizabeth Gray served the Hospital well for twenty-eight years. Working in the Outpatient and A & E Departments, she withstood the worst of the riotous 1970s, finding time to introduce a comprehensive appointments system for new and return patients. As senior nursing officer she weathered the storm of pressure to operate within a reduced budget, maintaining standards of nursing care in a situation where, in the new world of 'business' medicine, sentiment had little place. In the hurly-burly of hospital life she radiated an air of dignity and urbanity. In retirement, she has journeyed to Africa at her own expense to bring succour to leprosy sufferers.

PAEDIATRIC NURSE TRAINING

The first nurse tutor, Anne McGuinness, was appointed in 1949, and in the 1950s an area of the new Bostock House was set aside to accommodate the Children's Hospital School of Nursing. The last tutor based in the Bostock House School was Margaret Taylor, who was appointed in 1971 and retired in 1989. A popular and respected figure, she led the training course with quiet efficiency. She died suddenly in 1995 and the large attendance at her memorial service demonstrated the high regard in which she was held by her pupils and colleagues. In 1997 a lecture in her memory was instituted by the Eastern Area College of Nursing (Northside) and funded by a donation from the Taylor family. The lecture, entitled 'Nursing – The Future', was delivered on 23 May by Mary Uprichard OBE, president of the United Kingdom Central Council for Nurses, Midwives & Health Visitors.

Margaret Taylor, senior paediatric nurse tutor, 1971–89

Historically, a student could enter a three-year training course for the Register of Sick Children's Nurses in Northern Ireland, so it was with some dismay that the Medical Staff received a report from Rosabel McKay in 1977 that the Northern Ireland Council for Nurses & Midwives had decided to abolish direct entry to paediatric nursing, as of September 1978. Furthermore, the three-year General Training Course for the SRN Certificate would include only four weeks in paediatrics. McKay believed that these changes would have serious implications for the Children's Hospital, an opinion with which her medical colleagues concurred.

The deadline for the new arrangement passed with the announcement that the last intake for entry to the three-year paediatric training course would be August 1979. Following that date, nurses would be able to obtain paediatric training only through a post-registration training course of fourteen months.

There was a tense period in September 1980, when Elizabeth Gray reported the suspension of the arrangement whereby nurses finishing their training for the RSCN were automatically accepted at the RVH for general training. Nurses who had applied for SRN training at the RVH, at least one

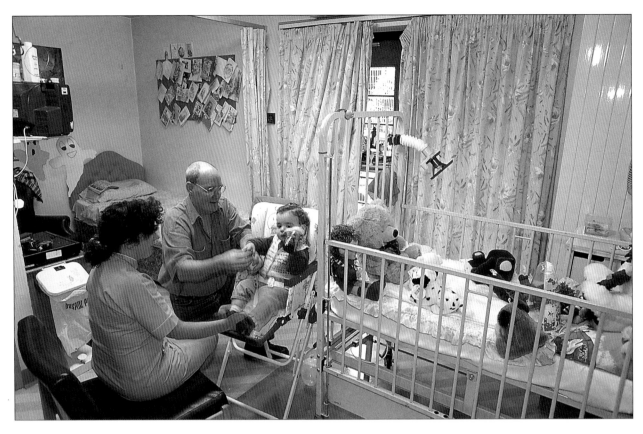

Co-operation between nurse
and parent is essential in the care
of the sick child.

year previously, had received letters to say that, due to 'difficulties', they
would not be taken in November of 1980 or in April of 1981. The impli-
cation was that they should try elsewhere. Feelings ran high at this abroga-
tion, by the Belfast Northern School of Nursing, of what was perceived as
a moral obligation to the nurses, and the suggestion was made that, in re-
taliation, the Hospital should refuse to take the RVH nurses for their four
weeks' paediatric training. Happily, such drastic action became unnecessary
as the ban on the RBHSC nurses was lifted some two months later.

In March 1981 the emotional temperature was lowered further when
word came that the Northern Ireland Council for Nurses & Midwives had
recommended to the Group Education Committee that the three-year
direct entry course to the RSCN should continue after 1 August 1981 and
that no new deadline should be set to cease recruitment. The last entry to
the course was delayed until August 1991.

All these difficulties and distresses must be seen against the background
of the progression of nurse training as a whole. Prior to 1970, there were
many small individual nurse training schools, of which the RBHSC was one.
Nurse education was led by the nursing service, the demands of which
took precedence over formal education. When the Northern Ireland
Council for Nurses & Midwives was given the responsibility of employing
and managing teaching staff, primacy was given to education. Group
Nursing Schools were created. The school at the Children's Hospital amal-
gamated with those at the RVH and the Mater Hospital, becoming the

Belfast Northern Group School of Nursing.

On the heels of these local changes came the development of certain European Community directives. At first these related only to nurses undertaking general training and specified the nature of the training and the types of experience required. It was in this context that the controversial suggestion of four weeks' paediatric training within the general course was introduced. Another problem arising from the European directives was that a nurse qualifying only in paediatrics, under the three-year direct entry system, had no standing as a specialist in paediatric nursing outside the British Isles. On the Continent, what was called generic training was a prerequisite of specialization. This progression culminated in October 1990 with the adoption of a new nursing training programme, Project 2000. The overall length of the programme was 160 weeks (80 weeks spent in common foundation training and 80 weeks in a branch programme), following which a student could decide to study in any other area of the profession, such as psychiatric nursing, community nursing or paediatrics.

Northern Ireland has led the way with the adoption of a modular system of assessment in the determination of an individual nurse's educational progress. Project 2000 meant that at last education had primacy over service. Henceforth, 99 per cent of the student nurses in training were made supernumerary to the ward staff. Furthermore, the concept of initial general training followed by various components, such as paediatrics, was consolidated, and student nurses' salaries were replaced by government-granted bursaries. Each course required approval by one or other of the two universities in Northern Ireland, and an end of training certificate was replaced by a Higher Education University Diploma. From September 1997 the School of Nursing at QUB became the leading provider of nursing education in Northern Ireland. The school is one of four in the College of Medicine and Health Sciences at Queen's, and offers nursing and midwifery diploma courses, with opportunity for students to proceed to a B.Sc. (Hons) in Health Sciences.

Mention must be made of the significant contribution made by State Enrolled Nurses over many years. This grade arose out of the original auxiliary grade, in an effort to meet a service need. Their training was of two years' duration and was orientated towards the acquisition of practical bedside skills. When the State Enrolled Nurses were phased out, individuals with the SEN qualification were offered so-called conversion training. Some chose distance learning, similar to that offered by the Open University.[3]

Over the past decades the permanent nursing posts have been filled by people from diverse backgrounds of upbringing, religion and political orientation. Some went about their duties with efficient unobtrusiveness; some mothered their junior staff, others terrified them; some welcomed those birds of passage, the medical students, others merely tolerated them. All, in their own way, contributed greatly to the varied colours of the life of the Hospital. It is tempting to single out such characters as Molly Rice, Annie McKenna, Kate Stevenson, Sheila Hammond, Gretta White, Christabel Hall (daughter of H.P. Hall) or Staff Nurse Scott for special mention, but that would be unfair to others no less worthy. Theirs was the era of the individual who directed nursing affairs within the ward and operating theatre untrammelled by directives or political correctness, answerable only to matron. Today's nursing sister or charge nurse is a manager with control of a budget, acutely aware that the 'business' has to pay its way. In addition, she or he must master the ever-changing complexities of medical technology, which some would allege places yet another barrier between patient and nurse, thus removing the personal touch of yesteryear. The 'Philosophy of Nursing' prominently displayed throughout the Hospital seeks to refute such strictures. It expresses in the official language of the day the high aims and ideals of current nursing practice.

PHILOSOPHY OF NURSING

The Royal Belfast Hospital for Sick Children will offer a holistic, child orientated, individualised and knowledge-based quality of care to children and their families.

Nursing practice will conform to the UKCC code of professional practice and will combine theoretical and practical skills in partnership with the child and his family to help each individual achieve optimum health and well-being. Nursing will be receptive and positive about changing practice, and will set standards, at an agreed level of performance, developing their own audit to evaluate, monitor and identify areas which need to be addressed and improved. Nursing, with other disciplines, will adopt ownership and responsibility for quality both individually and collectively and be fully committed to the individuality of planned care. Every child and his relatives will be treated with respect, dignity and a sensitive awareness of their needs, irrespective of race, religion or status.

More poetically, the moving words of Eddie Mulholland, a friend of the Hospital, touch what is still the heart of nursing – skill with compassion.

LOVING CARE

I have seen the beauty of the stars,
the sweetness of the spring flowers.
I have seen the highness of the Rocky Mountains,
the spraying of the Tivoli fountains.
I have witnessed the power of the Atlantic breakers
and the freshness of tulips in acres.
I have watched the lark soar high in the sky
and blackbirds sing their lullaby.
I have watched the bees as they search for honey
and little children play with their bunnies.

But nothing else so impresses my mind
as dedication of the human kind.
Your nursing work, so professional and rare,
shows experience and love beyond compare.
Those hands that treat little children with care
show hearts of gold and tenderness there.

Dedicated to Sister Eileen Bell and Staff Nurse Rita McAuley of the Royal Belfast Hospital for Sick Children, whose work for the young is priceless.

8

CHILD GUIDANCE
CHILD PSYCHIATRY

THE MENTAL WELFARE OF the young has always been a matter of deep public concern – a concern which was not diminished by the preoccupations of wartime. The Hospital Management Committee took the initiative in appointing a Child Guidance Subcommittee which met for the first time in the State Buildings, Arthur Street, on 25 May 1942. J.H. Craig occupied the chair and the attending members were Mrs F. Acheson, Mrs Gray, Dr Muriel Frazer, Dr F.M.B. Allen and J.M. McAuley. It was agreed that immediate steps should be taken to form a Child Guidance Council for Northern Ireland. To this end, a public meeting was summoned on 3 July, at which Dr Doris Odlum, a member of the Child Guidance Council for Great Britain, was invited to speak. Subsequently, six representatives were appointed to a new Child Guidance Committee, with Mrs Acheson elected as chairperson. F.M.B. Allen became the honorary director of the new Child Guidance Clinic and the Duchess of Abercorn accepted the invitation to be president of the newly formed Child Guidance Council for Northern Ireland.

Allen had previously gained the approval of the Medical Staff for the following ideas on how a child guidance service should be organised.

1 The Child Guidance Council for Northern Ireland should be formed of representatives of the Board of the Children's Hospital, the National Society for the Prevention of Cruelty to Children, the Belfast Council for Social Welfare, the juvenile courts, the Belfast Education Authority and other interested parties.

2 The Honorary Medical Staff of the clinic should be members of the Medical Staff of the Belfast Hospital for Sick Children.

3 The clinic would receive its direction from the Board of Management of the hospital and the Board should always retain a controlling influence on the Committee, and the Staff of the Clinic should consist of a whole-time psychiatrist, a medical psychologist and a whole-time psychiatric socialist worker [sic]. Furthermore, it was suggested that it might be possible to get a trained almoner and to persuade Miss Molly Hayward, who had previously lived and worked in Northern Ireland, to return to take charge of speech therapy.[1]

In fact, Molly Hayward did return in January 1944, to work at the Hospital for Nervous Diseases (Claremont Street) and at the Child Guidance Clinic on a sessional basis, at one guinea per session. However, she resigned in September 1945.

There are confusing reports as to the amounts and origins of the financial donations made to get the clinic started. A special meeting of the Medical Staff was held on 21 April 1942 to consider a letter from Professor W.W.D. (later Sir William) Thompson, Professor of Medicine at QUB, which contained an offer of £2,000 from an anonymous donor to establish a Child Guidance Clinic in connection with the Belfast Hospital for Sick Children. It was proposed by Allen, seconded by Dr Muriel Frazer and passed unanimously that the Board be advised to establish a Child Guidance Clinic and to accept the £2,000 towards this purpose. H.G. Calwell identifies the origin of the gift more specifically. The president of the Hospital, Lord O'Neill, was informed that Her Majesty Queen Elizabeth had allotted the sum of £2,000 from the Bundles for Britain Fund (a relief organization in the United States) for the special purpose of establishing a Child Guidance Clinic in Northern Ireland, and had entrusted this task to the Belfast Hospital for Sick Children.[2]

Dr Muriel Frazer's recollection is different:

A group in Canada wishing to show solidarity with the UK collected £1,500 and sent the money to Queen Elizabeth to be used for the benefit of children. It was decided to give it to Northern Ireland and Professor W.W.D. Thompson was asked to advise how it should be used. He asked me whether I had any ideas and I suggested the establishment of a Child Guidance Clinic, since I had seen something of the good work being done in England.

It may well be that the anonymous donor was indeed Bundles for Britain, whose gift was graciously directed to the BHSC by the Queen.

In August R.W. Harland, the Hospital secretary superintendent, wrote to Dr Odlum reporting that the financial position had been materially strengthened by the receipt of an anonymous donation of £1,000 towards the new clinic. His letter also underlined the difficulties of getting suitable staff to enable the clinic to make a start.[3] Doris Odlum, who apparently had ready access to the royal ear, replied that she had reported this situation to the Queen, whose response was a comment on Anglo-Irish relationships: 'An Irish or Scottish doctor or social worker would be desirable as they would understand the national temperament better.' Her Majesty's continuing interest in the clinic was demonstrated by a further gift of £30, which had its origin in the Sir A. Mackenzie Elementary School, Vancouver, and by a visit to the Hospital in the same year, 1942, by Her Royal Highness the Princess Royal – the first royal visit in its history.

It was recognized from the outset that to make the new unit viable, a consultant psychiatrist, as head of department, was essential. However, the search for such an individual proved fruitless and, as a compromise, it was decided to begin by appointing an educational psychologist and a psychiatric social worker, at annual salaries of £400–£450 and £275–£350 respectively. There were five applicants for the post of educational psychologist; one applicant was ruled out on the grounds that he was essentially a teacher and two others were excluded because they were of foreign birth. The person appointed, May Holt, withdrew her application and readvertisement of the post failed to produce further applicants. In the end, the original fifth applicant, Christina Mary Hadley of Burkhurst Hill, Essex, was appointed as a psychiatric social worker in May 1943.

Such was the somewhat tentative beginning of the first Child Guidance Clinic in Ireland. Its appearance was regarded with suspicion and outside bodies such as the NSPCC and the Poor Law Guardians declined to refer patients. The continuing absence of a psychiatric input was a handicap to progress and therefore, late in 1944, another attempt was made to acquire the services of a full-time psychiatrist. The Forces' Medical Services were informed and advertisements were placed in the *British Medical Journal* and the *Lancet*, as well as the *Scotsman* newspaper (shades of the Queen's observation on suitable staff nationality). Interview of the five applicants resulted in the appointment of Dr Louise Eichoff of Edinburgh. Such was the anxiety of the Committee to secure her services that, after the interviews, R.W. Harland was dispatched post-haste to the Belgravia Hotel on the Lisburn Road to inform Dr Eichoff of her success; her salary was set at £750. Dr Eichoff's tenure of office was not a totally happy one – she had some brushes with the management and difficulties with departmental relationships – and it was not a complete surprise when, in November 1946, she retired to East Anglia for health reasons, having stayed less than eighteen months.

Throughout the period from 1942 to 1945, the psychiatric side of the clinic's work had been kept alive by the participation on a sessional basis of psychiatrists from diverse locations. Among these were Majors Roberts and Malloy, who had wartime postings in Ulster. Dr M.K. Mellett, a psychiatrist from Portrane Hospital, Donabate, Co. Dublin, lent a hand throughout 1944, but his participation was curtailed by a severe illness which resulted in his untimely death in June 1945. Local doctors D.B.M. Lothian, superintendent of the Downshire Hospital, and D. Gardiner of Purdysburn Mental Hospital gave willingly of their services, so helping to keep the ship not only afloat but moving forward. It was felt that a further advertisement for a full-time psychiatrist would be a useless exercise and a locally based solution was sought.

The answer was found in the person of Dr M. Evelyn Lothian, wife of Dr D.B.M. Lothian, who stepped into the breach on a sessional basis. She commenced work in December 1946, with the status of clinical assistant. Dr Lothian turned out to be an excellent colleague with enormous funds of common sense as well as an intimate knowledge of childhood behaviour. In spite of other demanding duties, she increased her input into child psychiatry and as early as March 1947 was carrying out fifteen sessions each month. Her expertise and wise counsel were to prove invaluable, not only in the care of children but in the transition of child guidance into the wider and deeper sphere of child psychiatry. However, she was not invited to join the Medical Staff Committee until November 1954. The Staff were galvanized into this action by the appearance in the local press of an advertisement for a full-time psychiatrist for the Child Guidance Clinic, of which they had no prior knowledge. In the event, the applicants interviewed for this post were unsatisfactory, and Dr Lothian was requested to increase her sessions in an effort to reduce the waiting list of some 580 patients. Evelyn Lothian's contribution is all the more praiseworthy in view of her already heavy commitment at the Downshire Hospital and the travelling difficulties imposed by the continuing restriction on petrol supplies in the immediate post-war period.

Nevertheless, progress was made. Bulletins issued by the Northern Ireland Child Guidance Council in 1945 and 1947 outlined the early achievements of the Belfast Child Guidance Clinic.

Although situated within the precincts of the Belfast Hospital for Sick Children at 180 Falls Road, the clinic was a separate entity, as was pointed out in a notice published in 1945: 'Subscribers to the Belfast Hospital for Sick Children are reminded that the *Child Guidance Clinic* is not part of the ordinary hospital services. Arrangements for treatment and payments should be made with the Hospital Almoner or the Clinic Secretary.'

There were changes with the coming of the National Health Service. At the end of November 1948 the clinic became a department of the Hospital and an immediate request for a full-time psychiatrist was forwarded to the new Northern Ireland Hospitals Authority. The matter was deemed urgent in view of the fact that, despite the efforts of Dr Lothian and her colleagues, the clinic had a waiting list of 243 and rising.

On 5 January 1949 the Child Guidance Committee disbanded and the future control of the clinic became a matter of discussion and even contention at various administrative levels. The Medical Staff were told by R.M. Grieves of the Ministry of Health that child guidance work in the future might be the responsibility of the Mental Health Committee of the new Hospitals Authority. The Child Guidance Committee, in May 1948, had sent the following representation to the Executive Committee of the Northern Ireland Child Guidance Council: 'Without prejudice to the establishment of future Child Guidance Clinics in Northern Ireland, it is our opinion that this clinic should be regarded as a function of the Belfast Hospital for Sick Children, as we believe that Child Guidance Clinics should not be disassociated from paediatrics.' This resolution was approved by the Child Guidance Council and a copy forwarded to the NIHA. Seven years later, in April 1955, a government White Paper appeared recommending that child guidance should be placed under the control of Education Committees. The Medical Staff held to their strong view that major Child Guidance Clinics should continue to be closely associated with the hospital service. Dr Muriel Frazer put this viewpoint in trenchant terms in a letter to Dr W.A.B. Campbell in 1956:

> No one can now doubt that this work is an essential part of the Health Service. The only controversial point remaining seems to be the siting and control of the actual clinics – whether within the remit of a Children's Hospital, a Mental Hospital, or in connection with the School Medical Service.
>
> 'Behaviour problems' in children often have an organic foundation. Even when the physical element does not predominate, it may be the precipitating factor which determines whether stress and strain shall or shall not result in maladjustment. Very often, cure of a physical defect (for example, a disfiguring birthmark) enables a child to regain mental stability without any other treatment. It is therefore essential for every case to have a complete physical examination. This commonly involves radiological, biochemical and other investigations, for which facilities exist only in hospital. Referral from a clinic situated elsewhere results in delay and a sense of interruption of treatment which does not occur when departments of the same hospital are involved.
>
> The mental, intellectual, and physical health of the child form a most delicate equilibrium, necessitating harmonious co-operation between a number of experts, diagnostic equipment of the highest standard, and in-patient beds for a small proportion of cases. It goes without saying that the duplication of the facilities would be intolerably extravagant of both money and talent and that their availability should almost, of itself, determine the location of CGC at a 'key' hospital . . .
>
> I am unshakeably convinced that Child Guidance is an integral part of paediatrics, and properly forms one department of a Children's Hospital,

which indeed cannot be said to be fully, or even adequately, developed unless it can offer this service!

The concept of comprehensive child care, both physical and mental, required a change of name for the Child Guidance Clinic. The word from England was that this title was now reserved for clinics run by an Education Authority. Clinics held at hospitals, under the headship of a child psychiatrist, were being called Departments of Child Psychiatry. In proposing this change in April 1955, Dr Lothian felt that the time was now ripe to make clear once more the special nature of the unit in the Hospital, since it was hoped in the near future to provide in-patient facilities, in addition to the outpatient clinic. Furthermore, she reported that an attempt was being made by the School Medical Service to start a Child Guidance Clinic in Belfast. The change of name to the Department of Child Psychiatry did not happen overnight. Initially there was resistance from the Hospitals Authority, and full acceptance by all interested parties was not forthcoming until the appointment, in 1967, of the long-sought full-time consultant in child psychiatry. (Dr William McClure Nelson was the successful candidate.) The Staff had stated their case for this post in a memorandum produced by Professor Ivo Carré and Dr Evelyn Lothian, the matter being all the more urgent with the imminence of Lothian's retirement. They made a strong plea for the establishment of a consultant-led child psychiatry service within the Children's Hospital. This would encourage interchange of views between psychiatrists and paediatricians, train postgraduates and stimulate the interest of undergraduates in psychiatry during their period of paediatric study.

For twenty-one years, between the departure of Louise Eichoff in 1946 and the appointment of William Nelson in 1967, Dr Lothian was greatly assisted in her task of maintaining and developing child psychiatry by several colleagues who, in spite of commitments elsewhere, gave willingly of their time and talent, among them Dr W.S. McAuley (uncle of Dr Roger McAuley) and Dr J.R. Milliken.

During the formative years of child guidance/child psychiatry, the housing of the clinic was a continuing problem. Its first home was in a Quonset hut in the Hospital grounds. These less than ideal premises soon proved inadequate and it was suggested that a second hutted structure be built to increase available space. Nothing came of this, nor of the proposal for a sixty-bed unit within the Hospital with a psychiatric wing which would have provided both an outpatient and an in-patient facility. In 1954 a compromise solution was arrived at and the Child Guidance Clinic staff agreed (without prejudice to their demand for complete in-patient and outpatient facilities in the future) to move, together with speech therapy and audiology, to the recently purchased houses, Numbers 149–51 on Mulholland Terrace, Falls Road, directly opposite the Hospital. There the clinic remained until 1974, when, under the new management of the North &

West Belfast District of the Eastern Health & Social Services Board, the outpatient clinic transferred to the first floor of the RBHSC with Nelson as its director.

Throughout the period of the development of the child guidance/child psychiatry service there was a growing need for in-patient beds. For children not unduly disturbed, beds could be found by courtesy of colleagues within the RBHSC and at the City Hospital, but there was urgent need for in-patient accommodation for disturbed, noisy and destructive children whose hospitalization could last for up to a year. Three possibilities were considered: i) a unit attached to part of the Hospital but sealed off because of noise and so on, ii) a new in-patient and outpatient unit combined in an entirely separate building, to provide facilities for speech therapy and audiology, and iii) a unit specifically to accommodate in-patients in a large house with a garden. This third objective was attained, first in a country house near Lisburn, Co. Antrim, and later in the grounds of Forster Green Hospital. (See Chapter 9.)

9

LISSUE HOSPITAL

To discover the origins of the important part played by Lissue in the life of the Children's Hospital, it is necessary to look back to the outbreak of World War II.

On 13 September 1939 the Medical Staff met to consider a proposal put forward by the BMA regarding the provision of emergency services in wartime. Members of the medical staffs of the Belfast hospitals were to be summoned to duty immediately in the event of an air raid or other emergency. In the case of

Lissue House, Ballinderry, near Lisburn, Co. Antrim, which opened during wartime as a hospital with two wards in July 1940

The spacious entrance hall and grand staircase of Lissue House

the Belfast Hospital for Sick Children, Professor P.T. Crymble, Ian Fraser, J.S. Loughridge, Dr Rowland Hill, Dr Muriel Frazer and Dr Ivan McCaw were responsible.

Naturally, one of their main concerns was the availability of sufficient beds to cope with a major emergency. Therefore it was with gratitude and alacrity that the Staff accepted the most generous offer by Colonel and Mrs D.C. Lindsay to hand over part of their home, Lissue House, at Ballinderry, near Lisburn, as a convalescent or evacuation hospital, should the need arise. A preliminary inspection by Dr F.M.B. Allen and the honorary secretary of the Medical Staff Committee, Dr Ivan McCaw, reported that Lissue House would be ideal accommodation for up to thirty children. The house was ready to receive evacuation patients on 15 July 1940, and the first batch arrived the following day. This proved to be a timely provision, in view of the air raids which were to devastate Belfast early in 1941.

Dr Patterson, a Lisburn general practitioner, was asked to attend Lissue as a non-resident house surgeon, for which she would receive £75 per annum. In anticipation of their own remuneration for time and travelling to Lissue, Medical Staff decided to place a book at the Hospital recording their visits. Reminder letters regarding payment for such visits, sent to the Ministry of Home Affairs in March and April 1941, were not acknowledged; it was not until May 1942 that a response to repeated approaches was received. The Ministry conceded that Medical Staff were being put to extra inconvenience and loss of time in travelling to Lissue but offered only to defray travelling expenses at civil service rates. This worked out at 6s 8d per visit. Staff considered this derisory and resolved to bring the matter to the attention of the Parliamentary Medical Subcommittee, then sitting. Co-operation was also sought from the medical staff of the Ulster Hospital for Women and Children, who were in the same plight. This joint approach bore fruit for in September 1942 the Ministry agreed to pay a fee of two guineas for each staff visit to Lissue, to take effect retrospectively from the original date of transfer of patients. This rather tardy offer was accepted by Staff as satisfactory and Lissue continued to play a vital role as a convalescent facility throughout the war years.

With the cessation of hostilities, the Northern Ireland government stopped payment for the upkeep of Lissue, as of 30 September 1945, and ordered that all effects must be removed and the house vacated.[1]

The loss of Lissue House was a severe blow and the Medical Staff demanded the provision of a convalescent home to replace it, whether it be located inland or by the sea. The original Queen Victoria convalescent home, situated in the townland of Ballydollaghan on the outskirts of Belfast, had long since closed in 1908. (The house, now privately owned, can still be seen on the corner of the Saintfield Road and Beechhill Road, Newtownbreda.) The Board responded by purchasing Ballynascreen House, at Greenisland, Co. Antrim, for the sum of £4,500. However, by December 1946 Lissue was back on the agenda. Dr Muriel Frazer raised with Medical Staff the possibility of acquiring Lissue House as an ancillary hospital which would relieve the overtaxed accommodation on the Falls Road site. This possibility became a reality when, at its meeting on 12 August 1948, the Temporary Committee was able to announce that, through the great generosity of the Lindsay family, the Hospital was to acquire the whole of Lissue House for conversion to a branch of the Royal Belfast Hospital for Sick Children; no conditions were attached, except that the house must be occupied within nine months. Fortunately, the Board was able to sell the property at Greenisland at the original purchase price, and proceeded at speed with the necessary structural alterations to Lissue.

The first patients were admitted on 1 September 1948, and the official opening was performed by Mrs D.C. Lindsay on 21 January 1949.[2] A plaque to commemorate this important event was placed in the entrance hall.

THIS HOUSE WAS GIVEN BY THE
LINDSAY FAMILY
TO THE ROYAL BELFAST HOSPITAL FOR SICK CHILDREN
IN MEMORY OF
DAVID CECIL LINDSAY, D.L.
HIS SON
EDWARD WORKMAN LINDSAY
AND HIS GRAND-DAUGHTER
DEBORAH DAWN LINDSAY

For almost forty years Lissue House was to play a very significant role in the affairs of the Royal Belfast Hospital for Sick Children. Initially, it functioned as a convalescent hospital but by 1959 it had become a busy branch facility capable of caring for a wide variety of surgical and medical patients in seventy beds. However, the following ten years saw further change. There had been a slow but steady infiltration of psychiatric patients, and by the middle of 1966 the need for an in-patient child psychiatric unit was becoming a matter of urgency. For example, at the level of practical nursing, mobile psychiatric patients were interfering with other children confined to bed, and with numbers continually rising they became increasingly difficult to control. In response to this concern, a subcommittee of Medical Staff was appointed to decide how part of the Lissue accommodation could be converted to a psychiatric unit. In June 1969 the Ministry approved in principle a proposal to adapt the first floor of the house for this purpose, and in September 1970 a tender of £14,050 for the necessary building works was recommended and accepted.

The new unit opened in May 1971, and consisted of twenty in-patient beds providing residential care for children with emotional and behavioural difficulties. There were an additional five places for children attending daily. The unit was staffed by a multidisciplinary team comprising doctors, social workers, psychologists and Nursing Staff provided by the parent hospital in Belfast.[3]

William McClure Nelson, consultant psychiatrist and first director of the Child Psychiatry Unit, 1971–92

DR JOHN BARCROFT, son of Professor Henry Barcroft, past Professor of Physiology, QUB, was appointed as a consultant child psychiatrist at BCH in 1973. This service transferred to the Children's Hospital in 1974. Henceforth his remit covered the RBHSC, Ulster Hospital and Lissue Hospital. In 1978 Dr Barcroft took up a similar appointment in Cambridge.

The first director of the Child Psychiatry Unit was consultant psychiatrist Dr William McClure Nelson, under whom the treatment philosophy and general ethos was largely eclectic. The influence of Dr John Barcroft led to the inclusion of a psychotherapeutic approach, and with the appointment of Dr Roger McAuley in 1975 the philosophy changed to a new perspective of behavioural modification strategies. In 1976 this particular focus of treatment became the principal direction of care, with staff from all the disciplines adopting a behavioural philosophy in their work. At this time, the unit developed further with the advent of family admissions, providing a more accurate emphasis on family dynamic and the child management skills of the parents. To meet these criteria, it expanded in 1977 to provide parent accommodation with the conversion of additional adjacent rooms.[4]

While supporting the need for enhanced psychiatry facilities, Medical Staff became increasingly concerned at the possibility that all non-psychiatric beds at Lissue might be lost, in spite of assurances given by the Area Executive Team that such a dispossession would not occur until alternative accommodation was supplied. Dr W.A.B. Campbell, a paediatrician who took a great interest in Lissue affairs over many years, urged his colleagues to make as much use as they could of the Lissue beds. This situation contrasted with the attempts of Staff in the 1950s and 1960s to increase paediatric beds at Lissue, firstly to a figure of fifty, so that the appointment of a resident house officer could be justified, and then to eighty-five, as a final target. Efforts were made over the years to accomplish this increase by many internal architectural alterations. For example, in December 1961 the Works Committee was asked to give attention to three different needs, in order of priority: i) isolation facilities; ii) an infants' ward to accommodate twelve cots; and iii) alterations to separate the toddlers from the older children to allow easier nursing supervision. However, by January 1963 the push for more beds was losing momentum and the Staff's request to the Works Committee for more accommodation was not approved, on the basis that there was a substantial number of vacant beds throughout the area at the time. Accordingly, the request was changed to a plea for better distribution of the available beds, with no further increase.

It was not until May 1975 that Dr Campbell's fears were confirmed in a letter from the chief administrative medical officer of the Eastern Health & Social Services Board, Dr James McA. Taggart, asking the Medical Staff to address the following issues:

1 the long-standing low occupancy of paediatric beds at Lissue;
2 the possibility that the type of patient treated there could be accommodated elsewhere;
3 the urgent need for additional in-patient facilities for Child Psychiatry;
4 the Board's responsibility to ensure better utilisation of scarce resources.

The letter concluded:

> It would be appreciated if you would submit a proposal to your Medical Staff that the present paediatric beds be no longer used for this purpose and that all facilities at Lissue Hospital be utilised as a regional centre for Child Psychiatry.

The Board backed up its case with the quarterly statistics of Lissue Hospital, purporting to show the low occupancy of the thirty-eight paediatric beds. Pressure was duly applied for the relocation of twenty of these beds in the Allen and Musgrave Wards of the main hospital. The Medical Staff produced counter-occupancy statistics to demonstrate that such a transfer was not feasible.

Nevertheless, the persistent underusage of the convalescent beds at Lissue could not be ignored. The decreased demand for convalescent beds had several causes, among them the development of the nursing service in the community, with its emphasis on care and support in the home situation where possible, a trend continuing and growing today. Ironically enough, together with the greater demands of child psychiatry, another change was appearing: the paediatric beds were being occupied more and more by chronically sick and handicapped children. Furthermore, there was increasing recognition of the need to provide care for the carers, so that in 1977 an arrangement was made for the short-term admission of handicapped patients, with the object of giving their families periods of respite. In that year, only twenty-nine of the thirty-eight 'convalescent' beds were operational and seven of these were occupied by special care patients. This need to accommodate patients with multiple handicap went unacknowledged by the Eastern Health & Social Services Board, and throughout 1977 there was sustained pressure to remove all general patients from the ground floor of Lissue House and to use the vacated accommodation for psychiatric patients. This pressure was resisted, and by December 1979 the admission of special care patients to Lissue was a commonplace occurrence, largely at Campbell's instigation. Until Christmas 1988 the branch hospital at Lissue continued to serve the children of Northern Ireland through its paediatric and psychiatric units, and the new role of the paediatric unit as a facility for the care of the child with multiple handicap was emphasized further by the appointment, in November 1983, of Dr Elaine Hicks as consultant in paediatric neurology and, in June 1986, of Dr Agnes Elizabeth (Nan) Hill, as consultant with an interest in complex handicap.

Michael Swallow, consultant neurologist at the RVH, was encouraged by Ivo Carré and Claude Field to provide a service at the RBHSC in the years before Elaine Hicks was appointed. He established a weekly clinic and also took part on an ad hoc basis in a Genetic Clinic with Norman Nevin. Swallow was a strong supporter of the appointment of a full-time neurologist at the Hospital. He retired in 1989 to pursue his great interest in music, and in 1995 he was awarded an OBE for services to music therapy, art and disability.

The excellent work carried on at Lissue over so many years deserves particular credit given the difficulties which from time to time hindered the smooth functioning of the hospital. The house itself, while ideal for the care of short-term convalescent patients, was not architecturally suited to the ever-changing needs of an increasingly varied patient population, and its deficiencies as a major institutional facility were often exposed. Staff, planners and builders spent many hours making minor and sometimes major alterations to rooms, verandas, plumbing facilities and so on, in order to accommodate the demands of a wide spectrum of patients: infants, children – mobile and immobile – and those requiring education and behaviour control. This led the Nursing Staff to dub the house 'Legoland'. Some of the children called it 'The Zoo'.

In the early days tuberculosis posed a problem. For example, in July 1949 there was a case of open tuberculosis at Lissue, prompting the Medical Staff to adopt a policy stating that no open case of TB should be sent to Lissue or admitted into the main hospital. These words appeared to fall on deaf ears, for in May 1953 the Hospital Committee asked the Northern Ireland Hospitals Authority to take up with the Northern Ireland Tuberculosis Authority (NITA) the problem of the large number of cases of primary TB complex then in Lissue. In May 1955 there were twenty-four of these children at Lissue Hospital, there being no vacancies at the NITA establishment at Crawfordsburn.

Infections other than tuberculosis afflicted the hospital from time to time, and in September 1954 there was what was termed an 'explosive outbreak of enteritis', with no specific organisms found. In the same year, at a more mundane level, the ingestion of laburnum seeds by a few ambulant patients necessitated the felling of the offending tree. There is no record of any harm coming to the children.

There was the occasional brush with management at both local and area level. On 22 June 1964 a message was received from the Group secretary, R.T. Spence, who was proposing to transfer twenty-two orthopaedic cases from Greenisland Hospital to Lissue during the first week of July. This was the first notice that the Staff had of this move. Not surprisingly, they made urgent representations to the senior administrative medical officer of the Hospitals Authority, expressing deep concern at this lack of consultation before such a major step was undertaken. They pointed out the lack of space, the absence of treatment room facilities and poor sluice accommodation which should be upgraded prior to the transfer. Furthermore, the presence of so many adult-sized beds in the upstairs ward, with their necessary beams, pulleys and so on, would make it unreasonably cramped. The Nursing Staff were so perturbed that the matron, Molly Hudson, wrote to the Board in protest. Notwithstanding, by September 1964 the transfer of orthopaedic patients had taken place, with no improved hygiene facilities and no additional bed space.

Undoubtedly, the event which caused most concern and dismay to the Staff was the transfer, in 1973, of the administrative control of Lissue Hospital from the North & West Belfast District to the Lisburn District. In May of that year, the Ministry of Health (soon, with direct rule from Westminster, to become the Department of Health & Social Services) issued a memorandum to members of the EHSSB, the Central Services Agency and the Area Executive teams, concerning the overlap of services between Areas and Districts (Circular R16/73).[5]

In a section dealing with the 'Criteria for Management Arrangements', the document enunciated certain principles, among them:

1 The underlying policy in the administration of the Health and Personal Social Services is that the existence of administrative factors (Area or

District) should not place obstacles in the way of the provision of service to the public according to its needs, irrespective of the place of residence.

2 In so far as possible, facilities within the Area of the Board should be administered by that Board. This is important, as it makes for clear definition of managerial responsibility and avoids confusion in the minds of the public and Staff alike. Only exceptionally will there be a case for breaching this principle.

In the appendix, cases of overlap between Districts in an Area were set forth, with Lissue being quoted as an example:

Lissue Hospital, Lisburn Health and Social Services District. Beds 58, type: Convalescent and Child Psychiatry.

Hospital Management Committee: Belfast associations – is an annexe of the Royal Belfast Hospital for Sick Children.

Catchment area is predominantly greater Belfast. Comparatively few patients are normally resident in the Lisburn Health and Social Services District.

FUTURE ROLE: In view of its current links in the catchment area, there is a good case for this hospital to be administered and staffed by North and West Belfast Health and Social Services District, rather than Lisburn Health and Social Services District.

The Ministry's position was stated further in a letter, dated 31 May 1973, from Dr T.T. Baird, chief medical officer, to Dr J.M. Beare, chairman of the RBHSC Medical Staff Committee:

We have given considerable thought to this question of overlap between Districts within an Area and have recently issued a circular [the aforementioned R16/73] to Area Boards, giving guidance on this subject. Basically, we feel that in general, Area Boards should be responsible administratively for all the facilities within their area, but we do recognise that there are special cases, such as Lissue Hospital, where for very specific reasons the administration should continue to be the responsibility of a District other than the one in which the facility exists. We have asked Boards to look at the overlap problems and to keep us informed of their decisions. To me it seems that Lissue presents one of these exceptional cases and I feel that it would be very easy for the Eastern Health and Social Services Board to resolve it this way.

The Board did not agree and ignored this nudge from Dundonald House – Lissue Hospital was hived off to the Lisburn District. Staff concern that nursing and administrative posts would be downgraded and that laboratory services, records, X-rays and so on would suffer went unheeded, and repeated representations to have the decision reversed were of no avail. The Board continued to hold the view that no post would be reduced in status by this administrative change and that the function of the clinical nurses, and other staff associated with Lissue, would in no way be disturbed. Nevertheless, the infection control sister, Patricia Symmons, immediately found great difficulty in carrying out her duties in Lissue under the new regime and asked to be relieved of her post. This dispute rumbled on, and

in 1980 Dr Aileen Redmond was reporting to the Medical Staff Committee that the Nursing Staff at Lissue, who had strong loyalty to the main hospital, were feeling more and more isolated. Incidentally, the Board's opinion that the administration of Lissue could be better served by Lisburn District was not shared by the administrators and medical staff of that District, who made their contrary views clear on more than one occasion.

With hindsight, the decision to remove administrative control of Lissue Hospital from the North & West Belfast District of the EHSSB, while leaving the responsibility for patient care in the hands of the Medical Staff of the Children's Hospital, looks very much like a triumph of bureaucracy over common sense. Nevertheless, Lissue staff of that time were impressed by the efficient way in which essential day-to-day services were provided by the Lisburn District.

Children playing in the grounds of Lissue House, *c.* 1960s

THE MOVE FROM LISSUE

CHILD PSYCHIATRY UNIT

Throughout 1982 and 1983 rumours were circulating that the Eastern Health & Social Services Board was considering closing Lissue Hospital and relocating the psychiatric and paediatric units at sites yet to be decided. It is an oft-repeated charge that the first inkling clinicians get of major changes in the administrative structure is through the grapevine. This has happened frequently enough to create the suspicion that premature leaks are used by the policy makers to test the water.

Discussions eventually took place between the consultant psychiatrists and members of the EHSSB at which various reasons were given as to the desirability of a move from Lissue. The Board argued that the present unit was too expensive and too remote and that it would be more cost-effective to bring several services together on a new site. In a word, rationalization was its objective and it would not be deterred.

The news of the closure united the people of the Lagan Valley in a campaign to save Lissue. James Molyneaux, the local MP and Ulster Unionist Party leader, described the Board's decision as an appalling blunder, and the Alliance councillor Seamus Close dismissed the three-month consultative period as a 'complete and utter farce'. Albert Brown, chairman of the campaign committee, saw it as the 'old, old story of financial concerns taking precedence over parents' and people's wishes', and spoke for many in the community when he said that Lissue Hospital offered both an expert service and a loving unique environment that would be most difficult to replace.

The Save Lissue Campaign failed, and in mid-1985 the Medical Staff were invited to view various areas of Forster Green Hospital. After inspection, it seemed to them that the old Nurses' Home would be the most suitable in terms of accommodation, provided extensive alteration and refurbishment were carried out. They conceded that Forster Green had some undoubted advantages over Lissue; the site was nearer the outpatient unit at the Royal Belfast Hospital for Sick Children and was also in close proximity to the area of greater Belfast, whence the majority of patients would come.

Forster Green, a Belfast tea merchant, was a Quaker with an acute social conscience. In 1896 he purchased Fortbreda House on the Saintfield Road, Belfast, for adaptation to a sanatorium; the first patients were admitted the following year. In the 1930s TB was the main killer of young adults. It was responsible for 49 per cent of all deaths in the age group fifteen to twenty-five and for 38 per cent of those between twenty-five and thirty-five. The mortality rate was 20 per cent higher in Northern Ireland than in Britain.[6] Forster Green's own daughter was a victim. It was not until 1941 that the Northern Ireland Tuberculosis Authority was set up to find and treat the victims of what was then a dreaded disease of frightening morbidity and mortality. With the aid of new drugs, such as PAS and Streptomycin, and BCG vaccination, together with advances in surgical and anaesthetic techniques, by 1954 the incidence of the disease had been reduced by 15 per cent to the same level obtaining in England and Wales. NITA's success was such that it was dissolved in 1959.

For two or three years after 1985, consultant staff were involved in further negotiations with the Green Park Unit of Management and the EHSSB,

in drawing up plans for the necessary site alterations. The Board imposed financial restrictions, and the subvention of £150,000 covered only the cost of a new heating system, rewiring and redecoration of the existing building.

As the date of the planned move drew nearer, other potential teething troubles began to surface. Clinicians were worried that not only would there be a flow of Nursing Staff inexperienced in child psychiatry moving between the unit's hospitals, but traditional attitudes would involve nurses in the wearing of uniform – which was anathema to psychiatrists. Initially, they had to submit to this convention. Furthermore, mindful of the Lindsay family's past beneficence, Dr Nelson and Dr McAuley wished to have the new unit named the 'Lindsay Unit'.[7] This request was refused on the basis of the Board's stated policy not to name units after personalities, however distinguished: a decision viewed by the Medical Staff as an example of unnecessary bureaucratic insensitivity.

Less controversially, the transfer of the Lissue Hospital School to Forster Green proceeded smoothly under the aegis of the South Eastern Education & Library Board, which readily agreed to naming it the 'Lindsay School', thus ensuring that the name so long associated with the care of children would be perpetuated in at least one area of the new facility. Together with the Child Psychiatry Unit, the Lindsay School at Forster Green Hospital opened in March 1989.

From 1 May 1995, as a result of a patient survey, both the in-patient unit at Forster Green and the outpatient facility at the RBHSC (of the Department of Child Psychiatry) became known as the Child and Family

Dr Roger McAuley outside the Child and Family Centre inpatient facility at Forster Green Hospital, 1997. The building was formerly the Nurses' Home; at the rear is the Hospital School.

Dr Roger McAuley and patient pupil at a computer keyboard in the Lindsay School, 1997

Centre. In 1997 the consultant staff were: Dr Roger McAuley (appointed 1975); Dr Marie Therese Kennedy (appointed 1981); Dr Geraldine Walford (appointed 1994); and Dr Morna Manwell (associate specialist).

THE HOSPITAL SCHOOL AT LISSUE AND FORSTER GREEN

The school at Lissue House commenced and prospered under the leadership of Miss McConachie, by all accounts a formidable woman, held in some degree of awe by junior members of Staff. She and Ada Kirkpatrick, a keen assistant teacher, began their work at the bedside, and readily adapted to the increasing patient population over subsequent years. Their spectrum of pupils ranged from the educationally subnormal, through those with severe emotional and behavioural difficulties, to children who were capable of eleven-plus standard – indeed, success at that level has been recorded. Sometimes there was conflict of priorities between education and Hospital routine. In 1956 Dr W.A.B. Campbell met with Miss McConachie and the Nursing Staff to find the best way of reconciling medical requirements with teaching continuity. As a result, new classroom accommodation was made available, to cope with a mixture of ambulant children in a single area; bed patients would receive individual instruction as before. While recognizing the importance of children's education, Medical Staff felt that a period of fresh air in the spacious grounds would be beneficial, especially during the winter months. The teachers had no personal objections but were concerned about the consequences of the possible unheralded arrival of a school inspector while the children were outside. It was suggested that in such an unfortunate eventuality the outdoor activity could assume the guise of nature study. In the face of many vicissitudes, the Hospital school, through the selfless dedication of Miss McConachie and her staff, provided educational facilities for hundreds of Lissue children throughout the years.

Miss McConachie retired in 1975 and was succeeded by Mary Murphy. Joyce I. Moran, who took over as head in 1984, had the task of organizing the move from Lissue to the new accommodation at Forster Green. The Lindsay School now provides education for the children who are patients at the Child Psychiatry Unit at Forster Green Hospital. A member of its staff also teaches at the Ulster Hospital. The pupils on the roll are aged between three and a half and fourteen years and the high staff/pupil ratio allows for individual teaching, more than is possible in the mainstream of education. A child can be referred to the unit from anywhere in Northern Ireland by a psychiatrist, a medical officer, a GP, an educational psychologist or a head teacher. Parents are closely involved with the Hospital Staff in the work with their child, and the professional team concerned with each consists of a psychiatrist, a clinical psychologist, the school principal, the social worker and nurses. On Joyce Moran's retirement in 1993, Phillip Doherty became principal, with Patricia Aust as vice-principal. (See Appendix 6.)

The school's advice to parents could be taken to heart by parents of children without any identifiable psychological handicap:

PLEASE –

TALK to your child – children love to 'chat' and have things explained to them.

READ to your child – daily, if possible.

TAKE your child on visits – to the park, to the leisure centre, to the library, etc.

PLAY games with him/her indoors and outside.

ENCOURAGE your child – give praise and appreciation when it is appropriate.

SPEND TIME WITH YOUR CHILD – ENJOY EACH OTHER'S COMPANY

The Lindsay School continues to build upon the pioneering work of Miss McConachie and her colleagues, to enable children with handicaps to climb the tree of knowledge to the best of their ability. Lately, patients have been admitted from a wider catchment area, including Donegal, Limerick and the Isle of Man. Among the subjects taught are English, mathematics, science and technology, the environment and society, and creative and expressive studies.

The character and ethos of the school are excellently set out in a pamphlet issued by Phillip Doherty and his staff:

As an integrated all ability school, we aim to provide a happy, secure environment in which children can learn effectively to realise their full

Phillip Doherty, principal
of the Lindsay School at
Forster Green, 1993–

potential as unique individuals. This aim permeates the ethos of the school, the teaching styles and approaches, the pastoral care and the discipline policy of the school. As children have different abilities, aptitudes and needs, their performances will vary from their peers and every opportunity is given for children to experience success. Positive encouragement and praise for all pupils, regardless of gender, colour or creed, enables them to develop intellectually, socially, morally and spiritually and become full contributing members of the school community. The school provides an opportunity for children from the two main traditions in Northern Ireland, as well as those from other traditions and cultures, to develop a knowledge, understanding, appreciation and respect for their common culture. All pupils are encouraged to explore and value their own particular tradition so as to encourage the education together of children of various beliefs, cultures and traditions. A happy and caring environment is promoted, centred on the needs of the child in preparing him or her for a creative and satisfying life in a plural society. The right of parents to be involved in the decision making and community life of the school is protected, while respecting the role of staff as professional teachers. All pupils are equally cherished, nurtured and respected without discrimination based on sex, religion, ethnic origin, class or ability. The Lindsay School aims to –

1 create a happy, stimulating environment in which pupils can learn
   effectively;
2 nurture the pupils' sense of self esteem so that they can accept others
   whose ideas and beliefs are different from their own;
3 develop skills and knowledge to become independent thinkers whose
   attitudes and opinions are based on rational judgement;
4 provide a broad and balanced curriculum by implementation of the
   programmes of study of the Northern Ireland curriculum;

5 help pupils develop personally, spiritually and socially and recognise the importance of fulfilment, irrespective of ability;

6 foster in children the skills needed to develop and maintain healthy relationships;

7 encourage all children to give of their time and talents with generosity and with good grace;

8 promote the supportive, respectful partnership between the school, the home and the wider community.

THE PAEDIATRIC UNIT

In 1988 the Respite Unit at Lissue House was providing a service for up to one hundred families and over one hundred children, seventy of whom came from the Eastern Health & Social Services Board area, although patients from the Northern and Southern Area Boards still made up a significant minority. The accommodation offered as the new home for the paediatric unit was the ground floor of Belvoir Park Hospital, Pavilion 2, with the proviso that no structural alterations should be made. Dr Elaine Hicks and her colleagues, Dr Nan Hill and Dr Mark Reid, considered this accommodation unsuitable for the children concerned. Their anxieties were compounded by a suggestion from the EHSSB that immediate steps should be taken to reduce the number of beds from twenty to fifteen to fit the new accommodation.

On 18 March 1988 Dr Hicks wrote to Dr Angela Greer, acting administrative medical officer of the Board:

You will not be surprised when I say that I do not think I can support a suggestion that we undergo a decrease in beds from the autumn of this year to fit the offered accommodation. I feel the temporary nature of this accommodation to be unsatisfactory and, while I quite accept that in the long term we wish to have most of this service community based, there is no possibility of this coming about to any significant degree in the shorter intermediate term . . . we are talking several years before we can really start to see a community based programme with significant numbers.

Change, with its close companion uncertainty, is an unsettling, often traumatic experience for patients, parents and staff alike, so it is not surprising that Dr Hicks's letter ended on a rather despairing note:

The morale of the staff in the paediatric unit at Lissue is at an all-time low. Together with the parents, they are deeply concerned at the uncertainty of the [future] of the unit. The lack of substantive communication from the Board as to their definite plans and, above all, the suggested decrease in bed accommodation at the new location is not helpful.

The fears and concerns of the paediatricians at Lissue were shared by the members of the Paediatric Division at the Children's Hospital. They were worried about the fate of those patients residing outside the Eastern Board who had been receiving respite care in Lissue, now that the bed accommodation was to be reduced. The Board replied that the number of beds which would be available in Belvoir Park had been considered with regard to the needs of the Eastern Board children, who would take precedence over children from the other Board areas. In the EHSSB's view, respite care did not require a regional resource and other areas should be encouraged to set up their own units.[8]

The Board's determination was irresistible and on 3 August 1988 Dr Hicks informed the Division of Paediatrics that in January 1989 the paediatric unit at Lissue was to move to refurbished accommodation at Belvoir Park, Pavilion 1 (this having proved more suitable than Pavilion 2, originally offered). The cost of upgrading the accommodation came to £86,000 plus VAT.

The new unit, named Forest Lodge Children's Respite Care Unit, became part of the Green Park Trust, which includes Belvoir Park, Forster Green and Musgrave Park Hospitals. It has a complement of fifteen beds and cares for children up to the age of fourteen. The ward is staffed, as at Lissue, by nurses who have paediatric training and are under the charge of Sister R. Lloyd, who moved with the unit from Lissue Hospital. The medical care is provided by Dr Elaine Hicks (who assumed a regional role in 1992), Dr Nan Hill and Dr Paul Jackson. There are ninety-five to one hundred children on the books at present.

The appointment of Dr Nan Hill in 1986 was another step in the evolution of the neurodevelopmental service at the Royal Belfast Hospital for Sick Children. Eighty per cent of her work was hospital-based – at the Children's Hospital, Musgrave Park Hospital and Lissue House – with the balance involving responsibilities at the two regional schools for children with physical disabilities, Fleming Fulton and Mitchell House, and at schools for children with speech and language problems, namely, Thornfield and Seagal House (Mencap Nursery). (This situation is now reversed as she is almost entirely based in the community.) Dr Hill's work has been built on the labour and dedication of colleagues who preceded her, Dr Chris Green, Dr Maurice Savage and Dr Claude Field.

Dr C.M.B. Field wrote a report in 1948 on the types of illness in children admitted to a typical twenty-six-bed children's ward in that year. There were 94 children with lobar pneumonia, 63 with various strains of tuberculosis, 129 with rheumatic fever or chorea and 29 with heavy infestations with various kinds of worm. Writing in 1982, he noted that these illnesses had almost completely disappeared and that handicapping disorders of children were becoming a large and important part of paediatrics. Furthermore, he observed that children were rarely afflicted by a single handicap, most having several additional problems. Dr Field recognized that a special clinic was required where children with complex problems could be seen at leisure, not only by the paediatrician but by other

Nurses Linda Williamson and Sandi McTrusty consult a patient's notes at Forest Lodge Children's Respite Care Unit, 1997

personnel skilled in speech therapy, occupational therapy, physiotherapy, orthoptics, psychology and social work. He found these skills available at Fleming Fulton and Mitchell House, and a start was made by the seconding of these therapists to his clinic one day each week. The Belfast Education & Library Board provided an educational psychologist who had special skills. Dr Field had started his assessment clinic in 1976 in a suite of rooms in the Wakehurst House annexe of the BCH, in what used to be the Child Guidance Clinic. He held strongly to the belief that a clinic entirely devoted to the needs of children should be a centre not only for the assessment of handicap but for treatment. This far-seeing, pioneering work culminated in the opening of the new Child Development Centre at the Royal Belfast Hospital for Sick Children in 1991.

The years after Dr Hill's appointment saw continual development in the care of children with complex handicaps. The referrals to the Child Development Centre at the Children's Hospital became more complicated with the proliferation of community-based child development clinics. The work involved children with very complex problems or those for whom a second opinion was being sought. The investigative facilities on the Royal Hospitals site became increasingly important in the areas of neuro-imaging, neurochemistry and neuropathology. There was ongoing endeavour to unfold for worried parents the exact nature and causation of the different problems afflicting their children.[9] In more recent years, however, a volte-face has occurred. The new orientation towards a community-based service has resulted in the running down of the centre for complex handicap at the RBHSC.

The two former Lissue units are now settled in their accommodation at Forster Green and Belvoir Park, but the horizon is somewhat obscured by clouds heralding more change in the administrative climate. Indeed, in the case of the psychiatric unit, the recent change to Trust Status has resulted in the child psychiatry service being split between the RBHSC and Forster Green Hospital, run by the Royal Hospitals Trust and the Green Park Trust respectively. There is anxiety that such arrangements might result in administrative complexity, which could be detrimental to the efficient running of the service. The future of the paediatric unit remains uncertain in view of the planned closure of Belvoir Park Hospital.

Its forty years of service over, Lissue House was left empty to become run-down and overgrown, until its destruction by fire in 1996. The plaque commemorating the gift of the house to the RBHSC now resides in Lindsay House at Seymour Hill, Lisburn. Many would argue that a more appropriate home would have been within the precincts of the original object of the Lindsay family's generosity – the Royal Belfast Hospital for Sick Children.

The Haematology Unit was awarded a Charter Mark at a gala reception in London in 1997; admiring the motif with patient Conor O'Neill, is the Lord Mayor of Belfast, Dr Ian Adamson, Paul McWilliams, Elaine Hicks and Sister Barbara Carlisle.

10

THE LABORATORY

In 1896 JAMES LORRAIN SMITH, a lecturer at Queen's College, was appointed honorary pathologist to the Children's Hospital, Queen Street. Over the next half-century this post was held by various individuals, whose tenure of office was often of uncertain duration. Sometimes years elapsed between one appointment and the next. The pathology service was perforce low-key with wardside room accommodation and only basic equipment. From time to time the idea of having a pathologist with greater commitment to the Hospital was mooted, but the only positive action taken was to order some more equipment. In 1936 it was agreed to appoint a nurse with an interest in pathology, whom Professor John S. Young undertook to train at the Royal Victoria Hospital laboratory, free of charge. Miss Abernethy was appointed for a probationary period of three months with the status of sister. In a gesture of pastoral care, two members of Staff (T.S. Kirk and Dr J.A. Smyth) were deputed to interview the matron regarding the arrangements for Miss Abernethy's sustenance and the suitability of her quarters.[1] There is no further record of the outcome of this appointment.

Not surprisingly, in view of the way that the laboratory was staffed and equipped, the resident house surgeons and physicians performed the simpler tests; anything more complicated was sent to the laboratory at the RVH. After the appointment of John Henry Biggart as honorary pathologist to the Hospital in March 1939, the Staff remained content with these arrangements and re-emphasized that all specimens should be examined and reported on by the house doctor in charge of the case, with the proviso that those specially selected by the staff physician or surgeon should be sent to the RVH laboratory or to the Belfast City laboratory, where a free service was provided. Biggart's estimate that it would cost £15,000 per annum to maintain a fully equipped laboratory with a full-time pathologist did nothing to encourage the Medical Staff to change their policy.[2] They were undeterred even when the Hospital secretary superintendent, R.W. Harland, conveyed the management's concern that the increasing number of specimens being sent to the RVH was incurring undue expense. This was a reinforcement of the stance they had taken in the 1930s, when 'they wished the Board to know that the present laboratory service was being carried out most economically and that 5% of hospital expenditure was a reasonable amount to spend on laboratory investigation'.[3]

There was very little change in the scope and status of the laboratory in the run-up to the National Health Service. A proposal in March 1947 that a clinical pathologist should be appointed on a full-time basis, though sharing work with the RVH, was deferred. However, in May of the same year, Biggart endeavoured to impress upon his colleagues the desirability of decentralizing the laboratory service, and as part of this process he recommended the reopening of the clinical laboratory at the Children's Hospital. This accommodation, situated in the basement, had been converted into a protected operating theatre during the war. An adjacent preparation room had continued to function as a small laboratory. On 15 July 1940 a joint meeting of members of the Medical Staff and the Property Committee of the Board reported that various drastic alterations would be necessary to satisfy the Ministry of Home Affairs in connection with the proper protection of the patients and the building during air raids. Many windows were to be built up, the Bass Capper Ward was to be made splinter-proof and the basement converted into a shelter, with the present laboratory in the basement converted into a fully protected operating theatre with emergency lighting and so on. Any expense incurred in excess of £1 per bed would be met by the Ministry.

The Medical Staff Committee minutes record that this proposal to reopen was accepted and a further decision was taken to appoint a part-time clinical pathologist in charge on a yearly basis, at a salary of £250–£350 per annum. It is not clear whether this appointment was ever made and in any case the formation of the NHS was imminent.

Another milestone was reached when Dr M.G. Nelson, later honorary professor, returned from distinguished wartime service with the RAF. In 1947 he was appointed as consultant clinical pathologist to the RVH, with responsibility for providing a clinical pathology service to all the hospitals in the Belfast group, including the Children's Hospital. Initially, progress was slow, though some more basic equipment was acquired in the shape of a centrifuge, a microscope to perform white cell counts and a colorimeter.

The provision of suitable technical and medical staff was more of a problem. Initially, Albert Lamont, senior chief technician in the haematology laboratory at the Royal Victoria Hospital, visited the RBHSC when need arose, to carry out fairly rudimentary tests. Inevitably, increasing demands on his time in the main laboratory meant that further technical assistance was called for, and it was becoming evident that trainee clinical pathologists would be required to deal with more complicated matters, such as bone marrow pathology and difficult differential blood counts. At the same time, F.M.B. Allen had a vision of a biochemistry research unit at the Children's Hospital, and the appointment of a whole-time biochemist for routine work and research was proposed.[4] This was opposed by Dr J.A. Smyth, physician/biochemist at the RVH, who thought that all the work could be done in his laboratory. Nevertheless, during these early years, as the load grew, it became necessary to have more continuity of staff at the Children's Hospital laboratory. Accordingly, trainee clinical pathologists, as well as technicians from the main RVH laboratory, rotated through the Children's Hospital as part of their duties. The first trainee clinical pathologist to be appointed to work in the RBHSC was Dr Richard McCorry, who had developed an interest in biochemistry which he would sustain throughout his career. Among other trainee pathologists who rotated through the RBHSC laboratory were Doctors Nina Carson, Mabel Stevenson, Betty Nicholl, Ferry Hillman and Joe Lowry.

In 1950 a move was made to start providing research facilities in the laboratory, with the money to come from Free Funds of the Hospital. Unfortunately, the expected support from the Northern Ireland Hospitals Authority for the funding of the required staff did not materialize. Nonetheless, Allen purchased mahogany laboratory furniture, under the guise of scientific equipment, together with a flame photometer facility.

The year 1953 heralded significant advances in both the service and the research functions of the RBHSC laboratory. As Professor M.G. Nelson records in his history of clinical pathology on the RVH site, 'in that year, two people were appointed who were to have a profound effect on the development, evolution, and the service provided. They were Dr Nina Carson and Mr T.W. Macfarlane.'[5]

Dr Carson worked in both haematology and biochemistry in the course of her biochemical investigations on mentally retarded children. Using two-dimensional paper chromatography, she isolated an unusual amino acid, which led, in collaboration with Professor Dent of University College Hospital, London, to the discovery of a new inborn error of metabolism associated with mental deficiency, namely homocystinuria. As a result of this important discovery, Dr Carson became involved in the general problem of mentally retarded children, and in a massive screening for the congenital metabolic disease phenylketonuria, which occurs in one in four thousand live births in Northern Ireland, compared with one in ten thousand in the rest of the UK. This programme was an outstanding success and gave rise to the early dietary treatment of this distressing disorder which, if untreated, causes cerebral deterioration. Dr Carson became a world authority on mental deficiency associated with amino aciduria. Soon biochemical research was her full-time occupation. She held research fellowships in the university Department of Child Health, and in 1976 she was appointed senior lecturer and consultant paediatrician at the RBHSC.

By October 1952 there was renewed pressure for the implementation of the resolve by Medical Staff, in 1947, to provide a biochemistry facility. On 2 December Dr Payne of Great Ormond Street Hospital, London, visited Belfast to advise on the layout for a new biochemistry laboratory, to be housed in a store next to the existing laboratory, with a syringe service in the adjacent 'soap store'. (Prior to the plastic revolution, the glass syringes and metal needles were boiled up.) Syringes and needles were packed and dispatched by two worthy ladies, Mrs Murphy and Mrs Leacock, their service covering the RBHSC and the RMH Nursery. The idea was floated that a syringe service would work best in association with the expanded biochemistry laboratory, and some tentative decisions were taken as to its location and administration. The latter proved to be the stumbling block and the symbiosis with biochemistry was never a happy one. The coming of the Central Sterile Supplies Department in 1967 was a boon, not only to the RBHSC but to all the hospitals of the Royal Group. Dr George Gibson, a bacteriologist, had a large input into the new sterilizing service. Unhappily, he was lost to Belfast when he returned to England soon after the onset of the Troubles.

Throughout the 1950s the numbers and complexity of the laboratory tests performed at the RBHSC continued to grow, and by 1961 70,000 tests were carried out each year. The biochemistry section of the laboratory had opened for business in 1953, and in the same year an advertisement appeared in the press for a senior Medical Laboratory Scientific Officer (MLSO). The successful candidate was Tom W. Macfarlane. He had trained for nine years in the Belfast City Hospital, where he made his first attempts at microanalysis, and he at once set about developing these methods in his new environment. The scene that met him was not prepossessing – a bare room with no bench units or shelves – but undeterred, and aided by a junior MLSO, he made a tentative start. Macfarlane spent the next number of years bringing in new techniques, each one using less blood for analysis than its predecessor. In about 1960 Dr Manuel C. Sanz, of Geneva, published a series of articles, under the title of 'Ultra Micro Analysis'. This method was to prove to be of profound benefit, especially to newborn babies with low blood volume, as 50 microlitres (0.05 of a millilitre) of blood was sufficient to carry out detailed analysis – a far cry from the potentially exsanguinating methods used heretofore. With commendable foresight, Dr W.G. Wade, a trainee pathologist, nominated Macfarlane to be sent to Geneva to acquire the necessary knowledge of ultra micro methods.

SUMMARY OF TESTS AND SPECIMENS, 1951–1961		
	TOTAL SPECIMENS	TOTAL EXAMINATIONS
1951	6,117	14,396
1952	7,505	15,926
1953	8,809	18,551
1954	8,311	19,134
1955	12,666	25,965
1956	14,130	32,471
1957	23,909	44,875
1958	23,495	54,705
1959	22,808	49,327
1960	19,030	47,247
1961	20,773	68,304

Macfarlane's one-month sabbatical leave in Geneva had immediate effect. On his return, the biochemistry department closed while it was retooled with precision micro method equipment: micro pipettes, micro burettes, micro colorimeters and so on. His work attracted great interest, visitors coming from far and near to look, to learn and to wonder that so much could be done with so little. Simultaneously, the main laboratories were starting to acquire high-technology analysers, culminating in the Sequential Multiple Analyser Computer (SMAC), giving the so-called block analysis facility. These instruments removed the time-consuming drudgery of manual operation and were a welcome innovation in view of the rapidly increasing workload. Nevertheless, Macfarlane's proud claim was that 'they couldn't beat us for sample size'.

A demand by Allen for the determination of the levels in certain patients of the liver hormone transaminase required the acquisition of a spectrophotometer, at a cost of £1,500, and, not for the first time, the Endowment Funds of the hospital came to the rescue. Coincidentally, the importance of transaminase as an indicator of myocardial ischaemic heart disease was being recognized. Inevitably, Frank Pantridge heard about the pioneering work being done in the RBHSC laboratory and very soon Macfarlane and his colleagues were swamped by demands for this test to be carried out on the blood of adult patients with cardiac disease in the RVH. Macfarlane's somewhat plaintive response was, 'What could we do when he was demanding that they should be done?' – a cri de coeur that would strike a chord with many colleagues.

It speaks volumes for the skill and dedication of the laboratory staff that, throughout the 1960s and 1970s, they continued to cope with the manual operation of ultra micro techniques, in spite of the increasing demands placed upon them. Concern was expressed that repetitive pipetting steps could lead to inaccurate results, due to fatigue. By 1975, the work burden was growing at an average of 15 per cent per annum, reaching in 1979 a high of 33 per cent over the previous year. Since 1975 the overall increase had been 52 per cent.

Clearly, the time was overdue for the acquisition of automated equipment. Over the years, the Children's Hospital laboratory was never at the head of the line when new equipment was coming on stream. The main laboratory had first call on the available money, and the RBHSC had to be content with morsels from the remainder of the budget. However, in the late 1970s Macfarlane acquired a Coulter Kem-O-Mat Analyser, at a cost of £14,000, which turned out to be a useful tool but eventually became obsolete. Notwithstanding, the service continued to expand in various fields, for example in the early diagnosis of fibrocystic disease (CF) of the newborn (in association with Dr Aileen Redmond), the investigation of cot death and the early diagnosis of Reye's syndrome, special interests of Dr John Glasgow.

Dr M.D. (Dennis) O'Hara, consultant pathologist, was invited to join the Medical Staff in May 1976. In that year, his interest in the pathology of children was stimulated when Garth McClure informally sought his help with a paediatric pathological problem, and since then he has developed a comprehensive pathological service for the Hospital. He undertakes a whole range of paediatric autopsy pathology, including the malignant tumours of childhood and complicated congenital abnormalities.

THE CLINICAL COMPONENT

The established policy of assigning medical registrars from the RVH laboratory proved less and less satisfactory, especially in times of staff shortage. The main laboratory had first claim on their services and all too often the input to the children's laboratory was less than ideal. Accordingly, a case was made for the appointment of a consultant clinical pathologist, with a particular interest in both the clinical and the laboratory management of patients with haematological disease. The person appointed, in 1963, was

Dr John Moore Bridges, senior registrar in clinical pathology at the Royal Victoria Hospital.

The arrival of John Bridges in the RBHSC coincided with important changes in the academic structure and the clinical practice of pathology as a major discipline. The three elements of clinical pathology – biochemistry, bacteriology and haematology – began to separate. M.G. Nelson concentrated more and more on his expanding haematology practice while George Gibson supervised the bacteriology component. (Biochemistry on the RVH site had been the charge of Desmond W. Neill, the first graduate scientific officer in Northern Ireland, since before the inception of the National Health Service.)

The Royal College of Pathologists was founded in 1962 and was soon to establish its fellowship examination in single elements of pathology, signalling the emergence of the unidisciplinary pathologist. Heretofore, an MD or MRCP had been the passports to consultant status.

From the outset of his appointment John Bridges directed his attention to two of the most tragic diseases of childhood, leukaemia and haemophilia. Prior to the advent of chemotherapy, leukaemia was a fatal disease with no effective treatment. Gloom surrounded the whole subject, and his initial discussions with senior colleagues as to how to treat these children aggressively with the new drug therapy were not received with unalloyed enthusiasm. The usual response was to question the ethics of subjecting children to treatment which carried with it unpleasant, distressing side effects, when in six months or so they would be dead. Bridges was not discouraged by the prophets of doom and, underneath his quiet manner, manifested a vision, compassion and determination which was to transform the lives of many children and their parents.

Backed up by the Medical Research Council's trials that started in 1965–6, the highly successful treatment of childhood leukaemia gradually evolved. John Bridges had no allocated beds in the Children's Hospital, but he was greatly assisted by enlightened colleagues, such as Ivo Carré and W.A.B. Campbell. His early work eventually led, in 1970, to participation in a group haematological service in which the RBHSC laboratory was incorporated into the Department of Haematology and Bridges was redesignated consultant haematologist. Nelson retired in 1979 and Bridges was appointed to the first substantive chair in haematology, funded by the Northern Ireland Leukaemia Research Fund, whose subvention amounted to some £100,000. In August 1980 John Bridges passed on his torch to Dr S.I. Dempsey, in whose hands the service in haematology has continued to develop in tandem with the surgical and chemotherapeutic treatment of solid tumours of childhood.

THE HAEMATOLOGY UNIT

In 1983 the Northern Ireland Children's Cancer Unit Committee was

Professor John Bridges CBE, consultant haematolgist, 1963–94

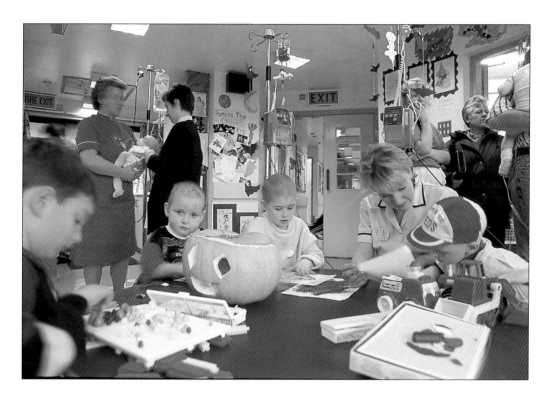

formed and meetings were sought with representatives of the Eastern Health & Social Services Board. The Children's Cancer Unit Committee was represented by Raymond Wade (chairman and parent), Nicola Rainey (secretary), Alan Cooke, William Elliott and Eunice McNeill (all parents). Representing the EHSSB were Sir Thomas Brown, J.V. Simpson, E.J. McCullagh and Dr J. McKenna. Patrons included Dr Lindy Burton, Professor N.C. Nevin, Dana, Mr V.E. Boston, Lynda Jane, Charlie Daze, Dr Barbara Lowry, Pat Seed, Willie John McBride and Alf McCreary.

The Committee expressed great optimism as to its ability to make a significant financial input and this turned out to be no idle boast. The Children's Cancer Unit Fund was launched on 30 April 1984 and raised over £1.2 million, demonstrating the generosity of Ulster people when their hearts are touched.

The new purpose-built Northern Ireland Children's Cancer Unit, usually called the Haematology Unit, was opened by Sir Thomas Brown, chairman of the EHSSB, in October 1987. It consists of eight single rooms capable of accommodating patients and, where necessary, the parents of very ill children. Many of the young patients stay in hospital for prolonged periods, and school and play facilities are provided. Dr S.I. Dempsey is the consultant in charge and Dr Carol Cairns is the clinical medical officer. The nursing sister, Barbara Carlisle, is assisted by fourteen staff nurses, one enrolled nurse and one auxiliary. Other staff include a teacher, a play specialist, a Malcolm Sargent Social Worker and a Macmillan Paediatric Nurse, the first in Northern Ireland.

The unit, now the Regional Centre, owes its existence to the perseverance of parents and friends who motivated so many people to contribute

Activity and colour in the Haematology Unit, 1997

Dr Sid Dempsey, consultant haematologist, 1980–

The Ryan Phillips Memorial
certificate, 16 May 1988

to a most worthy cause, the treatment of children suffering from leukaemia and malignant tumours. The adjacent Malcolm Sargent House provides support and accommodation for parents.

One of the most pleasing features of the last fifty years has been the continual flow of public generosity to the RBHSC, from parents and friends, small groups and larger organizations. Even the loss of a loved child has been the catalyst for effort on behalf of other children. The memorial to the short life of baby Ryan Phillips is but one example of many such selfless and heart-warming endeavours.

Twenty-seven tile pictures have also been donated to the Hospital, fourteen in Barbour Ward and thirteen in Musgrave Ward, most of them bearing the names of their donors. The tiles were manufactured by Minton Hollins of Stoke-on-Trent and supplied and fixed by a local firm, Norman MacNaughton and Sons Ltd. They include nursery rhymes, fairy tales, children's pastimes and biblical scenes. In recent times the trend in wall decoration is less formal and stylized; posters and wall murals abound, and Little Boy Blue and the Goose Girl have given place to Paddington Bear and Wallace & Gromit.

Throughout the 1980s the threat of closure hung over the Children's Hospital laboratory. A Government Working Party of 1980, under the chairmanship of Dr Robert Weir, chief medical officer at the DHSS, concluded that there should be six laboratories to cover the whole of Northern Ireland. This was open to various interpretations. One seized upon by the local administration was that the RBHSC laboratory should be closed – a proposal greeted with consternation and anger.

Five years later, in the autumn of 1985, the Pathology Ad Hoc Committee of the EHSSB continued on that road, suggesting that the Children's Hospital laboratory should be reorganized, or closed, as part of a planned development of laboratories on the Royal site. The Group Laboratory Division joined in by stating that a major laboratory redevelopment to start on the Royal site in 1986 would be providing facilities for cytopathology, microbiology, bacteriology and biochemistry. The chairman of the Laboratory Division, Professor N.C. Nevin, intimated that if work currently undertaken in the RBHSC laboratory was transferred to the main laboratory area, £80,000 per annum could be saved. Naturally, S.I. Dempsey and his colleagues were particularly concerned to maintain the status quo, especially with regard to haematology. A subcommittee was formed, consisting of Dr Dempsey, Dr Savage, Dr Carson, Dr Redmond, Dr Halliday, Mr Boston and Mr Macfarlane, to make a case for the preservation of the laboratory, in association with the Laboratory Division. Before the meeting took place, Staff were privately advised to concentrate on making a plea for retaining specific areas of biochemistry and haematology, as a comprehensive service at the Children's Hospital was out of the question.[6] Staff reluctantly accepted the loss of 'some' bacteriology and biochemistry.

The uncertainty as to the fate of the laboratory continued, with no definitive decisions taken, and in April 1990 Aileen Redmond, then chairman of the Medical Staff, wrote to the director of the laboratory services, Professor Peter Toner, expressing the Staff's dismay at the potential loss of all the biochemistry, haematology and bacteriology services provided at the Hospital. She also argued for the relocation at the laboratory of the facilities for metabolic screening, particularly for amino acids. This service was re-established, albeit temporarily, with the support of Professor E.R. Trimble, Professor of Clinical Biochemistry. With a budget continually overspent, further retrenchment was inevitable and the axe fell on bacteriology and biochemistry in 1995–6, leaving a much reduced haematology service dealing only with specimens originating in the Haematology Unit. Just one and a half technical staff equivalents remain. A portering service between the RBHSC and the main laboratories was designed to prevent logistical problems.

However, in the Department of Clinical Biochemistry in the newly refurbished Kelvin Building, all the complex biochemistry associated with paediatric diagnosis and monitoring is carried out in a paediatric laboratory with dedicated staff, under the general supervision of Geraldine Roberts, a consultant clinical biochemist. The more routine investigations, such as electrolyte measurements, can be performed on the same machines as those used for adult patients, because of the general change to the use of much smaller specimen volumes. Despite reduced budget and staffing levels, new techniques have been introduced which allow a much broader diagnostic menu. Since the paediatric laboratory provides a Regional Biochemistry Service for complex tests, it has been possible to bring in such techniques as gas chromatography and mass spectrometry for measurement of organic acids. As in all innovations, it remains necessary to assess what is technically possible and give priority to those cases requiring rapid turnaround times for adequate patient treatment. In rare and non-urgent cases it is more cost-effective to send the specimen on to a specialist centre elsewhere in the UK.

The purchase of a tandem mass spectrometer is currently being considered, which would allow for the diagnosis of inborn errors of fatty acid oxidation, since the prevalence of some of these defects is believed to be similar to that of phenylketonuria and the techniques now available in Belfast can usually make the diagnosis only when the child is acutely ill and in severe metabolic decompensation. There is already a very close collaboration with the Department of Medical Genetics, as the diagnosis of several inborn errors of metabolism is obtained by a combination of techniques involving biochemistry and genetic analysis.

THE RBHSC laboratory has had ups and downs in the hundred years of its history. Often there was a feeling of isolation from the mainstream, of uncertainty, coupled with fear of closure. In an atmosphere of constant change, it is tempting to indulge in bouts of nostalgia, to long for the individuality and proximity offered by the immediate availability of a laboratory service, staffed by loyal medical laboratory technicians. Traditionalists wince at what is perceived as increasing commercialization, with cost curtailment the operative words.

It is for others to record the effect of further technological advances and administrative changes. The day may not be far off when a robotic machine in a corner will be able to analyse and report on all manner of specimens; alternatively, a central analytical laboratory factory may be linked to the clinical area by a vacuum tube railway line, reminiscent of those in the emporia of old. (A modern version can be seen in Reid's Shoe Store in Sandy Row!)

The laboratories on the Royal and City Hospital sites were joined in administrative matrimony in 1996.

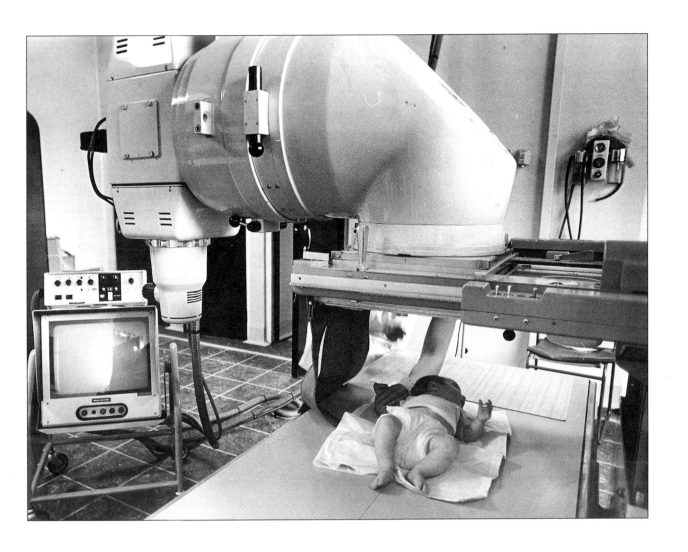

11

RADIOLOGY

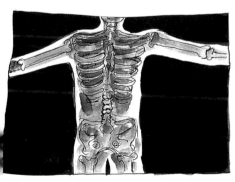

THE EARLIEST MENTION OF children being examined by X-rays at the Children's Hospital was at a meeting of the Medical Staff at Queen Street in 1911, at which T.S. Kirk informed his colleagues that Messrs Lizars, the Belfast optical and photographic firm, had decided to give up the X-ray component of their business; he mentioned the possibility of getting some work done in the Hospital.[1] There was no X-ray department in Queen Street, but the

The cumbersome X-ray apparatus of the 1960s

Medical Staff recognized the necessity for the appointment of a radiologist who might advise the architect on the planning of such a department in the new Hospital on the Falls Road. At their first meeting in the new Hospital on 20 April 1932, the first business on the agenda was radiology. A letter was read from A.S. Atkinson, secretary of the Board, asking the Medical Staff to obtain competitive estimates for the installation of X-ray apparatus. With some confusion as to terminology, the matter was referred to the 'radiographer', Dr Richard McCulloch. McCulloch, a former tuberculosis officer and private radiologist, was appointed physician-in-charge of the new department. Any worries there may have been as to the cost of the necessary equipment were allayed when Mrs McCormick, of Cultra, donated the entire amount in memory of her daughter Elizabeth and her father-in-law. Her generous gift of £1,000 was acknowledged by a brass tablet affixed to the east wall above the consultant's reporting desk, which reads:

IN LOVING MEMORY OF
ELIZABETH
30 MARCH 1932
AND HER GRANDFATHER, HUGH McNEILL McCORMICK,
8 AUGUST 1914

On the advice of Dr McCulloch a Schall two-valve generating unit with control trolley, together with the necessary overhead high-tension distribution gear, was installed, along with a Potter Bucky couch, a teletechnique chest stand and a complete set of darkroom equipment. None of it was shockproofed and a nurse received a severe shock when her head came in contact with a tube pole while she was trying to restrain an unruly child.

McCulloch died within a year of his appointment. The Staff hoped that the post would be filled by Dr James Gillespie, who, as F.M.B. Allen reported to his colleagues, 'was desirous in taking up radiography'. At the Staff meeting on 29 November 1933, several items of X-ray interest were on the agenda. The attention of the Medical Staff was called to the resolution of the Board that 'a fee of two guineas is to be charged for any emergency X-ray photograph taken to oblige a surgeon'. More seriously, it was reported that another nurse had received a bad shock while working in the X-ray Department, in similar fashion to her colleague. The Staff advised that a fully qualified lay radiographer be obtained to take charge of the department pending the appointment of Dr Gillespie. A letter was written to Messrs Schall reporting the incident and asking for advice as to the possibility of protecting the tube poles; the danger of washing the floor of the X-ray room was pointed out.

Tragically, Gillespie, who was undergoing training in radiology in England, was killed in a motor accident. Two members of the Nursing Staff were assigned to carry on the work, an arrangement which led Kirk to describe the X-ray facilities at the Hospital as the best in Belfast.

Furthermore, he expressed the fear that a radiologist might attempt to curtail the hours during which the services would be available! Others of contrary opinion, among them T.H. Crozier, initiated an informal discussion regarding the possible appointment of a radiologist, and soon afterwards an extract from the Board of Management minutes intimated that Dr Douglas Boyd had made a formal application for that position. The Board referred this to the Medical Staff for a decision as to his suitability, at the same time asking them to draft regulations for the running of the department. On the proposal of P.T. Crymble and Ian Fraser, Boyd was appointed, the vote being nine to one in his favour. A previous amendment moved by Dr Rowland Hill found no seconder.[2]

The rules for the X-ray Department on Boyd's appointment reveal the caution with which the new speciality was accepted by the medical establishment.

> 1 The X-ray department shall be available for work at any time.
>
> 2 The radiologist shall be a specialist in his work.
>
> 3 There shall always be two trained members of the nursing staff capable of taking radiograms.
>
> 4 The radiologist shall be responsible for the upkeep and condition of the apparatus.
>
> 5 The radiologist shall attend each morning with the exception of Sunday.

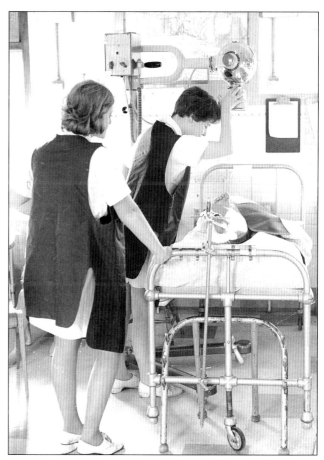

Boyd prevailed upon the Board to shockproof the hitherto unprotected X-ray tubes and to have none other than qualified technicians responsible for the radiography. The first full-time non-resident radiographer, Miss Whiteside, took her membership of the Society of Radiographers examination from the Hospital. There was no extra remuneration for the radiographer for work undertaken outside normal working hours, and calls to take photographs which did not constitute genuine emergencies were a source of concern. In a ruling on this matter, it was emphasized that the house surgeons may, on their own responsibility, call a radiographer for a suspected depressed fracture of the skull, for severe fractures involving joints or to locate swallowed foreign bodies causing embarrassment or shock, but for no other condition unless the urgency was confirmed by a member of the Medical or Surgical Staff. In 1938 a small shockproof portable unit was added to the equipment and the house staff were allowed to take X-ray photographs for themselves, a privilege which they enjoyed.

An early portable X-ray machine, c. 1960

DOUGLAS BOYD, consultant radiologist, 1935–72, was a cultured man with wide and varied interests. His radiological practice was not confined to paediatrics; he was also radiologist to the Benn Hospital, a special centre for ENT and ophthalmology, and the Belfast Ophthalmic Hospital, as well as running a thriving private practice, which included referrals from several of the local vets. Dr Boyd was extremely interested in the physical production of X-rays and he combined theoretical knowledge of physics with expertise in electrical engineering. If the X-ray equipment malfunctioned while he was in the department, he regarded this as a challenge rather than an inconvenience, and his reaction was to reach for a screwdriver and attempt to rectify the fault, rather than call out the engineers.

Dr Paul Thomas,
consultant radiologist, 1968–

In the same year the scope of the department was increased by the acquisition of a superficial therapy X-ray tube and stand, to be used in the treatment of ringworm. (A new therapy tube of improved design and free from the faults of its predecessor was installed in 1947.) A gift from *Uncle Mac's Children's Hour* of the BBC allowed the purchase of a Solus ward unit costing £220. In the period 1934–47 the number of diagnostic examinations rose from 2,642 to 5,855, an increase of over 50 per cent. Allowing for the sharp reduction in the demands for X-ray during 1941, the year of the air raids and the mass evacuation of children from the Belfast area, Boyd estimated that at the end of the next five years, the total of diagnostic examinations would be between 8,855 and 9,855, a figure that in his view would necessitate a completely new X-ray Department, together with an increase in staff, both in radiology and radiography.

Boyd is remembered for his skilled and innovative contribution to the radiological investigation of 'blue babies'. During the 1950s he was involved in the first angiocardiograms performed in Ireland and had a prototype rapid film changer designed to his specification which was used for these examinations. It was never produced commercially, as a similar but superior machine was brought out shortly after by one of the major X-ray equipment manufacturers. (See pp. 24–5.)

Paediatric radiology developed swiftly as a sub-speciality in the 1960s and the work in the Children's Hospital became too much for one part-time radiologist. Dr Paul Thomas, trained at University College Hospital and the Hospital for Sick Children, Great Ormond Street, London, was appointed in 1968 with a commitment to the Children's Hospital. When Boyd retired in 1972, he was succeeded by Dr D. Beatty Crawford – the only candidate to apply for the post. As he was not trained as a paediatric radiologist, Crawford went to the USA for a year's training at the Johns Hopkins Hospital, Baltimore. However, the attractions of the New World were so irresistible that he decided to stay permanently. When it became known that Crawford was not returning, Thomas transferred his adult sessions at the RVH to paediatric radiology. However, he remained single-handed until 1979, when Dr Cyril Morrison was appointed to the Staff. At this time, ultrasonography was expanding rapidly and with the introduction of suitable transducers it became an ideal imaging technique for paediatrics. Dr Morrison, a graduate of Trinity College Dublin, who had paediatric medical attachments prior to training in radiology, was particularly interested in the applications of ultrasound. He made a considerable contribution to the development of this method of diagnosis in the Hospital, but succumbed to the temptation to return to his family roots in the north of the province when a post became vacant in Altnagelvin Hospital, Londonderry, in 1983.

Dr Thomas was left alone again until the appointment of Dr Louise Evelyn Sweeney in 1985. She was a graduate of Queen's University who had worked as a paediatric senior house officer in the RBHSC prior to training as a radiologist. In addition to her radiological training in Northern Ireland, she had spent time in neuroradiology in Bristol and in paediatric radiology at Great Ormond Street, London, and Alder Hey in Liverpool. She was appointed to a post split between the RVH and the RBHSC and had responsibility for paediatric imaging procedures carried out on the Royal site outside the Children's Hospital, such as Computerized Tomography (CT) scanning. She also had special expertise and interest in ultrasonography, which continued to expand in scope and improve in quality. Although initially it was performed by a radiologist and one or two specially trained radiographers, the growing demand could be met only by training all radiographers for the task.

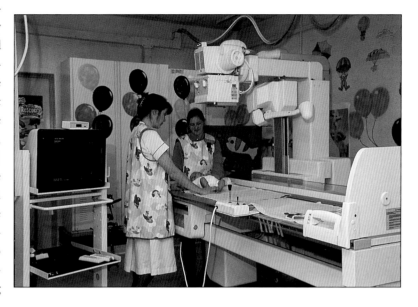

X-ray apparatus, 1997

The Children's Hospital has been extremely fortunate in the calibre of radiographic staff. Deirdre Capper, superintendent radiographer for some twenty years until her retirement in 1985, was always alert to the needs of patients, parents and members of Staff and was a skilled communicator. She carried the service with efficiency and good humour through the difficult 1970s, with increasing workload and static Staff levels. The most significant rise was in out-of-hours work. This meant that the old system of a radiographer being on call from home during the night had to give way to the presence of a radiographer in the Hospital at all times. Deirdre Capper was succeeded by her long-time deputy, June Barker, until she, too, retired in 1988. Jeanette Robinson then took over but in 1991 she moved to Daisy Hill Hospital, Newry, and was replaced by the current superintendent, Jennifer McKinstry.[3]

Urgent demands for extension and upgrading of the department were accepted in principle by the NIHA in 1973, but it was not until a decade later that they became a reality. The refurbished department opened without ceremony in April 1983.

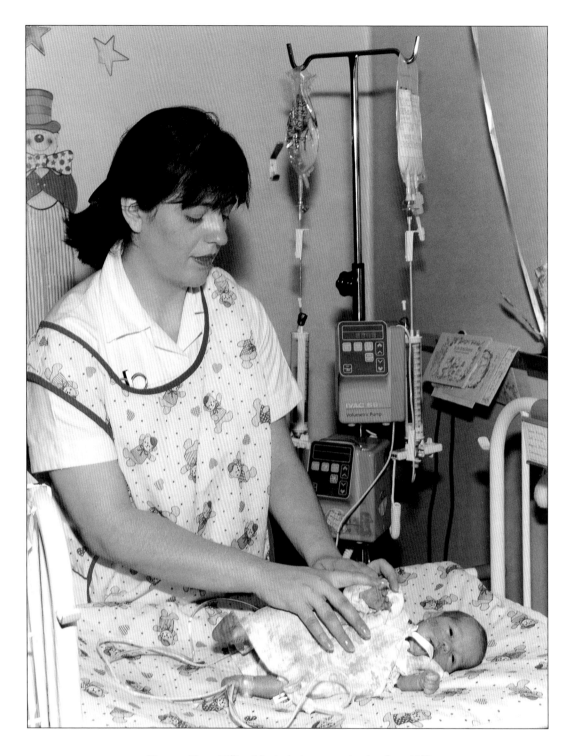

Nursery Nurse Gillian Martin laying on caring hands, *c.* 1995

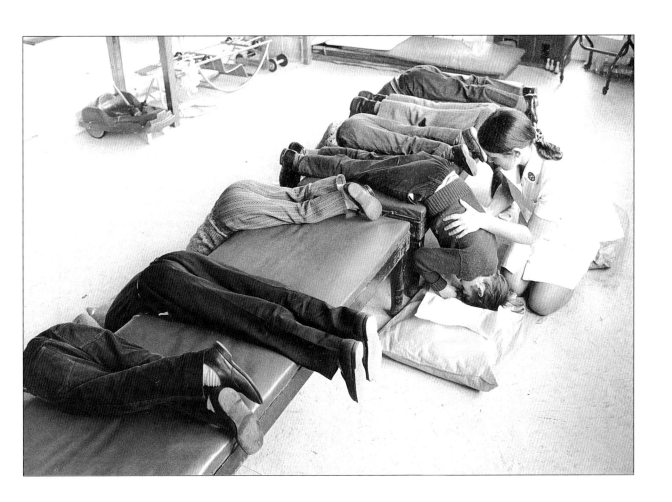

12

THE CLINICAL SERVICES

PHYSIOTHERAPY

In 1920 Joseph Boyce was appointed masseur to the Hospital. Boyce had served in the army during World War I and lost his sight in action at Arras in April 1917. Trained at St Dunstan's Institution for Blinded Soldiers and Sailors, he held the certificate for massage and electrical treatment. In November 1927, with the move to another location in view, the Staff at Queen Street concluded that among the essential features of any new hospital would be a separate gymnasium,

Group physiotherapy –
an asthma class in the 1960s

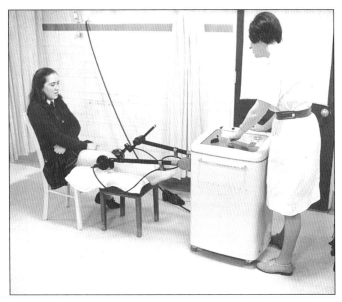

Senior physiotherapist Marie Kennedy applying deep heat treatment to a patient's knee, c. 1962

facilities for ultraviolet light and massage rooms. The new physiotherapy department on the Falls Road was at first called the Light Department, presumably due to the importance attached to ultraviolet radiation in the treatment of tuberculosis – a major problem of the day. Ivan McCaw was given charge of the light treatments and the assistant surgeons took control of massage and remedial exercises.

With increasing development of the service, the appointment of a full-time physiotherapist was considered and information was obtained from England concerning the organization of similar departments. In December 1945 Kathleen Yarr was appointed as a full-time physiotherapist on the recommendation of two surgeons, J.S. Loughridge and H.P. Hall. This evoked a letter from Joseph Boyce stating he had been honorary masseur/physiotherapist to the RBHSC for twenty-three years and wished to have his status clarified. It was agreed that his position should be confirmed as a part-time physiotherapist on a salary scale of 10s 6d per session (three sessions per week).

When the department located in 1949 to an area adjacent to the Paul Ward, Dr George Gregg, consultant in physical medicine at the Royal Victoria Hospital, made himself responsible for equipping it, an action perceived by the Staff as the first move in a takeover bid. Such was the esteem in which physiotherapy was held that it was suggested that a physiotherapist should have charge of the department and be given equal rights to other consultants on the Staff. Apparently, some one was confused between medical consultants in physical medicine and physiotherapists.

In 1950 the department came under the charge of the Department of Physical Medicine, RVH, and Dr Gregg requested teaching facilities, so that trainees in physical medicine could gain experience with children. While agreeing to this request, Staff stipulated that Kathleen Yarr's position should remain under their direction. When, in 1957, Dr Gregg was appointed to control the physiotherapy departments in the whole Group, the Staff continued to reserve the right to make direct physiotherapy appointments to the RBHSC and insisted that the new Group superintendent physiotherapist should not have overriding authority. George Gregg responded that he did not wish to upset the status quo at the Children's Hospital and, in a spirit of mutual respect and goodwill, quiet diplomacy prevailed and Dr Gregg was invited to join the Medical Staff of the Children's Hospital in October 1959.

The poliomyelitis epidemic of the 1950s was a stimulus to the art and science of physiotherapy and it was in this decade that the first hydrotherapy pool in Northern Ireland was established in Whiteabbey Hospital. In the

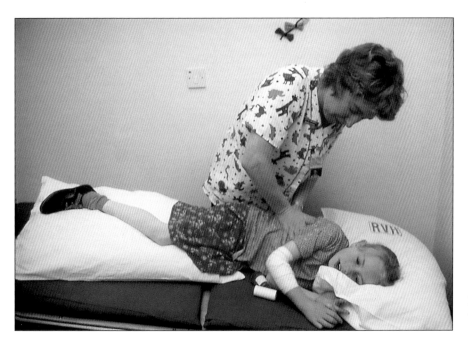

Physiotherapist Joyce Murray
with a cystic fibrosis patient, 1997

1960s physiotherapy for chest complaints was a routine procedure and classes for asthma sufferers were established in the Outpatient Department. Orthopaedic rehabilitation was another important branch work. Since then there has been a progressive, evolutionary expansion of paediatric physiotherapy. In the 1970s the department met the challenge of cystic fibrosis and the increasing requests for help from the Intensive Care Unit, where physiotherapy's ability to help newborn and very small babies with respiratory distress syndrome was of vital importance. A twenty-four-hour on-call emergency system to cover acute diseases of the chest, post-operative cardiac care and the treatment of haemophiliacs further extended the work of the department. It is noteworthy that this extensive service was carried on in spite of less than adequate Staff levels. This decade saw the emergence of more formal training for physiotherapists, with the establishment, first, of a university pass degree, followed by an honours course. When a Child Development Clinic was established in the Hospital, the service had an important part to play, assisting, successively, Dr Christopher Green, Dr Maurice Savage and Dr Nan Hill.

In the 1980s multidisciplinary teams brought a wide range of expertise to patients suffering from cardiac disease, neurological conditions, cystic fibrosis and spina bifida – ironically, at the same time as pressure was being exerted to contract the service. However, there was general satisfaction in 1987 at the opening of an enlarged and upgraded department, including a hydrotherapy pool. Children with orthopaedic problems, childhood arthritis, neurological conditions or severe burns greatly benefited from the therapeutic effects of hydrotherapy. Pain was relieved and relaxation induced; the range of limb

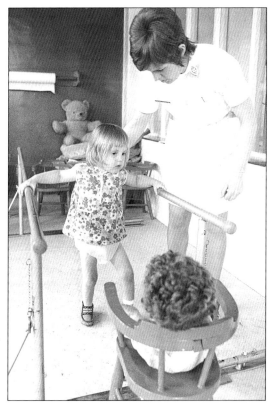

A young patient learns to walk
after injury, c. 1960s.

A mother and daughter enjoying the
hydrotherapy pool, opened in 1987

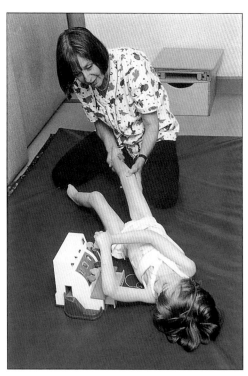

Dama O'Neill, superintendent
physiotherapist (1985–), performing
the therapeutic version of the
'leg pull', *c.* 1997

movement and muscle power were maintained. With the appointment of
Dr David Webb in the mid-1990s, a Head Injury Unit staffed by a multidisciplinary team was established, necessitating a high input from the
Physiotherapy Department in the acute post-injury phase. In addition to a physiotherapist, the team includes a speech therapist, an
occupational therapist, a psychologist, a social worker and a liaison
nurse.

OCCUPATIONAL THERAPY

Occupational therapy was established on the Royal Hospitals site in
1968, with the opening of the new Outpatient Department at the
Royal Victoria Hospital. It was located within the Department of
Rehabilitation (Physical Medicine) under the control of Dr George
Gregg. When Gwenda Dunlop was appointed head occupational
therapist at the Royal Group of Hospitals in 1972, she made
enquiries regarding the need for occupational therapy at the RBHSC.
The response was that the Hospital had adequate therapy using the
'army of Toy Ladies' – indicating the confusion in some minds
between occupational play and occupational therapy – and the matter was not pursued. In 1976 Dr Aileen Redmond suggested that an
occupational therapist would be most valuable in the Hospital during the school holidays.

However, in 1979 Dr Christopher Green asked Gwenda Dunlop to
provide a service in the newly established Joint Therapy Clinic for

handicapped children. A preliminary review of some one hundred children revealed that assessment, followed by advice to parents, was no substitute for adequate treatment, and so in spite of scarce resources a programme was organized, together with instruction sessions for parents. A so-called 'clumsy group' was set up, consisting of children who were attending normal schools but were handicapped by severe perceptual problems.

The straitened circumstances of the early 1980s had a serious effect on the occupational therapy service. In 1982 a request for further input into the Joint Therapy Clinic was turned down by the Area Board, and in 1983 the occupational therapy establishment allocated to the RBHSC ceased to exist, and the therapist seconded from the RVH was withdrawn. Nevertheless, Dunlop agreed to provide for three specific categories of patients at the Hospital: i) individual patients by special request; ii) severe burns; and iii) patients transferred from the Neurosurgery Department of the RVH to the RBHSC.

Significant relief of the unsatisfactory staffing situation did not come until 1991, when Dr C.M.B. Field's original child assessment clinic at the Musgrave Park Hospital transferred to the RBHSC, to become the Child Development Clinic. In December Ruth Page was appointed full-time occupational therapist at the Children's Hospital, the first substantive appointment in this clinical speciality for nearly a decade. Yet another directional change in the service took place in 1996, when the Child Development Clinic left the Hospital to relocate in the community.

The Hospital's Occupational Therapy Department is now part of the paediatric neurology service. Marlene Pickett, appointed 1 October 1996, is concerned with the relief of neurological problems of childhood sustained as a result of either neurological disease or trauma. Plans are afoot to extend the service to burns and plastic surgery. The Departments of Physiotherapy and Occupational Therapy work in close harmony, each complementing the work of the other. The physiotherapist's skill is directed towards the establishment of muscle joint movement, with the object of achieving in the patient a quality of independent mobility. Occupational therapy, through activity and play, aims to help the patient to gain independence in skills for daily living.

SPEECH AND LANGUAGE THERAPY

In December 1938 Molly Christie (neé Hayward) opened a Speech Clinic at the BHSC – the first of its kind in Ireland. The majority of her first cases were 'stammerers', 'lallers', retarded speakers, the deaf, 'lispers' and patients with neurological disorders. She returned to England in 1945 and was succeeded by Joyce Mitchell, just demobbed from the Auxiliary Territorial Service, who stayed until 1952. In 1950, with the coming of plastic surgery, the service was extended to care for children with harelip and cleft palate, marking the beginning of a significant expansion. Outreach clinics were established in the City and County Hospital, Londonderry. Children came by ambulance to the Children's Hospital and referrals began to arrive from the neurosurgeons and neurologists, including adult patients following laryngectomy.

In 1954 Bettina Kay from Lincoln became senior speech therapist, establishing assessment and treatment techniques for children and adults with communication problems until her untimely death from leukaemia in 1977. From 1963 the Northern Ireland Hospitals Authority's policy was to form a pool of therapists based in the RBHSC, with Bettina Kay allocating staff to clinics with greatest need. Muckamore Abbey and Lisburn Special Care School were among the first to benefit. The contracts for student speech therapists provided by the NIHA, to encourage recruitment in Northern Ireland, were abolished in 1968 and Kay was left to work an expanding service virtually single-handed. In order to cope with the many patients referred, she organized group therapy for pre-school 'stammerers' and adults with dysphasia, as well as being involved in the Regional Joint Cleft Palate Clinic and individual therapy sessions for both children and adults.

Formal training for speech therapists did not begin until 1975, when the first intake of students commenced their course in the Northern Ireland Polytechnic, now the University of Ulster at Jordanstown.

In the 1990s the six speech therapists covering the Royal Hospitals are based at the RBHSC – clinical specialists delivering a service to Paediatrics, ENT, Medical and Neuroscience Directorates. The emphasis is on multi-disciplinary activity, with more and more babies and very young children being referred, together with a large number of in- and outpatients with developmental and acquired speech and language disorders.

The Hospital currently has one full-time and one part-time therapist to provide a service to the Regional Child Development Clinic, the Regional Joint Cleft Palate Clinic and to in-patients with communication difficulties due to head injury and neurological disorder.[1]

ELECTROENCEPHALOGRAPHY (EEG)

The EEG Department opened in 1972 with Jean Aiken the operating technician in charge. After only six months in post she emigrated to Australia, resulting in the closure of the department for two years. The service was reopened in 1974, with the appointment of Hilary Todd at the age of nineteen. She had trained in the EEG Unit attached to the Neurosurgical Department of the Royal Victoria Hospital, under the tutelage of Alison Brown and Dr Harold Millar.

The RBHSC EEG Department was originally located in the reception room of the Clark Children's Clinic (then the private wing of the

Nurses preparing feeds, *c.* 1950s

Hospital), but the proliferation of records and the increasing size of the equipment necessitated a move to an office which had been the original home of the Intensive Care Unit. Patients were taken from within the Hospital, but soon requests for the facility were received from other hospitals in Belfast and from as far away as Londonderry.

The transistorized EEG machine was replaced in 1991 by digitized equipment, less subject to extraneous electrical interference. Multichannel recordings of abnormal brain activity are an indispensable diagnostic tool in neurological diseases where seizures are a feature.

A second technician, Claire Anderson, joined the department in 1995.

NUTRITION AND DIETETICS

Dietetics is the application of the science of nutrition to the construction of diets and the selection and preparation of food. The first dietician to the Hospital was Jean Stevenson, appointed in 1948. Her input was on a part-time basis as the principles of dietetics and nutrition were still in the process of development. A significant step forward was taken with the appointment in 1960 of Mary E. Beck, who began to place diet and nutrition on a scientific rather than a domestic basis. Her book *Nutrition and Dietetics for Nurses*, published in 1962, ran to five editions and became a standard reference work. At first the staff had to cope with primitive accommodation, until the building works necessary to provide accommodation for the Intensive Care Unit and the Hospital canteen created more space for the diet kitchen.

Mary Beck, chief dietician, 1960–82, serving dinners

Traditionally, the milk room for babies was the responsibility of the Nursing Staff, and with the evolution of special diets these too became the responsibility of the nursing auxiliaries and student nurses. In 1985 the Catering Department took over the preparation of special diets and in 1991 it assumed full responsibility for the milk room, making up feeds prescribed by the dietician. Since that time the milk room has been staffed by catering assistants.

A feature of the department's work has been the enteral feeding, in which the feed is administered via a fine bore stomach tube, in a single bolus or continuous drip. Until 1989 the feeds were 'home-made', later to be replaced by commercially produced preparations such as Paediasure (Ross) or Nutrison (Cow & Gate).

The dieticians have an important role in the Hospital team, dealing with inborn errors of metabolism such as phenylketonuria, where an accumulation of the amino acid phenylalanine leads to mental retardation, unless treated by a diet low in that ingredient. Feeds are made up of protein containing all the amino acids (except phenylalanine) carbohydrate, fat, vitamins and minerals. This regime, together with the wider variety of commercially produced protein-free foods, has greatly improved the quality of life for children with this disorder. The needs of the Hospital population not on special diets has not been forgotten; children with normal digestive processes are similarly in need of nutritious meals.

Teaching and research have continued to be an important part of the Nutrition and Dietetic Department of the Hospital. Attachment to the unit has always engendered a lasting interest in paediatric nutrition. Several students have returned to work in the department as members of the senior Staff; more have gone to join paediatric departments elsewhere or to set up units in other hospitals.[2]

The present department staff consists of two part-time and two full-time dieticians. The part-time members are Janet Mercer, appointed in 1989, and Ruth Thom, appointed in 1992 (having previously held a post from 1979 to 1984). Christine McCabe, appointed in 1995, and Hilary Morrison, appointed in 1996, have full-time posts.

SOCIAL SERVICES

The first social worker, J.S. Binns, was appointed in 1943, and given the title of certified hospital almoner. The word 'almoner' conjures up a picture of charity to the poor, and indeed a considerable proportion of the work of the early social workers was concerned with the assessment of the ability to pay, the degree of need and the distribution of funds to the impoverished. The Institute of Almoners was set up in 1945, and in 1964 they became medical social workers.[3]

J.S. Binns resigned in 1946, to be succeeded by Helena Eves and M.Y. Brown. The period of Helena Eves's service, 1946–83, was one of rapid development and expansion of the social services within the Hospital. The department became involved not only in practical financial help to the needy but, increasingly, in the solving of complex social and emotional problems. This functional change continued under a series of senior social workers. Mary Gallagher was appointed after Helena Eves and she in turn was followed by Joan Donnelly. The present incumbent is Sandra Ker.

Stained-glass window in the Chapel of Rest, 1992

The modern department is a branch of the North & West Belfast Health & Social Services Trust and has links throughout the Hospital. It has an important statutory function in the sensitive area of child abuse and neglect. Social workers are attached to units such as haematology, cardiology and nephrology and are involved with any child with a complicated medical or surgical complaint. The service interdigitates with the Department of Clinical Psychology in cases of behavioural and emotional problems.

Parent counselling forms a significant part of the department's work. This is especially valuable at a time of bereavement or during a protracted traumatic experience – for example, parents who suffer the agony of watching a beloved child so near and yet so remote in the unfamiliar and, to them, threatening world of the Intensive Care Unit. The annual interdenominational service of remembrance, conducted by the Hospital chaplains, regularly attracts a congregation of five hundred, including representatives of the Medical and Nursing Staff. The present chaplains with their colleagues are as follows: Church of Ireland, Reverend Gary R. Shaw; Presbyterian, Reverend Derek J. Boden; Methodist, Reverend David J. Kerr; Catholic, Father Paul Byrne; and other denominations, Reverend James A. Lemon.

On 7 October 1992 a Children's Chapel of Rest was dedicated by the Reverend Sydney Callaghan.

Can I see another's woe,
and not be in sorrow too.
Can I see another's grief,
and not seek for kind relief.
WILLIAM BLAKE

The transformation of the old mortuary into a chapel of rest has been carried out in response to the vision of the Accident and Emergency Personal Services Initiative Team. The death of a child is inevitably a very sad event for the parents. Members of the team felt that it might bring some comfort to bereaved parents to know that their child was surrounded by beauty, even in death. Many people have given of their skills, others have given of their resources . . . All have given with love and with a sensitive awareness of the ultimate sadness in the death of a child. To all of you who gave of yourselves, we say 'Thank You' for the generous spirits that saw 'another's woe' and sought to give relief.

In 1996 the Bereavement Quality Group, consisting of representatives from a wide range of Hospital activity, provided a Book of Remembrance, ensuring that little patients who, in spite of all the resources of modern medicine, did not survive are still lovingly remembered by parents, relations and Staff.

The department's influence extends into the community, liaising and negotiating with the statutory bodies responsible for the provision of housing and family support.

CLINICAL PSYCHOLOGY

Clinical and educational psychology formed part of the child guidance service established in 1943. In the 1970s, with the merger of the Department of Child Psychiatry at the Belfast City Hospital and the child guidance service forming a Regional Child Mental Health Service, clinical psychology began to establish a wider service within the Children's Hospital. During the 1970s and 1980s clinical psychologists worked alongside child psychiatrists, social workers and throughout the paediatric specialities. In 1988 the role of the psychologist expanded with the appointment of Nichola Rooney to a post in paediatric cardiology. Further expansion occurred with the transfer of the Regional Child Mental Health Service from Lissue House to Forster Green Hospital and with the provision of a psychology service to the Intensive Care Unit and the general paediatric specialities. Until 1991 clinical psychologists had been organized as an area service within the Eastern Health & Social Services Board, under the direction of Dr Desmond Poole, and managed by the medical administration in the Royal Group of Hospitals with the other non-medical clinical services. The Department of Clinical Psychology was formally established in 1991 with the appointment of a services manager, Patricia Donnelly, and in 1994 she also became the first clinical director of the reorganized non-medical specialities, as the Directorate of Clinical Professions.[4]

13

THE BELFAST HOSPITAL SCHOOL

IN NORTHERN IRELAND at any given time there are several hundred children whose general education is at risk due to prolonged hospitalization. Hospital schools exist to deal with this problem. Ministry of Education Acts in 1927 and 1947 recognized the need for maintaining children's educational standards while they were in hospital, stating that 'it shall be the duty of every local Education Authority to ascertain what children require special education treatment'. Education in hospital has two main aims: i) to ensure that children do not fall behind in their school work, so that when they return to their ordinary schools they will be able to continue with their peers; ii) to assist children, especially young children of nursery and

Joan Hennessy teaching in
Paul Ward, 1996

reception class age, to develop mentally in an orderly and harmonious manner. A child's removal from the normal home environment is a traumatic experience, and the continuation of school, even in hospital, provides stable conditions with which the child is familiar.

Computer technology is part of the curriculum, 1996

The education of children in hospital in Northern Ireland was first undertaken in the Belfast Municipal Sanatorium in Whiteabbey. During World War II a number of hospital schools appeared, at the Children's Hospital, Greenisland, Cushendall Cottage Hospital, the Ulster Hospital and the Dufferin & Ava Hospital. These were followed by the Musgrave Park Emergency School, set up in November 1946 with a staff of a principal teacher and one assistant teacher. Less than ten years later, this school had thirty-seven pupils on its roll and a staff of three teachers. In the 1980s, with an enrolment of forty pupils, six teachers and two classroom assistants were in attendance.

The Dufferin & Ava Hospital School came into being in April 1943. This school functioned in the Belfast City Hospital and the Royal Belfast Hospital for Sick Children. Over the next ten years it flourished, increasing its staff to a principal, vice-principal, nine assistants and one temporary teacher, with a total enrolment of sixty-three hospital children and sixty-two home tuition pupils by the middle of 1957. The next significant chapter in the history of the Dufferin & Ava Hospital School was the establishment in September 1969 of a teaching unit in the RBHSC, at the request of Dr Wilfred Campbell. Initially, there was one teacher, N. Murphy, later to be joined by E. Murphy; they shared in the task of teaching children throughout the Hospital.

The Belfast Hospital School was set up in September 1991 with the amalgamation of two of the oldest established hospital schools in Belfast, the Dufferin & Ava School and the Musgrave Park School. This amalgamation coincided with the introduction of the Northern Ireland Common Curriculum, the equivalent of the new Common Curriculum for England and Wales, which is intended to give children a broader education base with the introduction of science into the school system as a third element of a compulsory core, along with mathematics and English. The educational logic behind the amalgamation was the ability of one large school with a combined staff to offer the best and widest possible education to sick children. At the end of the 1980s, with paediatric medicine being concentrated more and more at the RBHSC and with the imminent closure of the Ava Hospital, the decision was made to vacate the school premises at the Belfast City Hospital and move entirely to the RBHSC. With the good offices of Gordon Clarke, the Directorate manager, and Dr Dennis Carson, chairman of the Board of Governors of the Hospital School, accommodation was secured for the teaching staff, who required a permanent base from which to plan and prepare for further progress.

The school caters for the educational needs of children as young as pre-school and as old as those studying for A levels. The only restrictions placed upon the school are the physical limitations of the pupils; therefore, physical education, drama and some field trips are excluded. Many scientific experiments are also excluded due to safety and other Hospital regulations. The school's daily enrolment is 130 to 140 pupils, with approximately 30 per cent of the children on home tuition. In 1993 the school had its first general inspection, which it passed with flying colours. A letter from the senior education officer of the Belfast Education & Library Board was complimentary:

> The Inspectorate as you know was very impressed by the quality of the teaching in the school and the spirit of co-operation which you have established amongst your staff. You will appreciate that I have read many general inspection reports and, in my experience, the Inspectorate seldom makes such favourable comments about the quality of teaching in a school. Such consistently positive remarks from the Inspectorate is praise indeed and something of which the school can be justly proud.

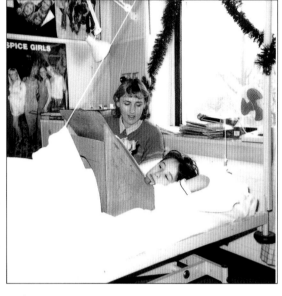

Confinement to bed is no obstacle to learning – Marian Slevin gives a one-to-one teaching session, 1997

The school has been supported most generously by the Ladies' League, the Working Men's Committee of the Royal Victoria Hospital, the Friends of Musgrave Park Hospital and individual parents, who have donated computers and other equipment in appreciation of the school's value to their children. The staff have an excellent working relationship with their medical and nursing colleagues, who have always been available to help in any way possible in encouraging and promoting educational normality within the Hospital. Two medical consultants sit on the Board of Governors and take a full part in all matters concerning the school. While there are certain restrictions for staff working within the Hospital environment, they are not plagued with probably the two greatest problems which face many schools today: unsupportive or apathetic parents and discipline problems with children. It is satisfactory to observe a child who has kept abreast of the school curriculum and is enabled to return to mainstream education ahead of classmates in most areas of the work.

Bruce Comfort, the principal, sums up the work of the school in these words: 'I can safely say that every member of staff is not only fulfilled in what they do but, also, feel a great privilege in helping children to continue their education with the constant support of parents, even in times of imminent pain, suffering and sorrow.'

Bruce Comfort, principal teacher in the Belfast Hospital School, was appointed in 1991.

Delighted expectation
on the faces of the
children when
Christmas parcels are
delivered by pupils
from various
Belfast schools

14

THE LADIES' LEAGUE

Since its beginning in 25 King Street, the Hospital has greatly benefited by the efforts of public-spirited ladies who have given of their time and substance to improve the care and welfare of patients. The value placed upon such voluntary assistance was made clear in the rules of the Hospital issued in the *1st Annual Report of the Belfast Hospital for Sick Children* in 1874. Under the heading of a Ladies' Committee, the following appears:

It shall be in the power of the Board of Management to avail themselves of the assistance of such ladies among the contributors as may form themselves into or be nominated by the Board of Management as a Ladies' Committee for the purpose of organising and carrying out a plan of aiding in the collection and augmentation of the funds of the Institution; and for providing articles of household use for the Hospital or of clothing for its poor inmates; and generally for supporting the interests of the Institution by the act of exercise of their influence in their several circles of society.

The Ladies' Committee shall appoint from among themselves lady visitors not exceeding three at any one time whose duty it shall be to visit the Hospital, to examine into the efficiency of the arrangements, and to inscribe in a book, to be kept for that purpose, any observations or suggestions which may occur to them, for the consideration of the Board of Management. It shall be the duty of the lady visitors to revise, half yearly along with Matron, the stock of household and cooking utensils, bed clothing, etc., within the hospital in order to ascertain whether or not they may be sufficient in quantity, in good order, and to report accordingly to the Board of Management.

The first president of the Ladies' Managing Committee was Mrs Henry Smyth.

A hospital devoted totally to the care of children caught the public imagination, and the evident enthusiasm of the ladies was matched by a surge of generosity. Over thirty city and outlying districts were assiduously canvassed and money began to flow in from individual subscribers and from the business community. Mothers contributed in gratitude for the preservation of a child's life, and in day schools and Sunday schools the children themselves responded to the need. Three ladies gave five shillings each to keep a convalescent child for a week at the seaside, and another individual gave a penny to each child in the Hospital. The food supply was continually augmented by gifts of bread, fresh vegetables, biscuits, jelly, buttermilk and beef tea. More unusual items such as wine whey and Brand's Essence were gratefully received. Among other gifts, in 1873, were a remnant of scarlet flannel and a piece of calico from Mrs Richardson, a canary bird from Master O'Brien, and from Mr Chittenden a cask of porter – it is not clear for whose delectation this gift was intended. Nothing was wasted; even milk left over from a soirée in the museum found its way to the Hospital. Extra clothing for the children became a top priority and the ladies saw to it that the clothing cupboard was never empty. This service was placed on a more formal footing with the formation of the Clothing Guild and the Linen League.

The Ladies' Committee first became involved in the clinical field when in 1881 a splint fund was set up by Ethel MacKenzie. Several ladies met on a weekly basis to knit, mend, patch and darn children's clothing and other household items, an activity which survived into the 1970s. Alexandra Day and Pound Day were occasions when special collections were taken. On Pound Day of 24 November 1932, the Duchess of Abercorn graciously attended, to receive gifts and to declare the new Hospital on the Falls Road open. (The Hospital admitted its first patients on 11 April 1932.)

In 1929 a junior branch of the Ladies' Committee was set up. It consisted of some ninety members who, with youthful enthusiasm, provided toys at Christmas and roses on Alexandra Day, and organized golf competitions,

The opening of the refurbished Musgrave Ward, Paul Ward and physiotherapy complex, 28 October 1992.
Left to right:
Mrs P. Robb, Ladies' League, Dr J.F.T. Glasgow, chairman of the Medical Staff, Mrs M.J. Graham, nurse manager,.Professor J.A. Dodge, Professor I.V. Carré, Mrs Dama O'Neill, superintendent physiotherapist, and Mrs A. Scott, chairperson of the Ladies' League.

gymkhanas and other fund-raising activities. (In 1902 a 'ping pong' tournament was the first sporting activity to augment the Hospital's coffers.)

In 1946 the Ladies' Committee moved further to support the clinical field by purchasing an electrocardiographic machine (the first in the Hospital) at a cost of £260, together with the 'newest' type of anaesthetic apparatus, costing £157 10s, and an instrument cabinet, at £67 15s.

The last formal meeting of the Ladies' Committee took place on 5 January 1949, and on 30 June of the same year a special meeting was called, with Mrs A.T. Boyd presiding. The ladies agreed that a sum of £991 5s 9d, standing in the Belfast Hospital for Sick Children's Ladies' Committee Comforts Fund, and lodged in the Belfast Savings Bank, should be transferred to the Royal Belfast Hospital for Sick Children's Ladies' League. Another £308 10s 3d, lodged in the Northern Bank, should be similarly transferred.

The first meeting of the new Ladies' League was held on 15 June 1949 at 3 May Street, the home of Lady Clark, who was invited to take the chair. In her opening remarks, Lady Clark referred to a letter she had written to Dr F.P. Montgomery, chairman of the newly established Northern Ireland Hospitals Authority, asking advice as to the propriety of such a Ladies' League being formed in the Hospital, now under state control. She had received a reply expressing Dr Montgomery's personal approval and the consent of the Hospitals Authority. There was only one proviso: the League was to be self-supporting and correspondence in connection with any of its activities was to be sent from a private address and not from the Hospital. Lady Clark added that 'there was still much important work to

be undertaken by voluntary helpers, in maintaining the personal touch, in keeping alive the friendly spirit, so vital to comfort and general welfare of patients and staff'. She went on to say that 'the Ladies' Committee had served the Hospital faithfully and well for nearly three quarters of a century and the change of name from Ladies' Committee to Ladies' League would do nothing to blunt the enthusiastic dedication of ladies committed to the betterment of the Hospital'. This enthusiasm was somewhat tempered by the news that the Junior Committee was finally to disband. The Hospital Report of 1946 had given the first indications of its demise: 'While expressing the hope that new members will be found to enable the Committee to survive, this has been found to be extremely difficult, as ladies of leisure are a thing of the past. Most girls are pursuing careers or taking courses in domestic economy' – an apt comment on the changing role of women in post-war society.

Since 1949 the Ladies' League has raised money through coffee mornings, bridge evenings, wine tastings, sales of Christmas cards and musical events. The Hospital has been decorated at Christmas and the dressing of dolls by pupils from Methodist College and other schools has provided much-appreciated presents for the girl patients; donations have been made to provide presents for the boys. Several Hospital departments have received furniture, toys and sundry items. In 1967 a travel fund was established to enable Nursing Staff to further their education at specialist training courses. Early beneficiaries were Carol Crawford and Kay Duffin, who studied at the Hospital for Sick Children, Toronto, prior to taking up their posts as the first nurses in charge of the Intensive Care Unit. In 1973 furnishings for an interview room and a rest room for parents were provided in the Intensive Care Unit; a soundproofed room for audiology and the

An array of dolls presented by pupils of St Louise's Comprehensive College in 1991, received by Audrey Lockhead, nurse manager (*centre*); behind her is Mrs Anthea Smyth of the Ladies' League and on the extreme right is Jenne McDonald, play specialist.

Adolescent Unit would benefit in similar fashion.

As the end of the century approaches, the activities of the Ladies' League continue unabated. For 125 years the members of the Ladies' Committee and the Ladies' League have devoted themselves tirelessly and selflessly to the interests of the Hospital. Long-established and innovative methods combine to provide items and services which do so much to enhance the comfort and well-being of both patients and Staff. So many ladies 'zealous of good works' have served that it is quite invidious to single out particular names. It is appropriate, however, to emphasize one name as representative of the many. An oil painting donated by the artist, the late Inkerman Watson, hangs in the Hospital, the caption stating simply: 'To honour Loubelle Robb, Honorary Secretary, Ladies' League, RBHSC, 1962–1982'.

15

PLAY IN HOSPITAL

Toys have always been provided for patients in the Hospital but it was not until November 1947 that volunteers not only distributed toys but actively played with the children. The Annual Report for the year ending 31 December 1947 recorded that an 'occupational therapy scheme' had been started and was proving an outstanding success, largely due to the hard work of June Charley, honorary secretary of the Junior Ladies' Committee. The report stated: '5 members of the Committee visit the Hospital for an hour and a half two days a week. Their aim is to keep the children occupied and amused. The older patients are encouraged to do handicrafts.' Money to buy and replace equipment was given by the Ladies' Committee, a practice continued by the Ladies' League today. The so-called 'occupational play

Over many years the volunteer Toy Ladies gave dedicated service to the Hospital.

scheme' met with the approval of the Medical Staff, and by the end of 1948 more volunteers were being sought.

With the disbanding of the Junior Committee in 1949, occupational play became the responsibility of the new Ladies' League, and in 1950 its activities were extended to the branch hospital at Lissue. In 1952 Mrs Maurice Neill became the occupational play organizer and was required to give regular reports to the Ladies' League. The next step was the foundation of an Occupational Play Committee, which soon began to assert its independence by asking the League to provide 'Toy Ladies' and at the same time stating that it would report to the parent body only once a year. In 1957 Norah Totten OBE assumed the title of president of the Occupational Play Committee, a designation which seemed to imply independence with a hint of elitism. Indeed there was some overlapping with the work of the Ladies' League in the provision of clothing for the matron's cupboard, a Christmas Fair, gifts to nurses and so on.

In 1961 Mrs Maurice Neill resigned, to be succeeded by Mrs K.E. Waite, who had been a Toy Lady since 1953. An occupational play room was named the Norah Totten Play Room, in recognition of her enterprise and tireless work to make the play scheme a reality. Norah Totten was small of stature, but strong and sometimes aggressive in her endeavours to safeguard the place of voluntary workers in a state-controlled environment.

However, several unrelated factors would dictate subsequent events. In 1971 the streets of west Belfast were often dangerous and it was no surprise when the Occupational Play Committee ceased to function. In winding up its affairs, the Committee expressed its continuing support of the Hospital by handing over its remaining monies to the Intensive Care Unit for the purchase of a piece of medical equipment. In spite of this setback, a core of Toy Ladies bravely continued their work through bombs and bullets and mayhem.

In 1976 a circular was received from the Northern Ireland Play in Hospital Liaison Committee, inviting comments regarding the provision of facilities for play in hospital and suggesting an international standard for the training of hospital play workers. The response of the Toy Ladies, backed up by the Medical Staff, was that it was not necessary in the RBHSC to have a formal training programme for play with children.[1]

Punch and Judy still fascinates the children, c. 1996

However, this rather complacent attitude was not to prevail; change became inevitable. In May of 1979, the International Year of the Child, a symposium was held entitled 'Play and the Child in Hospital'. The consensus was that play in hospital required more structure, with a trained staff. Subsequently, liaising through Dr John Glasgow, the Hospital approached the Save the Children Fund and invited it to provide a play worker. The appointment was for two years, in the first place, on the understanding that ways and means would be found to support the worker once that period had elapsed.

The first SCF play worker, Nan Halliday, was appointed in 1979 and assigned to the Musgrave Ward. When she retired, partly for health reasons, in January 1984, simmering tensions came to the surface. The play worker had not been treated as a full member of the ward management team and taken into the confidence of the doctors and nurses. She was not allowed access to clinical details, in spite of the fact that she was working with the children alongside the nurses for eight hours daily. With regard to the Toy Ladies, there was lack of co-operation both in terms of the ward areas in which each worked and the times at which they gave their services. The position of the Save the Children Fund was put succinctly in a letter of 23 January from Professor Richard C. Whitfield, its director of child care, to John Glasgow:

> I am sure you are aware SCF in the UK has endeavoured over the past decade, or more, to foster various play schemes in a large number of hospitals. In

Officers from the RUC traffic branch hold regular road safety seminars, *c.* 1996

these developments the fund has sought to collaborate fully with hospital staff and, where present, volunteers. They believe that they have generally helped to reflect good child care practice in their work, though, whatever the quality of our staff, we have found that good practice depends very much upon the hospital's own framework of support and encouragement . . . As far as your Hospital is concerned, we have invested our resources for some four years and our professional judgement is that we are not prepared to continue such investment unless there is some change in the overall framework within which our worker operates.

A meeting was arranged between Glasgow, Whitfield, and Margaret McGuigan, regional officer of day care, at which specific areas of difficulty were raised, detailed in a subsequent letter to Glasgow, dated 29 March:

a) Access to confidential medical information by SCF play staff. We endeavour to recruit appropriately qualified and professionally sensitive staff to all our projects whether in communities or more specialist sites. It is commonplace for our colleagues to be aware of personal information about clients. We would regard it as a matter for disciplinary action should any of our staff misuse confidential information.

b) Volunteer toy ladies – the ideal environment is in our view for these volunteers to be kept fully informed of the negotiations, rather than be presented with a fait accompli. [The work of the volunteers who had served the Hospital faithfully for so long ended in March 1984, when Mrs Waite and Mrs Appleby retired as Toy Ladies.] However, ultimately we recognise that discussions with them are not an SCF responsibility. As you

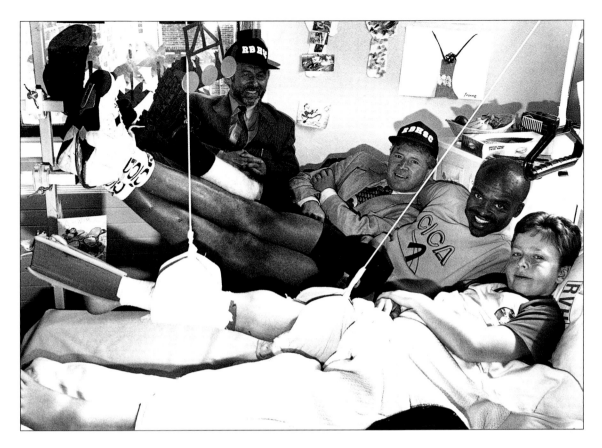

A visit from athlete Kris Akabusi brightens the day of both patient and staff, *c.* 1995

know, we are concerned for smooth working relationships all round should we renew any commitment to the Hospital. We feel that the widest possible consultation between Hospital personnel is still necessary regarding their commitment to the concept of a therapeutic play worker in the children's wards and to giving that worker appropriate status.

With the possibility that the generous support from the Save the Children Fund might be withdrawn, a subcommittee, consisting of Pat O'Callaghan, nursing officer, and Doctors Gerald Black, Sam Keilty and John Glasgow, made proposals to the Staff which were unanimously accepted:

1 Greater status afforded from senior medical, nursing and administrative staffs.

2 The worker should be treated in the same way as other paramedical departmental heads.

3 The worker should no longer be treated as a second-class person and should be given access to more information with regard to the cases with whom she is involved.

It had always been the aim of the Save the Children Fund that the RBHSC could eventually provide funding for a play worker, and in 1986 Jenne McDonald was appointed to a post funded through the Trust Funds of the Hospital, a situation which still obtains. Her remit was to plan and estab-lish a play service for the Hospital, with the main concern of the play specialists, as they were called, to be the emotional welfare of the children, especially those under five years of age.

The *raison d'être* of the play service was to improve the clinical and nursing management of the child and enhance his or her ability to cope, both in this and in further Hospital admissions; to help to shorten the Hospital stay, so that children could go home earlier; to occupy and supervise both patients and their brothers and sisters who could otherwise interfere with the work of Staff. The Hospital came to recognize that special people were required to organize and encourage play, play specialists who, unlike Nursing Staff, would not be diverted to other duties. In 1988 Karen McCormick was employed to work in the Clark Clinic and in 1992, due to increased demand, four nursery nurses were redeployed to work as play specialists. In 1996 the department had nine play specialists at its disposal.

The aim of the Play Department is to make the child's stay in the Hospital as happy as possible. Play facilities are provided appropriate to the age, medical condition and background of a patient. The play areas have sand, water, play dough, computer and construction toys, and everyone takes part in an extensive arts and crafts programme. The department arranges special visitors for the children, such as clowns, magicians, face painters and music specialists – all helping to create a positive image of the Hospital. Where possible, children are taken on trips to such places of interest as the transport museum and the cinema and they are encouraged to maintain their interests and hobbies. As Jenne McDonald has put it, 'If the lasting impression of being in hospital is having handled a snake or learned to perform a piece of magic and not about having injections and operations, then the play department feel that they have done a good job.'

Jenne McDonald, senior play specialist appointed in 1986, playing with a toddler, 1996

Play specialist Naomi Spence with two young patients in the Haematology Unit, 1995

In 1971 death and destruction came very close to the Hospital

16

'LIGHTEN OUR DARKNESS'

DURING THE TROUBLED 1970S, the care and compassion demonstrated within the Children's Hospital were in stark contrast to the death and destruction outside. In the winter of 1971 there was widespread civil unrest. The detritus of rioting littered the streets near the Hospital. Strewn across the road were the smouldering remains of hijacked buses, lorries and private cars. Even in the short periods of relative calm, the atmosphere was oppressive and menacing, compounded by the drone of army helicopters filling the night air.

With social life outside the Hospital difficult and sometimes dangerous, an answer was found in 'in-house' entertainment. A pre-Christmas concert was arranged in an effort to raise morale and shut out for two nights, at least, the disorder and destruction going on a few yards from the front

The RBHSC Miss World Contest, 1971: *left to right*: Jean Johnston, Miss Russia (M. McAlinden), Miss China (Doris Frizell), J. Mercer, 'compere', Miss Poland (Margaret Wilkin), Leading Lady (Martha Menza), Miss England (Marie Clarke), Miss Iceland (M. Craig), Miss Hungary (Alma Jenkins)

door. The programme ranged from the sublime to the ridiculous. In juxtaposition were Jimmy Gillespie, senior audiology technician, with his banjo, and the St Anne's Cathedral Boys' Choir. Mr Dormer gave a spirited rendition of 'Amazing Grace', and something called 'The Top of the Flops' contrasted with the offering of the semi-professional singing group The Sherwoods. Ten beauties were given the chance to show their style in a 'Miss World Contest'. The entertainment was rounded off by a 'potty panto' which, in the best traditions of hospital theatre, poked gentle fun at certain senior members of the Medical and Nursing Staff.

THE CAST

Cindy Cyanosis	– May Fay
Belly Button (ex-Naval Type)	– Sam Keilty
Penny Thrane	– Gerry Black
Annie Thesia	– Harold Love
Wolfish Willie	– Margaret Loughridge

THE CENTENARY: 1873–1973

As the date for the Centenary drew nearer, there was little enthusiasm for its planning. In the midst of such inauspicious social conditions, the wisdom of holding any sort of celebrations was doubtful. Eventually, a sense of history and native fortitude overcame the initial reservations, and preparations for the Centenary got under way, albeit later than was desirable. Two subcommittees undertook the planning of the arrangements for the clinical and social programmes. A widespread publicity campaign was

The cast of the Potty Panto, 1971

organized in which the local committees were generously assisted by the Hospital Management Committee, the Northern Ireland Hospitals Authority, the Northern Ireland Council for Postgraduate Education, the Ulster Medical Society and the Ulster Paediatric Society. Notice of the event was circulated to all general practitioners in Northern Ireland and advertisements were placed in the *Lancet* and the *British Medical Journal.* Two important publications marked the event: Dr Hugh Calwell's book, *The Life and Times of a Voluntary Hospital,* and *One Hundred Years of Caring,* a well-illustrated booklet by Alf McCreary, the prominent Ulster journalist. Particularly pleasing was the coming together in celebration of two old rivals, the RBHSC and the Ulster Hospital. A joint scientific meeting, entitled 'One Hundred Years of Paediatrics, 1873–1973', was held from 7 to 11 May. The proceedings opened at the Ulster Hospital with the Sir Thomas and Lady Edith Dixon Lecture, 'The Doctors' Dilemma', delivered by Sir John Peel KCVO. The programme indicates the wide scope of paediatrics in the early 1970s. (See Appendix 4.)

The Centenary Dinner opened the social programme on Wednesday, 9 May. In addition to representatives of the Hospital Staff, guests were drawn from the Ulster Hospital, Queen's University, the government and the judiciary. The toast of the Hospital was proposed by Peter Mills, Parliamentary Under Secretary of State for Northern Ireland, and replied to by J.S. Loughridge, the Group medical super-intendent and a respected past member of the Surgical Staff. Post-prandial entertainment was by the well-known singing group Canticle. Paying guests at the dinner were obliged to part with £4.00.

The Governor's Garden Party, on Saturday, 12 May, was attended by

In the early seventies, in spite of the chaos and mayhem within yards of the Hospital's front door, morale remained high.

The Royal Belfast Hospital for Sick Children, Belfast BT12 6BE.

On 7 April 1992 the RBHSC's diamond jubilee was marked by Rowel Friers's commemorative cover.

Front cover of *Under the Mackerel Sky*, a collection of poems by Consultant Surgeon Stephen Potts published in 1992; all profits were donated to the Hospital.

three hundred members of the staffs of the RBHSC and the Ulster Hospital. A continuous downpour throughout the afternoon failed to dampen the spirits of those attending. For the younger and fitter members of Staff and their guests, a Centenary Ball, in the 'Threepenny Bit' of the Royal Ulster Agricultural Society at Balmoral, was a highlight.

In other commemorations of the Centenary, the trustees of Rosamund Praeger's estate and the Ulster Museum granted permission for her sculpture *The Philosopher* to be adopted as the RBHSC logo, and with characteristic generosity Sir Ian Fraser presented a bronze replica of the statue to the Hospital, as 'a token of my appreciation of the friendship that I have had from the Royal Belfast Hospital for Sick Children in the 39 years that I was on the Staff'.[1]

THE DIAMOND JUBILEE: 1932–1992

The year 1992 marked the Diamond Jubilee of the Hospital on its present site. Largely due to the initiative of surgeon Stephen Potts, several events were organized to celebrate sixty years on the Falls Road. A commemorative cover was commissioned to coincide with the first issue (7 April 1992) of the Europa Collection of Stamps, marking the journey of Christopher Columbus to the New World. The illustration was by the well-known artist and cartoonist Rowel Friers. A birthday party and disco was held at the Dundonald Ice Bowl and the proceeds of a book of poems by Potts were donated to the Surgical Research Fund.

An Annual RBHSC Guest Lecture was established and inaugurated by Sir Roy Calne FRS, on Friday, 30 October 1992. Sir Roy presented to the

Hospital his own portrait of little Tamara Rainey, on whom he had performed a liver transplant at Addenbrooke's Hospital, Cambridge.

17

ADMINISTRATION AND MANAGEMENT

FIFTY YEARS WITH THREE MASTERS

NORTHERN IRELAND HOSPITALS AUTHORITY 1948–1973
EASTERN HEALTH & SOCIAL SERVICES BOARD 1973–1993
ROYAL HOSPITALS TRUST 1993–

THE MEDICAL STAFF OF THE Royal Belfast Hospital for Sick Children first came to realize that they were serving a new master when, at Christmas 1950, they received a memorandum criticizing the traditional method of appointing staff to the Hospital. The time-honoured procedure of Medical Staff recommendations, with management adding the rubber stamp, was about to disappear. While still a long way from the structured appointment panels of today, it was a first step towards greater accountability and administrative control. In rather terse terms, the Hospital Committee demanded that 'all appointments should, in future, be made to the staff of the hospital only after applications had been investigated by some, or all, of the members of the Hospital Committee, and, if necessary, after an interviewing panel had been set up by the Committee and had made its report'. It regarded the existing procedure as unsatisfactory, arguing that the Committee was responsible for making all appointments where the staff concerned were paid from the public funds allowed to the Hospital and so should exercise a greater measure of control. The Medical Staff opposed the change and, somewhat piqued, let it be known that they felt themselves capable of judging whether the candidates' qualifications were such as to make them likely to be helpful and agreeable colleagues.

In spite of these protestations, a new Establishment and Appointments Subcommittee was formed in January 1951, including the chairman and vice-chairman of the Hospital Committee, which would, 'with the head of department concerned, bring all appointments under close review, setting up an interviewing panel . . . and forwarding its recommendations to the Hospital Committee'.

J. Stuart Hawnt, whose report, published in 1966, recommended a restructuring of hospital management

THE HAWNT REPORT

The period 1950–65 was to be one of steady progress on the clinical front. Staff went about their business virtually unhindered by financial constraints; clinical freedom was the order of the day. However, in 1965, major changes in the administration of the Royal Hospitals were afoot. A Joint Working Party was appointed by the Minister of Health & Social Services and the chairman of the NIHA, with the remit 'to examine the administrative structure of the hospital service at the level of Hospital Management and Hospital Committees and to make recommendations designed to promote the most effective distribution and discharge of management functions'. The members were J. Stuart Hawnt, J. Andress, R. Garnsey, W. Harvey, W. Hawthorne, C.W. Kidd, R. Moore, R.T. Spence, S.E. Taylor, J.H. Copeland (secretary) and F.H. Orr (assistant secretary).

The Joint Working Party held its first meeting on 16 February 1965, and its recommendations were published in the latter half of 1966.[1] In January 1967 the Medical Staff Committee, consisting of thirty-three consultants of the Royal Belfast Hospital for Sick Children, considered the report and issued a memorandum expressing disquiet at several of the recommendations. Its first criticism was the constitution of the Working Party: it did not include a consultant and a medical administrator with first-hand, up-to-date experience of hospital work. Furthermore, the view of consultants closely affected by the proposed changes either had not been sought or had been disregarded.

Paragraphs 91 and 92 of the Hawnt Report recommended the setting up of a third functional committee of management, to be called the Medical and Allied Committee. The Staff considered this a retrograde step, in that it would increase the number of committees when the generally accepted view was that multiple layers of administration should be reduced. In their view:

> i) the introduction of another tier would have the effect of placing a barrier between the full Management Committee and the Consultant Staff, thus depriving the Management Committee of specialist medical advice at first hand; ii) medical policy and priorities amongst specialties must be determined by the Consultant Medical Staff who are best qualified to do so; and iii) matters which have been exhaustively investigated by the Group Medical Advisory Committee, after full discussion by the various Staff Committees, should not be delayed by an additional Committee.

The recommendation which generated most heat was the proposed abolition of the post of medical superintendent at the Royal Group of Hospitals (paragraphs 109–11). The Staff summarised their objections as follows:

> Problems of medical discipline, medico legal problems, professional matters and a multitude of day-to-day problems arising in wards and outpatient departments cannot be dealt with by a lay administrator. The Chairman of Staff with heavy clinical responsibilities and many committee commitments, has neither the time nor the detailed knowledge to deal with them. The loss of the Medical Superintendent would lead to frustration amongst Staff because problems could not be dealt with as they arose, minor problems would become major, due to delay, and medical and nursing staff would lose the support and guidance which they now have when difficult situations arise affecting patients and relatives.

They continued in the same vein in extensive minutes during January and February 1967:

> The Medical Superintendent is essential because he provides continuity of advice and can be approached for an impartial medical opinion. He coordinates the work of the various specialties and, because of his wide general knowledge, can help individual Consultant Staff Committees and Specialist Committees with their particular problems. The idea in the Hawnt report that administrators can take over the function of medical administration is completely erroneous. In a large hospital, the Group Secretary has more than enough to do in co-ordinating and supervising the non medical departments, such as finance, purchasing, maintenance and personnel, without attempting to run the medical side as well.

Two years later, in January 1969, the medical superintendent of the Royal Group of Hospitals, Colonel T.E. Field, resigned and the Group Medical Advisory Committee called a meeting to discuss the future of the post. The Children's Hospital was represented by Dr W.I. Forsythe. The Group secretary, R.T. Spence, argued that the medical superintendent was superfluous and that his work could be carried out by a relatively junior doctor with the assistance of an administrator. It was a surprising statement as the purpose of the meeting was to persuade the Management Committee to increase the salary of the medical superintendent and to raise his status to that of his counterpart in the Belfast City Hospital. This the Management Committee was reluctant to do, and it was suggested that a retired consultant should act as locum medical superintendent until the matter was resolved.

The Medical Staff were upset by Spence's attitude and unanimously agreed that the post of medical superintendent should be advertised immediately. On 27 March 1969 the chairman and honorary secretary, W.A.B. Campbell and B.T. Smyth, met the chairman of the Management Committee, Austen T. Boyd MBE, and impressed upon him the great need for a full-time medical superintendent. To their amazement, they were informed that R.T. Spence was now fully behind such an appointment, and also that the status of the post would be such that the medical superintendent would be able to stand up to the various pressures imposed by the job! The post did indeed survive, firstly in the person of J.S. Loughridge, as locum, and thereafter by a succession of medical superintendents, variously called administrators or directors. A former member of the Children's Hospital Staff, S.H.S. Love, held the post from 1984 to 1987.

Another Hawnt recommendation, that the Group secretary should attend Medical Committees as of right (paragraph 103), met with strong opposition from the Medical Staff:

> While accepting the view that there are occasions when a lay secretary should be asked to attend Medical Staff meetings, discussion often covers subjects of a professional and confidential nature. Consequently, the presence of a lay person would on occasions be unethical and inhibiting. The present Group Medical Advisory structure provides the necessary screening of proposals to ensure that no matter is put before management without due consideration and scrutiny. The advice of the Group Secretary can be sought if required, but Staff did not think it necessary or advisable for the Group Secretary to attend Medical Staff meetings as of right.

The Staff's final thrust was to draw attention to the enormous administrative pyramid which had risen rapidly in the Belfast Hospital Management Group without a comparable increase in patient services.

R.T. Spence reacted by sending a message to the Staff asking if they wished Miss M.P. Murray, executive officer, to continue to attend Staff meetings, in view of their memorandum. He was anxious to give all assistance in his power but felt bound to point out that Murray had been a senior administrative officer of the Group, was a member of his staff and therefore his representative in the RBHSC. The Staff felt that this presented no difficulty because they were satisfied with the present system, whereby the advice of the executive officer of the Hospital, and if necessary of the Group secretary, was sought when required. They reserved the right to invite the executive officer – and, in fact, any member of the lay administration – to help them in their deliberations. Murray continued to attend Staff meetings, as did her successors.

Since 1948 the Hospital has been served by a loyal group of executive officers. R.W. Harland was secretary superintendent at the changeover from voluntary to public control and was followed by J.A. Phillips, A.D. Cuthbertson, R.M. English, Moyna P. Murray, T. Crothers and Anne Allen. Diverse as they were in background and personality – some went about their duties with quiet diligence, others presented a higher profile – all in their own way contributed with courtesy and skill to the smooth running of the administrative affairs of the Hospital.

The Belfast Hospital Management Committee set up a subcommittee to consider the Hawnt Report. After consideration of the written and oral evidence submitted, the subcommittee recommended the acceptance of the report, with reservations – largely in line with those originally expressed by the RBHSC Medical Staff.

On 10 March 1969 the Group secretary wrote to the medical superintendent, T.E. Field, in the following conciliatory terms:

> You will be aware that the Management Committee, in adopting the Hawnt Report generally, with certain exceptions, have supported the expressed view that the attendances of the Group Secretary, or his representative, at meetings of committees, is to be commended. In case there should be any misunderstanding about this, I should like to make it clear that this does not in any way affect the situation currently operating between myself and the various medical committees in the group, whereby my attendance, or that of my representative, is by invitation only. I would not like the Medical Staff to think that the Management Committee's decision means that I have the right to attend Medical Committees in the Group. Would you please also assure the members of the Group Medical Advisory Committee of my continued co-operation and willingness to attend, or send a representative to, whatever special committee meetings you think desirable.

CHANGE AND TURBULENCE

The relative peace of the post-war years gave way after 1969 to ever-increasing civil unrest and violence. Prime Minister Edward Heath suspended the Stormont parliament, imposing direct rule from Westminster. The parliament met for the last time on Tuesday, 28 March 1972, and fifty years of Northern Ireland as a self-governing part of the United Kingdom came to an end.

Simultaneously, important changes were taking place in the administration of the Health Service under the newly designated Department of Health & Social Services. On 1 October 1973 four new Health & Social Services Boards were appointed for Northern Ireland. They would co-ordinate and assume responsibility for the duties previously undertaken by the Northern Ireland Hospitals Authority, the Health Services Board and the Health and Welfare Committees of local authorities. The Children's Hospital, together with the other Royal Hospitals, came under the aegis of the largest Board, the Eastern Health & Social Services Board (EHSSB), forming part of its North & West Belfast District. At local level, the Medical Staff acquired the added administrative designation of Paediatric Division.

In April 1971 the combined medical staffs had pre-empted local changes by introducing their own management structure based on 'cogwheel' principles. (See Appendix 3.)

The tensions engendered by this period of transition were reflected in the first Annual Report of the EHSSB North & West Belfast District (1974):

> It is hardly an understatement to say that despite the esoteric combined efforts of the Ministry of Health & Social Services and the consultancy firm of Booz, Allen & Hamilton, London, the first few months in the North & West Belfast District were somewhat traumatic. [The choice of the word 'esoteric' to describe the 'combined' efforts is intriguing. 'Esoteric' indicates that which is understood by only a small number of people, especially because they have a special knowledge, or, alternatively, that which is intended only for the initiated.] Severe working difficulties taxed to the full the patience of the staff brought together by the amalgamation. Happily the relationship improved as differing points of view mellowed, but the hostile civil situation, coupled with the hopelessly inadequate environmental conditions under which many of the field workers existed, brought no easement of pressure on staff at all levels and tribute must be paid to all for the tolerance and resource exercised.

R.T. SPENCE was a prominent victim of this somewhat turbulent period. A former secretary of the Royal Group of Hospitals, he became the first district administrative officer from the inception of the restructured system. He resigned in September 1974, having been appointed director general of the Northern Ireland Housing Executive. The loss of this able administrator was a severe blow to the Royal Group. His successor was J.C.G. Jackson, who assumed duty in February 1975.

Survivors of that time retain a certain nostalgic affection for the NIHA. Concerned as it was with hospitals only, it offered the individual clinician direct access to an officer with knowledge of, and interest in, his particular speciality.

In September 1981 a Review Body was set up, under the chairmanship of Dr John A. Oliver, a retired civil servant, to review the management of the Royal Group of Hospitals. Chapter 4 of his report caused the most stir. In particular, sections 88, 89 and 90 were music to the ears of many of the Medical Staff:

> From our point of view, as a Review Body examining the management of the Royal Group of Hospitals, we are absolutely convinced that it is essential for that Group to have strong and cohesive local management, with substantial delegated authority to manage the Hospitals within agreed strategic and operational plans. At the same time, however, we believe that the overall size and scale of the Royal Group, the diversity of the services which it provides, the range of its regional commitments and the complexity of its management problems are such that it will not function as efficiently as one amongst a large number of other units of management, all competing for the attention of the Eastern Board.
>
> Charged, therefore, as we are to make any necessary recommendations to promote efficient and effective management of the Royal Group, we have to conclude that this will most probably be best achieved by creating a new

Authority whose primary responsibility would be the Royal Group of Hospitals.

In this connection we considered very carefully the relationship between the Group and the other services, both Hospital and Community, in the present North & West Belfast District. Our investigations have indicated, however, that these interrelationships are desirable in principle and that they are beginning in some respects to prove worthwhile in practice. We believe therefore that it would be a mistake to separate them in administrative terms from the Royal Group. As a result, a new authority will be coextensive with the present North & West Belfast District, which we believe has a sufficient population, budget and range of services to make it viable in its own right. The outcome of the creation of a new Authority would, of course, mean that the Eastern Health & Social Services Board would be relieved of responsibilities for the largest of its present districts, thus reducing its span of responsibilities.

This perceived emasculation was not acceptable to the EHSSB. Nevertheless, it is interesting to reflect on these recommendations in the context of the present Trust Status.

RESOURCE MANAGEMENT

In spite of the rejection of the Oliver Report, the last word on administrative structures had not been heard. In 1984 the North & West Belfast District of the EHSSB was renamed the Royal Group of Hospitals, and the Community Management (Social Services) unit and the Mater Infirmorum Hospital were hived off to form separate entities.

In 1988 there appeared on the agenda a new subject – Resource Management. The vice-chairman of the Medical Executive Committee of the Royal Group, J.S. Laird, wrote to the Medical Staff:

It has become clear that the Government is committed to the introduction of Resource Management throughout England and Wales, within the next 18 months. Therefore it is very likely this will occur in N. Ireland. In effect this means devolving budgets downwards to clinical units etc. It is also apparent that the EHSSB is incapable of solving its own problems, let alone those of the Royal Group. For these reasons the Medical Executive Committee has decided to investigate the potential of Resource Management. This is based on the philosophy that the Royal Group has increasing problems and that we must make every effort to resolve these ourselves.

An accompanying paper entitled 'Good Clinical Practice is Efficient Medicine' outlined the proposals in some detail:

At a time of financial constraints in the Health Service it is very important to emphasise that good clinical practice is also the most cost effective form of medicine. Therefore it is proposed to provide clinicians with appropriate information to allow them to evaluate the clinical practices. In conjunction with this it is further proposed to set up a medical review and management structure which will promote good clinical practice. An important bye-product of this will be the reduction of costs for all components of diagnosis and treatment in each patient. This means that improvement in clinical practice will usually be associated with specific savings. Already in place in the Royal Group of Hospitals is a comprehensive speciality costing system based on previous resource management progress at the Freeman Hospital, Newcastle-on-Tyne, which has a highly developed information technology system and Guy's Hospital, London, which is most advanced in medical management structure.

Laird went on to develop another administrative innovation, the 'Diagnosis Related Group'.

This method has been invented by Professor Fetter of Yale University some 20 years previously to evaluate clinical practice. It examines the components of any individual patient's diagnosis and treatment, for example, the length of stay, the number of X rays, laboratory tests, operative procedures etc. Its original object was to provide a structured method of recording and comparing clinical practice and for some years it has been used as a method of payment for patient treatment by Medicare and Medicaid in the USA. The accumulated information should also be research orientated to allow comparison for types of treatment and to measure the outcome. Each clinician should be able to study his or her own treatment patterns and compare them with others.

In summary, Laird outlined the objectives of Resource Management as follows:

a) to promote the efficient practice of medicine in clinical terms with consequent increase in financial effectiveness;
b) to devolve budgets to appropriate clinical units in order to produce more efficient and responsive management;
c) to produce a corporate approach to long-term problems affecting the Royal Group of Hospitals.

The Medical Staff reacted to the prospect of Resource Management with mixed emotions. It had been reported to them that the budget would be a historical one, based on the previous year, and would be for nurses, medical records and clerical personnel, junior Medical Staff, paramedics and laboratories where they did not overlap with the main laboratory system. The Hospital would be in full control of its own budget at administrative level, and its Trust Funds would remain under the control of the Medical Staff. In November 1988 Laird attended a meeting of the Medical Staff to clear up points of difficulty and allay fears with regard to the new management structure. He stressed that in future all Hospital expenditure would be subject to increased scrutiny and it was unlikely that any additional funding would be available for growth of services. However, if the Hospital services could become more efficient, budgets could be devolved to unit level and the savings accrued would be used to benefit that particular unit. All the information required would be held on a microcomputer based in each ward in the pilot scheme.

In further correspondence during 1989 Laird explained the proposed changes and their implications:

The proposed new medical management structure required for Resource Management Initiative envisages that instead of the present divisional structure new clinical divisions should be constituted with clinical directors and devolved budgets. The Children's Hospital would become such a division with a devolved budget and this system would come into operation on 1 April 1990, when the Group Medical Advisory Committee would be replaced by a Management Board. This would be a major and fundamental change in the management of our medical affairs. This Board will consist of the clinical directors and the unit general manager. Each directorate will have a clinical director, nurse manager and a business manager. The Clinical Director will be responsible to the Unit Management Group on budgetary matters and to his own Medical Staff on the way the unit is managed. Each directorate will have the responsibility for the management of the resources of the unit, in manpower, goods and services. The only additional money will be for the Business Manager. There will be no additional support services for him. The capital cost of the computer systems will be met from a separate budget but there will be no help with the running costs. Two additional computer terminals will be installed in each ward by April 1992.

The Children's Hospital Directorate set out with the belief that the Hospital was one unit and that all its services should be managed from within. Nevertheless, a number of diagnostic and therapy departments opted to be managed on a functional basis from the Royal Victoria Hospital, as did the laboratories and X-ray Department.

By Christmas 1989 the RBHSC Clinical Directorate was beginning to take shape, although the business and nurse managers had not yet been appointed. In April 1990 Stephen Brown became the first clinical director of paediatrics. Medical Staff minutes outlined his responsibilities:

In 1990 Mary Graham was appointed first nurse manager under the new clinical directorate

1   promotion of the most efficient and effective clinical practice;
2   the actual management of the relevant speciality, outpatient clinics, waiting list and associated medical records functions;
3   management of in-patient facilities from the speciality with all the associated functions and staff directly related to ward units;
4   medical records facilities associated with in-patients;
5   most efficient provision of speciality service within the context of the hospital group.

On the financial side he was charged with

1   negotiation, administration and control of the budget for the speciality;
2   consultation of the clinical division, the identification of financial priorities for the speciality; and
3   through medical executive the overall control of the clinical budgets for the hospital group.

In December 1989 W.S. McKee was appointed chief executive for the Royal Group of Hospitals and a month later Stephen Brown introduced Gordon Clarke, the new business manager at the RBHSC. The first nurse manager was Mary Graham.

In April 1991 the Royal Hospitals applied for Health & Social Services Trust Status, claiming that 'the freedom and responsibility to manage the hospitals would be in the best interest of our patients, our community and the staff who serve them'. It was believed that Trust Status would assist in serving the fundamental purpose of the Royal Hospitals, which is 'to provide the highest quality cost effective health care, as an outstanding teaching centre, through exceptional service to our patients, staff and community, in an environment of education, teaching and research'. The RBHSC became incorporated in the Royal Group of Hospitals and Dental Hospital Trust in April 1993. This new association has inevitably led to some loss of individuality, symbolic of which has been the removal of the distinctive 'Philosopher' logo from the Hospital notepaper – a move vigorously opposed by the Medical Staff. An assurance given in 1993 that it would reappear when the logos had been agreed for all the hospitals in the group awaits implementation.

Stephen Brown, consultant surgeon, became first clinical director of paediatrics in April 1990.

Other concerns occupy the minds of Medical Staff under Trust Status. The imposition of new structures, incorporated in the administration of the Health Service, has imposed additional strains. While there have been improvements in the National Health Service – for example, in the delineation of standards of care to be given to patients as laid out in the Patients' Charter – there is a downside as well. The expansion of personnel, finance and contracting departments has pushed up the administrative costs by £1.5 billion per annum. At the same time hospitals are being pushed into so-called 'efficiency savings', placing severe demands on those aspects of the service delivering medical and nursing care to patients. Furthermore, the new internal marketing arrangements have resulted in a disturbing trend towards inter-hospital competition, rather than contributing to the co-operation enjoyed in the past. There is overwhelming evidence that the development of the new bureaucratic structures and the rigid control of finance are being given priority over the provision of a compassionate, caring and responsive service to patients.[2]

There is a widely held view that the original purpose of the National Health Service, 'that no person need lack health for lack of means', is in jeopardy. Such feelings of concern are not new. In every age there have been loud protests at the perceived commercialization of medicine. Many can identify with the sentiments expressed by Sir Samuel Garth three hundred years ago: 'How sickening Physick hangs her pensive head; what was once a science now's a trade' (*The Dispensary* [1699], quoted by Sir William Osler in *Aequanimitas*).

Gordon Clarke, business manager, RBHSC, 1990–

Architects' drawing of the main
façade of the new buildings – due
for completion in 1998

18

DEVELOPMENT AND REDEVELOPMENT

Hᴏsᴘɪᴛᴀʟ ʙᴜɪʟᴅɪɴɢs – once state of the art and seemingly ideally suited to the needs of the moment – are
soon found wanting, when faced with the unrelenting
pressure of medical progress. Such has been the case
with the Children's Hospital on all of its three locations.
This final chapter is the story of those who have striven
to improve and extend the estate on the Falls Road to a standard in keeping
with a modern centre of medical excellence. The splendid new buildings
opened in 1998 are lasting rewards for their efforts over half a century, the
first phase of a continuing programme of development and redevelopment.

The ability of the Hospital to cope with ever-increasing demands on its limited architectural resources has been a recurrent problem since the early days in 25 King Street. In 1932 the new Hospital on the Falls Road had space for seventy-four beds, compared with forty-five in Queen Street. Nevertheless, P.T. Crymble, the honorary secretary of the time, went on record to dispel the idea that the last word in accommodation had been provided. In his medical report of December 1932, he stated:

> Some of our supporters were in doubt as to whether this new Hospital would be fully utilised. After one year of working we can report that we were working to full capacity through the whole year. There is always a waiting list for our beds, in spite of the bed expansion produced by converting every available small room into a ward; we have today a waiting list of 35 surgical and 8 medical. We now have 63 beds and 10 swing cots and there is no doubt that many more beds could be filled with cases suitable for our Hospital. Daily we have to turn away acute surgical cases and it is becoming increasingly difficult to secure beds for the chronic cases met with in the outpatient department.

A rider was added that has resonance in the present day: 'All seriously burned children are to be admitted whether or not there is a vacant bed.'

The first major addition to the Hospital was the private wing. The Clark Children's Clinic was opened with a golden key on 15 March 1944, by Angela Doxford, a granddaughter of Sir George Clark, who, with his brother, Captain H.D. Clark, was its benefactor. The clinic consisted of two wards containing four beds each, six single rooms, a ward for infants with two swing cots and a suite with accommodation for a private nurse (the Rose Suite). It had its own operating theatre. A.S. Atkinson, chairman of the Board of Management, presenting Angela Doxford with a silver salver as a memento of the occasion, remarked that 'the clinic would fill a long existent gap, as it would treat children of a higher social class than those for which the Hospital was intended'!

The Clark Clinic continued as a private wing until the 1970s, when it was adapted to accommodate a variety of specialities: cardiology, ear, nose and throat, haematology, orthopaedics, plastic surgery and dentistry. Gradually cardiology came to occupy the entire lower floor with the exception of a small area housing the Electroencephalography Department. The operating theatre ceased to exist and the upper floor became the home of the Infant Surgical Unit in 1974.

In 1945 the Medical Staff made a formal plea to management for a greatly enhanced bed complement, as follows: 100 beds for acute medical and surgical cases, 25 beds for long-stay orthopaedic cases, 15 isolation beds for babies, 10 beds for nursing mothers and their babies, 10 dermatology beds and 10 eye, ear, nose and throat beds – a total of 170. These recommendations, not unreasonable from the perspective of the time, would be overtaken by future events.[1]

When Norman Hughes began the plastic surgery service at the RBHSC in

1950, in-patient accommodation was at a premium. Initially, a small unit in the surgical ward (Barbour) provided six or seven bed spaces and a bathroom for the treatment of burns, the cost being met by the Hospital's Endowment (Free) Funds. Plastic surgery in all its facets continued to expand and this unit soon became inadequate to cope with the rising number of patients, the overflow occupying up to half the beds in the main surgical ward. The general surgeons of the day, namely Ian Fraser, J.S. Loughridge, H.W. Rodgers and H.P. Hall, only occasionally, and in muted tones, suggested that this overflow into their territory should be curtailed. At a Staff meeting of 3 March 1953, it was proposed that the Plastic Surgery Unit be expanded by including the surgical ward balcony, but on reflection this was felt to be undesirable and Hughes was authorized to submit alternative ideas to the Works and Projects Committee. He started by measuring all the bed spaces and found that they were far below the statutory minimum of around 120 square feet per patient. Therefore he was able to produce a good case for expansion, by forty new bed spaces, to give more patient room. This simple exercise resulted in the eventual construction in 1959 of the Allen and Knox Wards, twenty beds in the latter being allocated to the Plastic Surgery Unit – a deserved reward to Hughes for his quiet industry and far-sightedness.

The building of the block housing the new wards was planned in co-operation with a well-known London architect, S.E.T. Cusdin (also the architect of the new Eye & Ear Clinic, Royal Victoria Hospital). The estimated cost was £109,000, but in fact the lowest tender submitted was £96,000, to be paid for out of the Free Funds of the Hospital. Plans were quickly drawn up and work started on the building with no alteration to the original plan. This was possibly the only hospital building in Northern Ireland completed within the tender price. The lesson drawn by Hughes was never to introduce a variation order as, immediately this is done, it gives the tenderer flexibility to let prices soar. (The estimate for the tower block of the Belfast City Hospital was £7.6 million; twenty years later this had risen to £80 million.)

This increase in bed accommodation came none too soon. When the Hospital opened on the Falls Road in 1932 there was provision for 74 beds. In 1946 this had risen to 97 beds, and in 1955 the figure of 141 was reached, an increase of almost 100 per cent. During these twenty-three years no additional floor spaces had been provided, making the RBHSC the most crowded children's hospital in the UK.

Hughes next turned his attention to the outdated and inadequate operating theatre accommodation. At that time one small room doubled as a waste disposal and sterilizing room. The tiered seating in the operating theatre was removed to allow the incorporation of an extra area, making space available for a separate sterilizing room. At the same time an anaesthesia induction room was provided and eventually piped medical gases were installed throughout the Hospital. This planning submission of Hughes's was the start of his major involvement in administration and planning, resulting in an appointment to the Children's Hospital Management Committee, the Royal Group Management and the Northern Ireland Hospitals Authority, together with the Royal Victoria Hospital Planning Team and the Ministry of Health Advisory Committee.[2]

In 1954 F.M.B. Allen issued a paper setting out his view on measures which he considered necessary to enable the Hospital to function properly as an integral unit of the Nuffield Department of Child Health. Although it was written from the perspective of the Professor of Child Health, his colleagues could not disagree with the general thrust of Allen's argument, set out as follows:

> The developments at the Royal Belfast Hospital for Sick Children during the past 20 years have established the hospital as the recognised centre for teaching the principles of child health and for the treatment of sickness in infants and children. The necessary and desirable expansion of child health services at other hospitals, especially at centres outside Belfast, is a parallel picture and cannot be regarded as providing a service to replace what is regarded as necessary at the RBHSC. In fact, were developments to take place elsewhere, the demands upon the RBHSC would increase and make calls upon its facilities far beyond its present capacity. To fulfil its proper function, the hospital must have a representative sample of all kinds of illness and injury in childhood. It is neither necessary, nor desirable, that it should carry an undue share of routine everyday work. On the contrary it is of great importance that the less common and more difficult types of injury should be dealt with at a special centre. In this way, the main volume of research may be carried out at one centre, thus economising on expensive equipment and highly trained personnel . . .
>
> The importance of geography must not be overlooked. The Royal Belfast Hospital for Sick Children, the Royal Victoria Hospital and the Royal Maternity Hospital are on the same site and closely associated, so that a particularly favourable position for continuing development has been created. The erection of a new University Institute of Clinical Science, beside the Institute of Pathology, on the same site, lends weight to this argument. [The Institute of Clinical Science, accommodating several academic departments – including the Department of Child Health – was opened by Lord Wakehurst KCMG, Governor of Northern Ireland, on behalf of HRH the Duchess of Gloucester, on 7 May 1954.] Perhaps nowhere else is there such a favoured proximity of services of all kinds and nowhere is there such an opportunity presented for really close and worthwhile co-operation between a great general hospital, a large maternity hospital and a progressive child health centre. [These remarks of over 40 years ago have had, until recently, a certain relevance when the sword of Damocles hung over the Royal Maternity Hospital. The decision to close the RMH was taken in March 1997 by Malcolm Moss, Under Minister of State for Health & Social Services, against overwhelming professional advice to the contrary. It would appear, from a clinical standpoint, that the nearer the sick newborn baby is to the medical and surgical facilities of a children's hospital, the better. Incidentally, the Court Report of

1972 restated Allen's concept that 'ideally a University Children's Hospital or department would be on a single site adjoining the Maternity Hospital and linked to the Medical School'.[3] On 13 November 1997 the decision to close the Royal Maternity Hospital was reversed by Health Minister Tony Worthington, following a spirited local and, indeed, worldwide campaign opposing the closure.] The RBHSC is capable of taking the 60 additional beds [which Allen was seeking] by virtue of its development, geographical situation and the fact that the present services, i.e. outpatient department, laboratories, radiological department, kitchen, operating theatres, etc., would not require expansion. The Chair of Child Health was founded in 1948 to provide what had been lacking in the past, namely, extended facilities for the teaching and study of the principles of child health and an adequate staff for the purpose. In association, there must be accommodation and equipment and ancillary services required to maintain the active University Clinical department. The present hospital comprises 187 beds distributed as follows – medical 52, general surgical 36, plastic 11, EENT 15, Convalescent (Lissue Hospital) 54, Private CCC 19, Total 187. These are accommodated in buildings designed to accommodate less than 100 patients. Sixty new beds are urgently needed.

From the outset of his appointment in 1959, B.T. Smyth, consultant surgeon, took a deep interest in the betterment of the Hospital's estate. He was soon to recognize deficiencies in the buildings and facilities which were inhibiting the Hospital's ability to keep pace with the rapid expansion and increasing sophistication of paediatric medicine and surgery. In January 1960 he produced a memo stressing the urgent need for changes in the Outpatient Department, provision for child guidance, an infant unit, isolation facilities, a lecture theatre and accommodation for Nursing Staff, Medical Staff and students. Two years elapsed before architectural advice was sought from S.E.T. Cusdin, who presented the following options:

A an entirely new development, with the outpatient department to be built on the lawn opposite the Clark Children's Clinic;
B demolition of the present surgical ward with a new outpatient department to go up on this site. This would also include the area occupied by the air raid shelter and necessitate building a new surgical ward on the south side of the hospital;
C extensive alteration to the present administrative block and to the nurses' and matron's living quarters, with a new outpatient department to be built there.

The Staff favoured plan B, since it was agreed that the surgical ward would need replacement in the near future, and this was the best place for an outpatient department, being close to the X-ray Department and main entrance to the hospital. There was general agreement that plan C was inherently bad. The only difficulty in plan B seemed to be that the new surgical ward would then be quite a distance from the present operating theatre. The surgeons made it plain that the theatre accommodation was already strained to the utmost and that additional accommodation was required. Ivo Carré suggested that, since Musgrave Ward was already convenient to the theatre, it could become the new 'surgical ward' and the physicians could then get an entirely new medical block. This suggestion found enthusiastic support from the physicians but not from the surgeons. It was finally decided to recommend to the Hospital Committee as follows:

1 Plan B of Mr Cusdin's letter should be adopted. This includes the building of a 2–3 storey block on the site of the present surgical ward, with accommodation there for all outpatient clinics, with the possible exception of the child guidance clinic, which presents special problems and might be better accommodated beside a new child guidance in-patient department.
2 A new surgical ward should be built on the south side of the Clark Children's Clinic with theatre accommodation appropriate to its needs.
3 A baby unit with 3 cots replacing the present medical and surgical cots . . . should be built along with the new surgical ward.
4 Consideration should be given to the provision of accommodation for the in-patient and outpatient child guidance department and, also, for audiology and speech therapy.
5 A small lecture theatre is desirable. It might be possible to provide one in the vacated accommodation.

The Medical Staff were anxious that the Hospital Committee should also give sympathetic consideration to the provision, in the future, of students' 'living-in' accommodation, which would include six bedrooms with bathroom and married quarters for house officers.

Advances in dermatology in the 1950s were hindered by lack of in-patient accommodation. In 1951 Ivan McCaw and Martin Beare made an urgent demand for a twelve-bed unit, separate from other medical cases. This aspiration was not fulfilled for another ten years (May 1960), when the annexe attached to the medical ward (Musgrave) was vacated, coincidental with the opening of the two new wards, Allen (medical) and Knox (plastic surgery). The medical annexe was officially designated the Paul Ward on Tuesday, 8 May 1962, named after Mrs T.D. Paul, a member of the Board of Management since 1932.

The Hospital now had five wards. The Barbour, the surgical ward, was named in recognition of the beneficence of the Barbour family. Musgrave Ward perpetuated the name of Henry Musgrave, whose generous donation of £10,000 in 1922 was such a stimulus to the planning of a new hospital. Allen and Knox, named after F.M.B. Allen and Annie Knox, owe their existence in great measure to the foresight and efforts of Norman Hughes.

In October 1962 Ian Forsythe wrote to his colleagues suggesting that, with minor modifications, an area at Lissue Branch Hospital could accommodate adolescent patients suffering from protracted illnesses such as cystic fibrosis. This proposal, although rejected at the time, was a seed sown, destined to germinate in the shape of an Adolescent Unit in the main

Hospital, nearly twenty-five years later.

In October 1963 the NIHA let it be known that it had proposals for a number of improvements to the RBHSC, including Outpatient and A & E, and the Child Guidance, Audiology and Physiotherapy Departments. It suggested seeking expert advice from several independent persons, an idea deemed highly desirable by the Staff.

The Advisory Subcommittee on Paediatric Services on the Grosvenor Road site met at the Hospital on Monday, 20 April 1964, under the chairmanship of Professor E.J. Wayne of Birmingham, who was reputed to have special experience in planning matters. His colleagues were Professor D.V. Hubble, also of Birmingham, and Professor Charles Wells, of Liverpool. Its findings, published later that year, began with some general statements:

> Ideally a children's hospital should be a children's hospital, should have an intimate, informal and friendly atmosphere. It should not be part of, or even too intimately related to, the general hospital buildings. Its wards should, as far as possible, have access to outdoor play space. If these features are not preserved, much of the case for a separate children's hospital falls to the ground.

The report went on:

> A children's hospital should A provide an atmosphere congenial to children; B provide facilities for the treatment of conditions peculiar to children, for example, neonatal problems; C provide facilities and amenities particularly suited to children, such as appropriate X-ray and laboratory equipment. All highly specialised paediatric work should be centralised and arrangements made for the amalgamation of services where necessary. Special provision within a children's hospital should **not** be made for procedures such as cardiac and neurosurgery and the treatment of severe burns and multiple injuries. Special provision within the main hospital (RVH) should, however, be made for the nursing of this type of case.

Lastly, the Wayne Report concluded that the Medical Staff of the Children's Hospital should be members of the Staff of the whole teaching Group and should have privileges and duties in the main hospital, the neurological and cardiac units and in the Maternity Hospital.

At the heart of the Wayne Report were the following recommendations:

A As and when possible the paediatric work and the paediatric staff of the City Hospital should be joined to and incorporated in the RBHSC [this finding was not accepted by the NIHA].

B The existing Children's Hospital should be upgraded to enable it to fulfil its functions, in particular, the following deficiencies need attention –
   B1 outpatient facilities;
   B2 facilities for child guidance and psychiatry including in-patients;
   B3 in-patient facilities for the mentally retarded;
   B4 upgrading of certain medical wards;
   B5 facilities for dealing with Infectious Diseases;
   B6 a new operating theatre suite;

B7   mother/child accommodation;

B8   provision for neonatal surgery;

B9   student teaching accommodation including a lecture theatre;

B10 additional residential accommodation for nurses and doctors including married quarters.

C The following activities should **not** be provided for in the Children's Hospital – Cardiac Surgery and Accident & Burns [the suggested amalgamation of the Children's A & E Department with that of the RVH was rejected].

D Provision for these specialities should be made either in the specialist departments or in the general hospital, as may be the more appropriate. The nursing of children so treated should, however, receive special attention and may be cared for by the nursing staff of the Children's Hospital.

E If the site plan lends itself to the construction at a later date of a new children's hospital in such a position that it can be linked by corridors to the main hospital and to the maternity hospital without sacrificing the above defined essential characteristics of a children's hospital, the appropriate area should be reserved for this purpose. By the time such a plan can be put into operation ideas may have changed. So far as can be perceived, the functions of such a hospital would not greatly differ from those of the Royal Belfast Hospital for Sick Children, as now envisaged. [This appears at variance with the statement in the preamble that a children's hospital should not be part of, or too intimately related to, the general hospital.]

F We express no strong views on the inclusion of a in-patient accommodation for orthopaedics, but in view of the need to accept a certain number of injuries, and in view of the teaching obligation of this hospital, it would seem desirable that some provision be made.

The Wayne Report fell far short of the Staff's hope for a completely new hospital. Nevertheless, they welcomed the proposals as far as they went, although they did point out several important omissions: for example, in the recommendations for neonates, no mention was made of the need for increased accommodation for infants in general.

They subsequently sought clarification on certain points from the NIHA, and Ivo Carré, Brian Smyth and Ian Forsythe represented the Hospital at a meeting in December 1964 with Dr John Andress, deputy administrative medical officer of the Authority. He dashed the hopes of Staff for a new Children's Hospital, intimating that it would be at least ten to fifteen years before a new hospital could be built and that it was therefore imperative to proceed at once with improving the present one. In the absence of any immediate implementation of Wayne's proposals, a make-do-and-mend policy was adopted for the next several years, including the transfer of patients to the City Hospital facilities, under the care of Dr Muriel Frazer and Dr Claude Field.

In June 1972 a memorandum appeared over the names of J.M. Beare, (chairman of the Medical Staff), G.W. Black, honorary secretary, and

T. Crothers, executive officer. It recommended that 'immediate consideration be given to the building of a new hospital which would provide for local and regional services in paediatrics. It should be physically linked with the Royal Victoria Hospital and the Royal Maternity Hospital.' The memorandum claimed that

> the present buildings were incorrectly sited and incapable of being restructured to meet the needs of a modern Children's Hospital. If plans were not made to provide these facilities, then hospital accommodation for children in Belfast would be obsolete within a decade. A Children's Medical Centre of some 350 beds would enjoy the advantages accruing from the concentration of all the services required by the sick child . . . We wish to put forward the concept of a general hospital for children with facilities and staff to provide for the physical, psychological and practical needs of the child. Such a concept is not possible in the context of simultaneous adult hospital planning. The new hospital would provide routine and specialist care in every aspect of paediatric medicine and surgery for patients aged from birth to 13 years of age.

The estimated cost was £3 million to £4 million. The document emphasized further the regional role of the Hospital in providing a referral centre for difficult clinical problems from all over Northern Ireland.

Staff asked for a meeting with the NIHA to discuss the recommendations of this memorandum. A preliminary meeting scheduled for 24 November did not take place and it was not until 12 February 1973 that Martin Beare and other members of Staff met with John Andress and NIHA secretary William Harvey. They were informed that the next review of the hospital plan for Northern Ireland would be presented in October 1973 and it was hoped that provision for a new Children's Hospital would be included.

In April 1973 a letter was received from Dr T.T. Baird, chief medical officer of the Ministry, which further complicated the situation. It contained comments on a booklet issued by the Academic Board of the British Paediatric Association, entitled *Paediatrics in the Seventies – Developing the Child Health Services*. Baird, while agreeing to circulate the document to all paediatricians for discussion and comment, made it clear that it was not a presentation of Ministry policy. He highlighted one section with the comment:

> In particular, there was an apparent difference of opinion over concentrating large numbers of children's beds in one place. An increasing number of sick children are cared for by a combination of hospital in-patients or day bed facilities and the Community services leading to a more intensive use of hospital beds in this speciality. Area hospitals will normally have children's departments and the need for special hospitals for children only is therefore likely to decrease.

This seemed to suggest that the Authority and the Ministry were travelling on two divergent tracks, the Authority cognizant of the need but without the means to meet it, the Ministry demonstrating little understanding of the form and function of a regional children's hospital, an attitude which caused the Staff deep unease.

Word then came that the Ministry was setting up a Working Party to study the future development of the total Grosvenor Road site, a project that would include paediatrics. The Staff decided on a direct approach to the Working Party and a letter dated 19 November 1973 from N.C. Hughes, chairman of the Medical Staff, to Dr D.J. Sloan, medical secretary to the Working Party, set out their case and instantly questioned the Ministry's interpretation of the Court Report (*Paediatrics in the Seventies*):

Last year the Division of Paediatrics gave active consideration to the future requirements of the Royal Belfast Hospital for Sick Children. At that time considerable discussion took place with all those likely to be concerned in such a venture and the outcome of this was a memorandum on the building of a new hospital comprehensively adapted to the needs of children. For your information I enclose a copy of this memorandum and a statement 'Hospital Services for Children in Regional Centres', from the British Paediatric Association to the British Association of Paediatric Surgeons and the Society of Paediatric Pathologists. This latter document points out that there was a serious omission in the British Paediatric Association publication *Paediatrics in the Seventies*, in that the latter dealt only with the setting up of children's departments in district general hospitals and did not refer to the situation pertaining to the needs of children's departments in regional and University centres.

Such a hospital would be responsible for the specialised paediatric services in Northern Ireland. It would also be the centre for training the consultants of the future and for research into paediatric problems. The present scattered distribution of children's beds in Belfast is both inefficient and uneconomical and it is difficult to provide satisfactory training programmes for junior medical staff. Already, the Specialist Advisory Committee in Paediatric Surgery has found the facilities available in Belfast unacceptable for higher training leading to specialist registration.

The Medical Staff are of the opinion that the provision of a new children's hospital is a matter of considerable urgency. As emphasised in the attached memorandum, the new hospital should be sited in close proximity to both the specialised departments in the Royal Victoria Hospital and the Royal Maternity Hospital. Dr Martin Beare and I would like to meet the Working Party, in order to amplify this submission and to answer any questions which the members may wish to put to us.

In response to this request, members of the Staff were invited to present oral evidence to the Working Party. The letter of invitation from D.J. Sloan contained a paragraph that hinted at the difficulties on the road to a new Children's Hospital:

There is complete agreement that the Royal Victoria Hospital and its associated hospitals on the Grosvenor Road site must retain its position as a major teaching hospital and centre of excellence. This makes it necessary to maintain a proper balance between the service needs of local and regional specialities and the needs of undergraduate and postgraduate teaching. At the same time the hospital service is faced with the reality of severely limited resources, notably staff and finance. The opening of Block A at the RVH will increase these demands. It will be necessary to meet the requirements of the Royal's several functions within these constraints.

These negotiations coincided with the winding up of the Northern Ireland Hospitals Authority and its replacement by the four Health & Social Services Boards, and not surprisingly, in the upheaval of the changeover period, the Staff's demand for a new hospital was not at the top of the agenda. Nevertheless, in September 1974, an urgent letter was dispatched to Dr James McA. Taggart, chief administrative medical officer of the newly formed Eastern Health & Social Services Board, asking what had happened to the Staff's memorandum, first submitted eighteen months previously. The honorary secretary, Desmond Burrows, wrote:

> Members are very concerned about the apparent lack of action and as the future development of the Hospital is uncertain, it is difficult to know what advice could be given about various projects that are in urgent need of attention. Members are also concerned that the memorandum . . . might never have reached the Ministry of Health [now the Department of Health and Social Services]. This matter comes up each month and there is nothing to report and it does tend to lead to increasing disappointment and frustration.

Taggart visited the Hospital on 2 December and informed the Staff that the document had been passed up with many others from the Area Board to the Department for consideration in the next five-year plan. He confessed that it had not yet been considered at Board level.

Meanwhile, a regional plan for the Health and Personal Social Services for 1975–80 had been issued by the DHSS. In the past, Hospital, Community and Personal Social Services had developed along separate lines, and in the Department's view it was now necessary to produce a balanced plan on an integrated basis. The upshot of this was that the capital development projects already put forward by the Royal Hospitals, including that for a new Children's Hospital, had to be resubmitted with a deadline of 20 September 1974. Over the years, the Staff had presented a united front in their demands for a new hospital, yet in their private discussions this was not a unanimous opinion. Some members believed that such a solution was out of reach and that energy should be directed towards refurbishment and piecemeal building. Nevertheless, the idealists and the pragmatists managed to maintain a satisfactory compromise in that, while pushing for the ideal, they seized upon any crumbs that fell from the master's table. These crumbs were not mere scraps, as is indicated by a letter, dated 7 October 1974, from R.M. English, the assistant district administrative officer, to G. Taylor, chief administrative officer of the EHSSB. English outlined the capital works either in the process of construction or completed at the Children's Hospital in the past five years:

1   intensive care unit/diet kitchen – £32,000 completed;

2   new theatre – £44,000 inclusive of £24,000 ex free funds, completed;

3   child psychiatry unit/Lissue – £14,050 completed;

4   upgrading of outpatient department to include child psychiatry outpatients and changing accommodation, lecture theatre, audiology department – £86,000 completed;

5   infant surgical unit (12 beds) top floor Clark Children's Clinic – £9,205 completed;

6   recovery room/intensive care unit store – £10,000 currently under construction;

7   upgrading of existing X-ray department – £73,000 (submission for monetary grant dated 7.7.74 to the EHSSB).

The EHSSB's first Annual Report (1974) also recorded some developments at the Children's Hospital:

> A new Lecture Theatre, Audiology Clinic and Psychiatric Outpatient Clinic are now functioning in the Royal Belfast Hospital for Sick Children and the improvements to the Outpatient Department are virtually completed. However, it must be stressed that if the hospital is to continue to attract the calibre of staff and remain in the forefront of paediatric treatment and research, a policy decision must be made soon as to whether it should be rebuilt possibly in closer spatial association with the neighbouring adult hospital or, failing this, the medical planners should be encouraged with a hope of realisation to ask for those much needed upgradings and facilities which they have sought for so long.

By January 1975 the upgrading of the X-ray Department had been given high priority but disappointment was expressed that there was still no mention of a new Children's Hospital in the draft regional plan. This disappointment was compounded when, in February 1975, the Board issued a summary of the proposed development in the North & West Belfast District for the following five years, which stated: 'Consideration of the proposal to erect a new hospital has been deferred but will be taken into account when the long term development of the Grosvenor Road site is being dealt with.' With these words the long-term hope and struggle by the Medical Staff for a new hospital seemed to have been extinguished once and for all. There was scant comfort in a proposal for the enlargement of the Physiotherapy Department and the establishment of a Cytogenetic Unit.

With admirable tenacity the Staff renewed their demand for a new Children's Hospital in 1978. William McClure Nelson, honorary secretary of the Medical Staff and the Division of Paediatrics, wrote to Dr T.T. Baird of the DHSS on the subject and requested an early meeting. Norman Hughes, Victor Boston, Aileen Redmond, Gerald Black and Mark Reid were nominated to represent the Hospital. However, before contact could be made, Baird retired and a meeting was arranged with his successor, Dr R.J. Weir, in August.

Two letters written by the incoming chairman of the Medical Staff, Brian Smyth, to Bob Weir illustrate well the Staff's increasingly pragmatic approach to the solution of the needs of the Children's Hospital. The first, dated 6 September 1979, was headed 'A New Children's Hospital for Northern Ireland'. In it Smyth outlined the remarkable growth over the past twenty years in specialist techniques and treatments in treating children's diseases, pointing out that most of these advances had been pioneered in the Children's Hospital. During that period, he wrote, there had been a striking consensus of agreement among all doctors treating children that there was an urgent need for a new central Children's Hospital to serve the growing requirements of the Regional Paediatric Service. He re-emphasized the necessity of direct communication with the Royal Victoria Hospital for specialized neurosurgery and cardiac surgery, and argued that, in association with the Royal Maternity Hospital, the RBHSC should provide a Neonatal Intensive Care Service for Northern Ireland. His concern was that the Hospital was not receiving evident recognition and that, while other hospitals had been rebuilt or had major extensions, 'no commitment has been given that anything will be done for the children of this province'.

He enclosed with his letter some of the regional services provided by the Children's Hospital:

1   The Royal Belfast Hospital for Sick Children is the Centre for the Department of Child Health of the Queen's University of Belfast and it is also the main teaching centre for Undergraduate Students and for Postgraduate Students studying paediatrics. There is also a Training School for Paediatric Nursing Staff.

2   A unit for plastic surgery in children was initiated in the Children's Hospital and is still the only one in the province. This unit also deals with all cases of severe burns.

3   This hospital was the first to have a Paediatric Cardiologist and it pioneered the first open heart operations in Northern Ireland. It continues to be a regional centre for Paediatric Cardiology. The present situation where cardiac surgery is carried out in the Royal Victoria Hospital and the children transferred to the Children's Hospital for post-operative care is unsatisfactory.

4   For many years this has been the main Accident Centre for children under the age of 12½ years. We are also a referral centre for children coming from other hospitals in Northern Ireland.

5   Provision of the first paediatric intensive care unit in the province and all the pioneer work of intensive care neonates has been done in this unit and it has been responsible for training other doctors in these techniques.

6   The Children's Hospital is the only hospital to have an Infant Surgical Unit. Infants requiring surgery are referred from all parts of Northern Ireland.

7   This Hospital has pioneered the use of intravenous alimentation in neonates and children. One member of Staff devotes her time entirely to this work.

8   The Children's Hospital has built up a large experience in the treatment of various forms of cancer in children and, in particular, progress has been made in the treatment of leukaemia and of Wilm's Tumour of the kidney. Patients in the province now come to this Hospital and, in future, all treatment will be carried out in this Hospital, with the exception of deep X-Ray Therapy.

9   This Hospital has been responsible for the development of services for children suffering from spina bifida and associated lesions, with a 'team' run follow-up clinic.

10   The Children's Hospital is the first to have a Department of Child Psychiatry and the only hospital with an In-patient Child Psychiatry Unit.

11   Whilst most major orthopaedic operations are carried out in Musgrave Park Hospital, in recent years Mr Piggot has found it advantageous to carry out orthopaedic operations in the Children's Hospital and Mr Halliday has expressed a desire to carry out spinal fusion operations in this Hospital because of the specialised post-operative facilities available.

12   The Biochemistry Laboratory in the Children's Hospital was the first in the province to develop the micro techniques for estimation of elements in blood.

13   The Children's Hospital provides a Paediatric Urology Service and the number of patients attending this service is greater than that attending any other hospital.

14   The Dental Department has been responsible for much original work in the treatment of deformed or injured teeth and also in the treatment of cleft palate. The contribution to the dental treatment of the handicapped has been particularly valuable in the provision of specialised and Day Hospital facilities.

15   The Ear, Nose and Throat Department has a specialised Audiology Clinic in which the latest techniques in audiometry are available. This unit is shortly to be enlarged.

16   The Children's Hospital pioneered research work in the diagnosis and treatment of Phenylketonuria.

17   The investigation and treatment of hiatus hernia has received particular attention and almost all children with this complaint now attend the Children's Hospital.

18   The Hospital Staff have initiated special work in the investigation and treatment of cystic fibrosis.

19   There are also specialised children's departments of Physiotherapy and Speech Therapy.

20   The Hospital provides a Regional Service in Genetic Studies and Genetic Counselling.

21   The Hospital is the only one which provides a Dermatological Service confined to children.

Smyth's second letter, dated 14 December, expressed the Staff's pleasure that 'there was a possibility of a new Central Children's Hospital in perhaps 10–12 years' time'. It is not clear from whose hand this carrot dangled but, adhering to the pragmatic route, Smyth highlighted the considerable work required to keep the service going in the interim period and reiterated the urgent major projects already outlined. As a result of these representations a Working Group – from the Eastern Board, the Department, the North & West Belfast District and the Hospital – was set up in January 1980. The chairman was Dr B.E. Swain, principal medical officer at the DHSS.

Its terms of reference were to produce a plan costing the minimum capital amount which would ameliorate the present physical defects and underpin viability for fifteen years, phased in such a way as to effect minimal interruption of clinical services. Another objective was to identify closely what might be done to improve accommodation and facilities to enable the Hospital to cope efficiently with the increasing workload, pending its eventual replacement by a new Children's Hospital in Belfast. Paediatricians at the RBHSC were given an assurance that whatever schemes were undertaken to keep the service running during the interim period would not prejudice major development regarding a new Children's Hospital in years to come.

As far as the surgeons were concerned, the Swain Committee did not come a moment too soon. In January 1979 they had presented a paper to the Division of Paediatrics, setting out their recommendations for the upgrading of the general Paediatric Surgical Department. At that time the surgical ward (Barbour) contained thirty-four beds for children from the age of six months to thirteen years. There were three single rooms and the remaining thirty-one beds were contained in the main ward. There was only one parent room and no facilities for the mothers to sleep next to their children. This was found to be a serious drawback, particularly when nursing children with cancer. The general aura of the ward was described as one of dilapidation and there were no satisfactory facilities for play or schooling. Access by the Orthopaedic Department to beds in Barbour Ward frequently resulted in twenty beds being unavailable for general surgical use.

The twelve-bedded Infant Surgical Unit on the upper floor of the Clark Children's Clinic, opened in 1974, soon became recognized as the regional unit for neonatal surgery and for the surgery of infants up to the age of six months. This vital service was carried on in less than ideal conditions. Storage space was inadequate to house the bulky equipment essential for the nursing of patients suffering from spina bifida and other neonatal problems. The nurse–patient ratio was unsatisfactory, resulting in post-operative neonatal patients being nursed in the intensive care area, thus overburdening the facilities of that unit. Gradually, many of these difficulties have been overcome, yet in the 1990s one deficiency still faces Sister Maggie Bonnar and her staff – the absence of accommodation for nursing mothers.

		INFANT SURGICAL UNIT		
YEAR	SPINA BIFIDA NEONATES	OTHER NEONATES	TOTAL NEONATES	ADMISSIONS 1/12–6/12	TOTAL ADMISSIONS
1974	47	46	93	95	188
1975	55	49	104	92	196
1976	32	64	96	99	195
1977	44	65	109	113	222
1978	47	71	118	120	238
1979	34	93	127	141	268
1980	31	80	111	126	237
1981	40	86	126	129	255
1982	35	93	128	154	282
1983	30	71	101	140	241
1984	28	69	97	136	233
1985	21	72	93	191	284
1986	33	86	119	159	278
1987	22	90	112	174	286
1988	16	110	126	197	323
1989	26	86	112	204	316
1990	12	75	87	252	339
1991	11	90	101	239	340
1992	10	81	91	261	352
1993	6	54	60	306	366
1994	9	81	90	264	354
1995	12	78	90	300	390
1996	5	104	109	309	418

The Swain Report outlined various proposals for the development of the Hospital, bearing in mind the constraints imposed by the terms of reference. It concentrated largely on schemes of new construction and improvements to existing accommodation, for example, a Day Care Unit, Outpatient/Accident & Emergency, the Barbour Ward and Operating/ Intensive Care Unit. The estimated total capital and revenue costs of the schemes were as follows:

	£
Day Care Unit	405,000
Outpatient Department/Accident & Emergency	321,000
Barbour Ward	156,000
Operating Theatre/Intensive Care Unit	1,803,000

It is clear that the proposals in the Swain Report were concerned with medium-term solutions, pending the provision of a new hospital. As there appeared to be no immediate prospect of this happening, the Board had widened the range of options being considered, in order to provide adequate facilities into the twenty-first century.

On 23 March 1983 the government announced a £4 million improvement scheme for the Royal Belfast Hospital for Sick Children. The accompanying press release stated:

> On a visit to the hospital today, Mr John Patten MP, Parliamentary Under Secretary of State for Health & Social Services, said 'work on improvements

would be going ahead as a matter of urgency. He said the improvements had been considered by his Department and the Eastern Board as a top priority and planning had been under way for some time. The physical constraints on the site and the need to maintain services throughout the period of reconstruction mean that improvements will be introduced step by step. It's a complex task which demands considerable planning.

The minister set out the main features of the improvements, which would include:

1 a £441,000 extension to the X-ray Department due to be opened in May 1983;
2 a new £65,000 Adolescent Unit for the treatment of chronically ill teenagers including those suffering from Cystic Fibrosis: this is due to begin in October and be completed by January 1984;
3 improvements to wards costing upwards of £600,000; the first scheme (£165,000) due to begin in the next financial year to provide parent/child accommodation;
4 a £409,000 Day Care Unit;
5 new theatres and an Intensive Care Unit costing almost £2 million;
6 an extensive £326,000 renovation scheme for the Outpatients and Accident and Emergency Departments.

Patten continued:

A Working Party from my Department and the Eastern Board, together with representatives of the Hospital Medical Staff, was established in 1980 [Swain Committee]. It has produced recommendations for the improvement of facilities at the Hospital which are now incorporated into a programme of action. I am satisfied that the work now in hand will ease the serious shortcomings in the Hospital's facilities. The Hospital will also be able to cope with its increasing workload until it can be replaced by a new Children's Hospital in Belfast.

Finally, the minister paid tribute to the work of the Staff at the Hospital:

I know conditions have not been up to modern day standards and I have the utmost admiration for the excellent work which the Staff have carried out in sometimes quite difficult circumstances. Real progress is being made towards upgrading the facilities . . . My Department and the Eastern Board will be working closely together to ensure that the full package of improvements is completed as soon as possible.

Items 2 and 3 in the minister's statement were examples of several projects which came to fruition through the persistence of individual members of Staff and magnificent public generosity. In March 1979 John Bridges had announced that the Malcolm Sargent Fund for Children was interested in providing parent/child accommodation at the Children's Hospital, to be known as Malcolm Sargent House. The accommodation would consist of an office, a kitchen/dining area, a lounge and a cloakroom on the ground floor, and on the upper floor three bedrooms with toilet and shower accommodation. The cost would be in the region of £35,000 to

The facilities of Malcolm Sargent House, opened in April 1981, are greatly appreciated by parents.

£37,000. The Malcolm Sargent Fund members demonstrated their commitment by being undeterred at the prospect of an overdraft. However, the Staff recommended subvention from the Free Funds to bridge any deficit. Further help came from the Mothers' Union of Ireland, particularly the Connor diocese branch. A Mrs Knox went round the pubs and clubs of east Belfast raising nearly £2,000, and more modest but invaluable amounts arrived, like £100 from the Aghalee Darts Club. The work went out to tender in March 1980 and the house was officially opened on 3 April 1981. Bridges received well-deserved congratulations for his initiative. Miss S. Murdagh was appointed the first Malcolm Sargent Social Worker.

In April 1981 Aileen Redmond submitted plans for an Adolescent Unit to be attached to the Allen Ward. With the great advances in the treatment of cystic fibrosis, children were living longer, and by the late 1970s teenagers were being cared for – those who in earlier years would not have survived. The lack of suitable accommodation for this age group had been causing increasing distress to parents and concern to the carers. The 'cut-off' age for transference to an adult ward was thirteen years, an action which amounted to early banishment from the circle of care. This deficiency was not rectified until 1996, when a unit dedicated to the care of adult CF patients was opened at the Belfast City Hospital.

Largely due to Dr Redmond's efforts, £20,000 was raised from voluntary subscriptions. The Hospital's Free Funds made up the difference, amounting to £30,000. The Adolescent Unit, cheerily called Cherry Tree House, was officially opened on 20 May 1986 by Sally Wrigley, chairwoman of the Cystic Fibrosis Young Adults' Association, but did not receive its first patients until December of the same year, due to lack of Nursing Staff. It was a source of satisfaction that the entire building and landscaped garden was funded by the general public, through the generosity of parents, relatives and friends and was the first purpose-built unit of its kind in the UK.

The cystic fibrosis service still relies largely on such generosity for its maintenance and, happily, public beneficence continues unabated. In 1991 Holywood (Co. Down) Round Table and local GP Tom Ryan organized a trip to Lapland for one hundred young patients from the RBHSC. With monies left over a decision was taken to upgrade three existing side rooms in Allen Ward. The money available was not sufficient to cover the total projected cost so the Ladies' League of the Hospital stepped in with a major donation and Dr Redmond 'found' the remainder. The Northern Bank Employees' Charity Group supplied the curtains and soft furnishings. The new rooms have full ensuite facilities and fold-down beds for parents wishing to stay with a sick child. A comprehensive subvention from the public purse is still awaited.

Other important units which opened while the campaign for a new hospital continued were the Day Care Unit, providing much-needed facilities of day care surgery and dentistry, and the Haematology Unit.

In May 1983 three members of Staff, Victor Boston, Maurice Savage and Sam Keilty, were appointed to represent the Hospital in negotiations with the DHSS and the EHSSB regarding the implementation of the Swain Report. Some progress was made and by November 1983 plans for the new theatres and the Intensive Care Unit were well advanced. The prospect of added theatres and intensive care facilities stimulated some individuals to reintroduce the age-old question of cardiac surgery at the Hospital, although it was realized that in that event further readjustment and expansion of the new development would be required. However, it was not until June 1987 that the Medical and Surgical Cardiology Division indicated a renewed desire to carry out closed cardiac surgery at the Children's Hospital. They wished to be involved in discussion of plans for the new operating theatres, and in May 1988 D.H. Gladstone requested one operating session to perform closed cardiac procedures in young children. There the matter rests.

By the spring of 1985 it was becoming clear that no permanent solution to the accommodation problem could be found within the buildings fronting onto the Falls Road. The radical suggestion was made that the Accident & Emergency Department and the Medical and Surgical Outpatients should be resited at the rear of the Hospital adjacent to the Clark Children's Clinic. Subsequently, Dr Keilty reported that he had met informally with Mr Cole, the architect at the Department of Health, regarding the possibility, but that Cole believed this would not be possible as it would encroach on the space for the theatres and ICU project, already in train.[4]

However, at a meeting some two years later with DHSS planners and architects and representatives from the EHSSB, it was agreed that the best option for rebuilding the Outpatient and Accident & Emergency Departments would be to combine them with the proposed theatre/ICU building, then at the planning stage. (It is salutary to speculate what might have happened to this project if a proposal of 17 April 1967 to erect a seventy-two-bed geriatric unit on this site, with a corridor link to the Hospital, had proceeded.) Happily, a later proposal to build a multistorey car park at the rear of the Hospital came to nothing.

By September 1985 the future of Paul Ward was in doubt; inadequate as it was, it had served the needs of dermatology for some twenty-five years. The combined medical staffs of the Royal Group of Hospitals recommended that Paul Ward should close and that a small children's unit should be provided on the balcony of ward 26 in the RVH, with the retention of a single bed for dermatology in the RBHSC. This scheme did not materialize, due to the absence of paediatric trained nurses in ward 26. The Paediatric Division raised strenuous objections to what they saw as the arbitrary closure of a twelve-bed unit without consultation of any sort, without regard to the needs of the children or the requirements of nurse training, or consideration of the ongoing plans for the refurbishment of Musgrave Ward and the Physiotherapy Department development, which were at an advanced stage. Desmond Burrows, then chairman of the Group Medical Advisory Committee, was the subject of some undeserved opprobrium for his perceived part in the closure.

In fact, the demise of Paul Ward was unavoidable for reasons both financial and clinical. Improved social conditions had led to the virtual elimination of some common skin conditions, such as scabies and seborrhoeic eczema, which often necessitated admission to hospital. Furthermore, the Royal Group of Hospitals was in dire financial trouble, a harsh truth not readily assimilated by the Medical Staff. In such circumstances, it appeared reasonable to close the most inferior accommodation in the Hospital – a philosophy which some members of Staff found difficult to accept. Nevertheless, as a reluctant first step, it was agreed that the bed complement in Paul Ward should be cut to four. By April 1986 the total closure was accepted and the dermatologists were granted identical admitting privileges to the general medical (Musgrave) ward as the other consultant paediatricians. Finally, agreement was reached that in future Paul Ward should become a general paediatric medical ward with a dermatological component. Eventually, six years later, a new, twelve-bed Paul Ward opened, housing neurology and dermatology, as did an expanded and refurbished Physiotherapy Department in a new area underneath an altered and revitalized Musgrave Ward.

The official opening ceremony of the complex was performed by Emeritus Professor Ivo Carré on 28 October 1992, a satisfactory conclusion to a scheme that had been on the agenda at the EHSSB since 1976.

When the reconstituted Paul Ward opened, the bed distribution was:

Dermatology	3
Neurology	6
Severe Handicap	1
Emergencies	2

The beds in the remainder of the Hospital were distributed as follows:

Cardiology	9
General surgery	33
Plastic surgery	21
Orthopaedic & Trauma	13
Paediatric medicine	51
Haematology	8
ICU	6
Total	153 approximately

As the 1990s approached, the new development programme at the
Children's Hospital began to falter. A letter from James McKenna, chief
medical officer at the DHSS, stated that 'the appraisal for the proposed new
development had yet to be considered by the Department of Finance and
Personnel', and warned that 'due to lack of funding the Department's
capital building programme was being restructured and many projects in
advanced stage of planning had been deferred. Developments such as those
at the Children's Hospital might well have to be considered in the longer
term.' McKenna continued: 'The Eastern Health and Social Services Board
are presently reassessing their priorities for capital building projects and will
be submitting a list to the Department within the next few weeks.' Not
unnaturally, members expressed their dismay and frustration that the

much-needed improvements at the Hospital appeared to be losing their priority, in spite of the minister's fine words of 1983. A direct approach was made to the Under Secretary of State for Health & Social Services, Richard Needham. He assured the Medical Staff that

> the Department remained fully committed to the need to complete the programme of improvements to the Hospital and would ensure that the importance and urgency of this scheme was taken fully into account in the ongoing discussions held with the Boards to identify their most pressing priorities in the capital building programme.

This response did little to allay Staff fears.

The Royal Unit of Management was still in severe financial difficulty. In the first two months of the financial year 1989–90 the Royal Group of Hospitals was overspent by £143,000. In 1989 the net annual running cost of the Children's Hospital was £7,784,205, the cost per patient per week being £1,295.81. Management decided to close the Ava I Hospital at the Belfast City Hospital, an action that would effect a saving of approximately £100,000. It was the opinion of the Unit of Management that patients from Ava I could be accommodated in the RBHSC, as the average bed occupancy in the Hospital was only 70 per cent. The proposed date of closure was 31 October 1988. The Medical Staff expressed their disquiet, stating that 'they did not think that the hospital would be able to cope with paediatric medical emergencies, especially during the winter months'. They were concerned that no assurance had been given that the newly refurbished Musgrave Ward would open with a full complement of beds and declared the decision to close Ava I unacceptable. At a further meeting on 27 October, the Medical Staff chairman, Sam Keilty, reported that, in spite of his dissent, the overwhelming majority of the members of the Medical Executive Committee of the Royal Group (MEC) had agreed with the proposed package of bed closures, including those in Ava I. The Unit of Management appealed to Medical Staff to try to accommodate this decision in spite of the difficulties that would ensue, as it was essential to reduce the current overspending on the Royal site. In view of the MEC stance, it was difficult to resist the closure of Ava, and Staff considered alternative accommodation for the patients usually admitted there. As is often the case in seemingly impossible situations, goodwill supplied an answer and recourse was had to a more flexible bed usage. Ava I closed in March 1990.

All was not doom and gloom. A new phase of the Hospital development was soon to dawn; idealism was being replaced by realism. The objective held so tenaciously for many years of a completely new hospital to serve the district and Northern Ireland was to give place to a compromise solution. In December 1993 Sir George Quigley, chairman of the Royal Hospitals Trust, welcomed the announcement by the DHSS of a £9.4 million funding for redevelopment at the RBHSC. The Trust chairman was speaking at a reception in Parliament Buildings, Stormont, at which the

The Duchess of Kent, Sir George Quigley, chairman of the Royal Hospitals Trust (*centre*), and William McKee, chief executive, at the plaque unveiling ceremony to mark the laying of the foundation stone of the new Hospital in October 1995

principal guest was HRH the Duchess of Kent, patron of the Royal Hospitals.

In October 1995 the Duchess of Kent unveiled a plaque to mark the laying of the foundation stone of a complex of new buildings on the southeast portion of the Hospital site. This will involve a complete reorientation of the Hospital through 360 degrees, with a new front door opening on to the Hospital Road, rather than the Falls Road. A range of new units will be accommodated: i) operating theatres and ii) Intensive Care Unit; iii) Accident & Emergency and Outpatient Departments; and iv) the Medical Records Department. In 1996 Belfast-based artist Rita Duffy was employed as creative director of the project. From the outset she worked alongside the Royal Hospitals Trust, Tim Geary and Andrew Spiers of Todd Architects and Planners, and builder Gilbert Ash to produce architecture and art works which promote a feeling of harmony.[5] The project as a whole was supported by a grant of £317,000 from the National Lottery, an excellent example of public money being spent on 'public good'. Artists were either directly commissioned or responded to advertisements and finally included John Kindness, Rita Duffy, Gavin Weston, Brian Connolly, Peter Rooney, Rhona Henderson, Eoin Crawford, Hilary Cromie, Margaret McGonagle, Vivienne Burnside, Helena Kanshal, Annette Hennessey, David Dudgeon and Anne-Marie Robinson.

The architects' specification describes the proposed new Hospital thus:

- The entire outside of the building is clad in white laminate rain-screen material and the roof is constructed of colour-coated aluminium.

The bright new buildings of the Hospital rise against the background of the Black Mountain

- Vehicular and pedestrian access is achieved by a new approach road.
- The majority of accommodation is located on two levels within two individual building blocks which are linked on both levels via a ten-metre-wide, seven-metre-high atrium street which extends the full length of the building. This should provide clarity of visitor orientation by the simplicity of design and layout.
- Medical records and secretaries are accommodated at basement level with a view of the garden.
- The A & E and Outpatient Departments are located at ground level. Within the A & E Department, emergency admissions and walking casualties will be separated by having different entrances, the ambulance entrance being close to the resuscitation room, which leads on to the major trauma area and thence to the bed lift with access to the theatres or Intensive Care Unit. The walking casualty entrance leads to a large waiting and play area. Adjacent are minor treatment rooms and a small observation ward. Both major and minor treatment areas lead separate routes to the satellite X-ray Department, which has an ultrasound facility.
- The Outpatient Department (OPD) consists of three independent suites, which share treatment, diagnostic and ancillary rooms, located as close as possible to the OPD main corridor. Each suite has its own waiting area with exciting play facilities.

Architects' impression of the new outpatient reception area, 1998

- An art gallery is planned for the main waiting area, where children's art will be displayed in a specially designed feature.
- The second level houses theatres and Intensive Care Units, which are interconnected.
- The Theatre Department has three operating suites, one of which is extra-large to facilitate 'ultra clean' procedures.
- From the theatre entrance, parents and children will be directed to a holding room with play facilities, prior to being escorted to the operating suite.
- The exit from the recovery room is discrete from the holding room, thus separating the flow of pre- and post-operative patients. A separate access corridor permits rapid transfer of patients to and from the ICU.
- The Intensive Care Unit contains twelve beds and is divided into two- and four-bed bays with generous single rooms for barrier nursing. Each bay can be easily supervised from the central staff base. Within the unit are two overnight rooms for relatives.

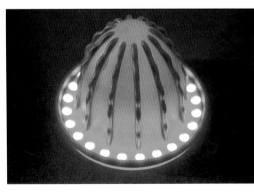

A Raymond Henshaw light box, which will hang from the ceiling in the intensive care area

Among the exciting art works are David Dudgeon's 'Alice in Wonderland' seats, John Kindness's fairytale museum and Hilary Cromie's updated grandfather and grandmother clocks. Rita Duffy has designed a series of storyboards, a recurring art project throughout the building which provides a continuous, engaging narrative, from the bright and inviting

'Welcome to the Hospital' sign at the entrance to the often tongue-in-cheek narrative of the others. A child-friendly sculpture of a stainless steel spaceship by Peter Rooney will also be situated at the entrance. Brian Connolly and Annette Hennessey have devised an audio sculpture that encourages the curious child or adult to place their hands on a 'whispering wall' and so discover a catalogue of pre-recorded stories and songs. Vivienne Burnside has designed an art-play sculpture comprising of stacked cubes – alpha blocks – each side of each cube revealing a different picture. Raymond Henshaw has designed a series of light boxes for the intensive care area. The boxes are made of suction-moulded plastic and will hang from the ceiling, giving the impression of alien torpedoes containing intriguing little pictures. The new building is connected via a glass corridor which curves and rises to join the present accommodation at Allen Ward, with a garden on each side. Artist Gavin Weston has planned the gardens to architectural specifications. In association with Tyrone Brick, he has designed a clever yet simple system of brick paths: nonsense poem narrative has been indented into the bricks, the whole forming a sort of story-path to a concentric seating area. A large specially commissioned sign is backlit and is visible from the West Link road.

Vivienne Burnside's alpha blocks

The integrated art works project shares the aims of the building project to provide an environment that promotes wellbeing. The patient, family and health professional will all spend time in this environment and it is vital that the surroundings are supportive, friendly and interesting. New standards have been set for art in hospitals, with the firm belief that architecture and art works, which are not viewed separately, should not be planned separately.

Since the early days on the Falls Road, the words 'isolation unit' or 'facilities for infectious diseases' have cropped up in discussions with monotonous and unproductive regularity. Finally, on 6 October 1997, an infectious diseases unit opened in an extension to a renovated Knox Ward. The official opening was performed by Phil Coulter, the well-known singer–songwriter. The unit consists of nine isolation cubicles, one of which has positive and negative pressure ventilation. At the level of Allen Ward, a further extension deals with suspected cases of viral haemorrhagic fever. The new unit has been named Belvoir Ward.

Singer–songwriter Phil Coulter officially declaring the Belvoir Ward open in November 1997

These new units will enhance the capability of all Staff to carry out their avowed aim of delivering skilful, compassionate succour to the sick children of Northern Ireland. They could readily take the words of one of their predecessors, Rowland Hill, who, on 1 March 1929, addressed the Hospital Management Committee as follows:

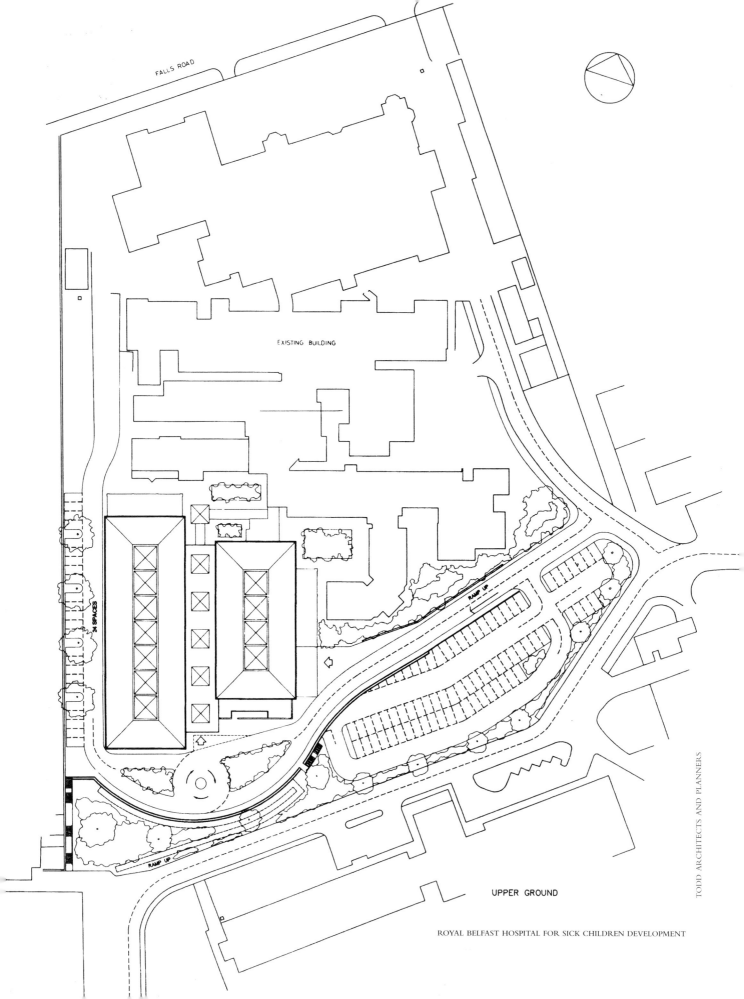

FALLS ROAD

EXISTING BUILDING

24 SPACES

RAMP UP

RAMP UP

RAMP UP

UPPER GROUND

TODD ARCHITECTS AND PLANNERS

ROYAL BELFAST HOSPITAL FOR SICK CHILDREN DEVELOPMENT

That your Hospital shows no diminution in its popularity and esteem as a refuge for the sick and ailing children of Northern Ireland is demonstrated by the fact that no less than 11,970 new patients sought treatment there during the year. It is therefore with great relief that the Medical Staff realises that the task of endeavouring to cope with diseases incidental to child life in the present buildings [Queen Street] is approaching its end and they look forward with eagerness to a sphere of much greater usefulness in the buildings of which the foundations are now actually being laid.[6]

The acquisition of these state-of-the-art buildings will show up in vivid relief the deficiencies of the remaining estate. It cannot be long before further development is set in train and the immemorial question arises, yet again: where are the resources to meet the challenges of the new century?

John Kindness's teapot spider

APPENDIX 1

APPENDIX 2

APPENDIX 3

EHSSB NORTH & WEST BELFAST DISTRICT

COGWHEEL MEDICAL ADMINISTRATION — ROYAL GROUP OF HOSPITALS

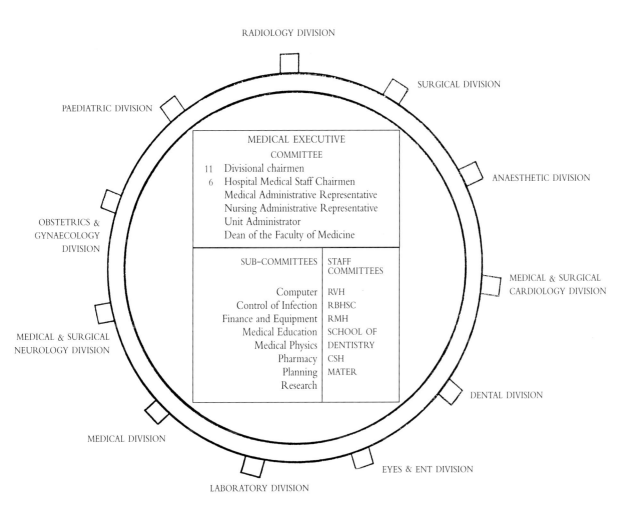

RADIOLOGY DIVISION

SURGICAL DIVISION

PAEDIATRIC DIVISION

ANAESTHETIC DIVISION

OBSTETRICS &
GYNAECOLOGY
DIVISION

MEDICAL & SURGICAL
CARDIOLOGY DIVISION

MEDICAL & SURGICAL
NEUROLOGY DIVISION

DENTAL DIVISION

MEDICAL DIVISION

EYES & ENT DIVISION

LABORATORY DIVISION

MEDICAL EXECUTIVE
COMMITTEE
11 Divisional chairmen
6 Hospital Medical Staff Chairmen
Medical Administrative Representative
Nursing Administrative Representative
Unit Administrator
Dean of the Faculty of Medicine

SUB-COMMITTEES	STAFF COMMITTEES
Computer	RVH
Control of Infection	RBHSC
Finance and Equipment	RMH
Medical Education	SCHOOL OF
Medical Physics	DENTISTRY
Pharmacy	CSH
Planning	MATER
Research	

APPENDIX 4

ONE HUNDRED YEARS OF PAEDIATRICS
1873–1973

Scientific Meeting, 7–11 May 1973

ULSTER HOSPITAL

Monday, 7 May 1973

5.00 p.m.	The Sir Thomas and Lady Edith Dixon Lecture: 'The Doctors' Dilemma' Sir John Peel KCVO

ROYAL BELFAST HOSPITAL FOR SICK CHILDREN

Tuesday, 8 May 1973

	Symposium: Highlights in Paediatric Nursing Chairwoman: Miss E.N.I. Lamb
8.30 a.m.	Introduction: Miss M.H. Hudson MBE
9.45 a.m.	'Development of Paediatric Skills' Miss S.M. Bates, Birmingham
10.30 a.m.	Coffee
	Chairwoman: Miss M. Rooney
11.00 a.m.	'The Low Birth-weight Infant' Miss B. Collins
11.30 a.m.	'Intensive Care Nursing' Mrs C.A. Crawford
12 noon	'Nursing Care Studies' Miss E.D. Girvan and Miss S. Simpson
12.30 p.m.	Discussion
12.45 p.m.	Lunch
	Chairwoman: Miss M. Taylor
2.00 p.m.	'Terminal Illness in Children – The Nurse's Role' Miss S.E.H. Allen and Mrs I.M. Sammon
2.30 p.m.	'Nursing in a Child Psychiatry Unit' Miss P.B. Cleary and Mr S. McClelland
3.15 p.m.	Afternoon tea
3.45 p.m.	Panel discussion: 'The Asthmatic Child' Miss M.J. Hurst (chairwoman) Miss I. Heaney, ward sister Miss M. Kennedy, physiotherapist Miss E. McCaughrain, health visitor Mrs J.G. Colville, teacher

7.00 p.m. | Robert Campbell Oration:
'The Campbell Heritage Lives On'
Sir Ian Fraser DSO, OBE

INSTITUTE OF CLINICAL SCIENCE

Wednesday, 9 May 1973

Symposium: Early Diagnosis in the Prenatal and
Perinatal Periods

Chairman: Professor I.J. Carré

9.30 a.m. | 'Prenatal Diagnosis and the Paediatrician'
Dr N.C. Nevin

10.00 a.m. | 'Prediction of Respiratory Distress Syndrome from Amniotic
Fluid'
Dr C.R. Whitfield

10.30 a.m. | Discussion

10.45 a.m. | Coffee

Chairwoman: Dr Joan B.T. Logan

11.15 a.m. | 'Prenatal Diagnosis of Genetic Defects'
Dr M.A. Ferguson-Smith, Glasgow

12 noon | Discussion

12.15 p.m. | Lunch

Chairwoman: Dr Muriel J.L. Frazer MBE

2.00 p.m. | 'Perinatal Environment as a Determinant of Handicap'
Professor N.R. Butler, Bristol

2.45 p.m. | 'Future of Early Diagnosis'
Dr C.O. Carter, London

3.30 p.m. | Afternoon tea

4.00 p.m. | Panel discussion:
Professor P. Froggatt (chairman)
Professor N.R. Butler
Dr C.O. Carter
Professor S.D.M. Court CBE
Dr M.A. Ferguson-Smith
Dr C.M.B. Field
Dr C.R. Whitfield

ULSTER HOSPITAL

Thursday, 10 May 1973

Miscellaneous Papers
Chairman: Dr W.A.B. Campbell

9.30 a.m. | 'Orthopaedic Problems in the Mentally Handicapped'
Mr W.V. James

9.50 a.m. | 'Congenital Malformations in Belfast'
Dr Maureen J. Scott

10.10 a.m.	'Timing the Correction of Congenital Defects' Mr J. Colville
10.30 a.m.	Coffee
	Chairman: Dr A.A.H. Gailey
11.00 a.m.	'Refractive Surgery of the Cornea' Mr E.C. Cowan
11.20 a.m.	'Non-penetrating Intra-abdominal Injuries' Dr J.M. Hood
11.40 a.m.	'Acute Leukaemia in Dublin' Dr J.N. Bell, Dublin
12 noon	'Intracardiac Conduction' Dr Patricia Morton
12.20 p.m.	Lunch Symposium: The Neonate Chairman: Dr S.H.S. Love
2.10 p.m.	'Neurological Examination of the Newborn' Dr N.J. O'Doherty, Dublin
2.30 p.m.	'The Ill Newborn Baby' Dr M. McC. Reid
2.50 p.m.	'Respiratory Problems in the Newborn' Dr G.W. Black
3.10 p.m.	'Nursing the Critically Ill Infant' Miss Kay C. Duffin
3.30 p.m.	Afternoon tea
4.00 p.m.	Panel discussion: Dr S.H.S. Love (chairman) Dr G.W. Black Miss Kay C. Duffin Dr N.J. O'Doherty Dr M. McC. Reid
4.45 p.m.	Interval
5.15 p.m.	Glaxo (Ireland) Ltd Lecture: 'Respiratory Insufficiency in Infants and Children with Special Reference to Congenital Heart Disease' Dr W.J. Glover, London
6.30 p.m.	Reception by courtesy of Glaxo (Ireland) Ltd
7.30 p.m.	Buffet supper

ROYAL BELFAST HOSPITAL FOR SICK CHILDREN

Friday, 11 May 1973

	Chairman: Mr M.H.H. Nixon, London
9.30 a.m.	'Epidemiology of Anencephalus and Spina Bifida' Dr J.H. Elwood
9.50 a.m.	'Early v. Late Closure of Myelomeningocele' Mr J. Piggot

10.10 a.m.	'Educational and Social Aspects of Spina Bifida' Dr C.M.B. Field
10.30 a.m.	Discussion opened by Mr E.J. Guiney, Dublin
11.15 a.m.	Coffee
	Miscellaneous Papers Chairman: Dr J.F.T. Glasgow
12.05 p.m.	'The Relationship of Granuloma Annulare to Diabetes Mellitus' Dr Grace E. Allen
12.25 p.m.	'Immuno-Fluorescent Studies of Warts and Water-Warts' Dr P.V. Shirodaria
12.45 p.m.	Lunch
	Chairman: Dr W. Bingham
2.10 p.m.	'A Measurement of Lead Contamination' Mr D.J. Stewart
2.30 p.m.	'The Diagnosis of Hereditary Galactosaemia' Dr Nina A.J. Carson
2.50 p.m.	'Bone Changes in Biliary Disease in Infants' Dr P.S. Thomas
3.10 p.m.	Afternoon tea

INSTITUTE OF CLINICAL SCIENCE

4.00 p.m.	Menary Lecture: 'The Allergic Child' Professor R.G. Mitchell, Dundee

APPENDIX 5

DEPARTMENT OF CHILD HEALTH, 1997

Professor J.A. Dodge	Nuffield Professor of Child Health (resigned September 1997)
Professor B.G. McClure	Neonatology (RMH)
Professor H.L. Halliday	Neonatology (RMH)
Dr J.F.T. Glasgow	Reader A & E
Dr J.M. Savage	Nephrology (SL)
Dr D.G. Carson	Endocrinology (SL)
Dr M. Stewart	Community services (SL)
Dr M.D. Shields	Respiratory medicine (SL)
Dr M.M.T. O'Hare	Lecturer in paediatric biochemistry

APPENDIX 6

GOVERNORS AND STAFF OF THE

LINDSAY SCHOOL AT FORSTER GREEN

CHAIRPERSON	Dr W. Nelson
VICE-CHAIRPERSON	Ms R. Lavery
HONORARY SECRETARY	Mr P. Doherty

GOVERNORS

	Dr K. Trew
	Dr R. McAuley
	Mr W. Graham
	Dr L. Mestel
Teacher/governor	Colin Campbell

SCHOOL STAFF

Principal	Phillip Doherty
Vice-principal	Patsy Aust
Assistant teachers	Sandra Glass
	Aidan McNally
	Colin Campbell
	Janet Dickey
	Sally Richardson
Classroom assistant	Meta Tease
Secretary	Mary Herd

APPENDIX 7

THE GOLD MEDAL

Final year medical students compete annually for a Gold Medal, awarded by the Medical Staff of the Hospital. In the event of no candidate achieving the high standard meriting the award of a medal, the best performers receive book tokens. The first recorded date for the award of the Gold Medal was 1885, when the winner was J.J. Redfern.

WINNERS FROM 1948

1948	Mr R.N. Beck	1971	Miss P. Young
1949	Tokens of two guineas each were awarded to Mr R.W. Harland and Mr R. Hurwitz	1972	Mr C.W.B. Corkey
		1973	Mr A.B. Atkinson (book token)
1950	No record	1974	Mr J.N. Patton
1951	No record	1975	Miss S. Creswell (£10 book token)
1952	Miss M. Watson (three-guinea book token)	1976	Mrs C.P. Gilmore
1953	Mr I. Johnston (three-guinea book token)	1977	Mr P. Watt
1954	Miss L. Loughbridge and Mr B.S. Kidd (joint medallists)	1978	Mr R.F. Houston
		1979	Mr P. Gray (£10 book token)
1955	Miss M. Boyle and Miss A. Dorman (joint medallists)	1980	No record
		1981	Mr T. Patton
1956	Mr G.W. Johnston	1982	No award
1957	Mr R. Gibson	1983	Miss J. Forsythe
1958	Mr R.G. Shanks	1984	Miss M. O'Connor
1959	Mr T.A. McNeill	1985	Miss S. Grey
1960	Mr N.C. Nevin	1986	No record
1961	Book tokens awarded to Mr Kahn and Mr W. Wallace	1987	Miss C. McIlroy
		1988	Mr P. Johnston
1962	Mr D. McDevitt	1989	Miss F. Small
1963	Mr J.J. Connor	1990	Mr J. McAteer
1964	Miss R. Imrie	1991	Miss A. Gregory
1965	Mr P.J. Pemberton	1992	Mr M. Duddy
1966	No award	1993	Mr B. Mullan
1967	Mr P. Kennedy	1994	Mr S. Houston
1968	No award	1995	Miss S. Maynard
1969	Mr H.P.S. Campbell	1996	Miss U. Mason
1970	Mr J.M. Elwood	1997	Miss C. O'Kane

APPENDIX 8

This scholarship is awarded for original research into diseases of children.

WINNERS

1935	Dr E.W. McMechan
1937	Dr J.S. Matthews
1938	Dr J.E. Morrison
1939	Dr J. McMurray
1949	Dr A.W. Dickie
1950	Dr M.G. McKeown
1953	Dr N. Johnston
1974	Dr J.B. McConnell
1976	Mr R.A.B. Mollan
1978	Dr J.M. Savage
1985	Dr M.D. Shields
1988	Mr R.J. Stewart
1990	Mr M.M.J. Quinn
1992	Dr F.A. Casey
1994	Mr W.B. McCallion

APPENDIX 9

CHAIRMEN OF MEDICAL STAFF
1932–97

1932–8	Dr T.S. Kirk	1971–3	Dr J.M. Beare
1938–42	Professor P.T. Crymble	1973–5	Mr N.C. Hughes
1942–5	Dr R. Hill	1975–7	Dr S.H.S. Love
1945–9	Mr H.P. Hall	1977–9	Professor I. Carré
1949–52	Dr F.M.B. Allen	1979–81	Mr B.T. Smyth
1952–4	Dr I. McCaw	1981–3	Dr G.W. Black
1954–7	Mr I. Fraser	1983–5	Dr W.Mc. Nelson
1957–9	Dr D. Boyd	1985–7	Dr P.S. Thomas
1959–61	Mr D.H. Craig	1987–9	Dr S.R. Keilty
1961–3	Mr J.S. Loughridge	1989–91	Dr A.O.B. Redmond
1963–5	Mr J.A. Bingham	1991–3	Dr J.F.T. Glasgow
1965–7	Dr M.J.L. Frazer	1993–5	Professor J.A. Dodge
1967–9	Dr A.A.H. Gailey	1995–7	Dr M. Reid
1969–71	Dr W.A.B. Campbell		

CHAIRMAN ELECT – MR V. BOSTON

APPENDIX 10

1949–53	Dr. D. Boyd
1953–5	Dr W.A.B. Campbell
1955–7	Mr N.C. Hughes
1957–9	Mr D.H. Craig
1959–61	Mr J.A. Bingham
1961–2	Dr A.A.H. Gailey
1962–3	Dr J.M. Beare
1963–5	Dr S.H.S. Love
1965–7	Dr W.R. Dickie
1967–9	Dr W.I. Forsythe
1969–71	Mr B.T. Smyth
1971–3	Dr G.W. Black
1973–5	Dr D. Burrows
1975–7	Dr J.M. Bridges
1977–9	Dr W.McC. Nelson
1979–81	Dr P.S. Thomas
1981–3	Dr S.R. Keilty
1983–5	Dr A.O.B. Redmond
1985–7	Dr J.F.T. Glasgow
1987–9	Mr I.D.F. Saunders
1989–91	Dr R. McAuley
1991–3	Mr V.E. Boston
1993–5	Dr J.M. Savage
1995–7	Mr S. Brown
1997–9	Dr S.I. Dempsey

APPENDIX 11

PAUL WARD	Sister U. Eddie
MUSGRAVE WARD	Sister J. Frazer
	Sister E. Collins
BARBOUR WARD	Sister A. Colhoun
ALLEN WARD	
CHERRY TREE HOUSE	Sister A. Pollock
KNOX WARD	Sister J. McCollum
BELVOIR WARD	Sister J. Ramage
DAY CARE UNIT	Sister L. Surgenor
INTENSIVE CARE UNIT	Sister C. McCormick
	Sister P. Haslett
	Sister H. Tough
	Sister M. Chapman
INFANT SURGICAL UNIT	Sister M. Bonnar
HAEMATOLOGY UNIT	Sister B. Carlisle
CLARKE CHILDREN'S CLINIC	Sister A. Kearney
	Sister J. Darragh
MEDICAL OUTPATIENT	
DEPARTMENT	Sister B. Moneypenny
ORTHOPAEDIC OUTPATIENT	
DEPARTMENT	Sister E. Bell (retired June 1997)
ACCIDENT & EMERGENCY	
DEPARTMENT	Sister M. Hawthorne
THEATRES	Sister M. Jackson
	Sister J. Devine
NIGHT DUTY	Sister D. Martin
	Sister I. Kinkead
	Sister D. McMullan

From July 1996 Sisters Jackson, Moneypenny and Surgenor, in addition to their nurse manager duties, functioned as an administrative triumvirate.

NOTES

NB: There are no notes for Chapters 1, 13 and 14

CHAPTER 2

1   H.G. Calwell, *The Life and Times of a Voluntary Hospital* (Belfast 1973), p. 103
2   *75th Annual Report of the Belfast Hospital for Sick Children* (1947), p. 17

CHAPTER 3

1   Medical Staff minutes, March 1948
2   Sir Ian Fraser, personal communication
3   R.S. Allison, *Lancet*, 22 January 1972
4   Dr Sara Campbell, personal communication
5   *Ibid.*
6   Dr Douglas Boyd, personal communication
7   Dr George Patterson, personal communication
8   Dr H.C. Mulholland, personal communication
9   Dr Fiona Stewart, personal communication
10 Dr P. Froggatt, Dr M.A. Lyons and Dr T.K. Marshall, 'Sudden Unexpected Death in Infants ("Cot Death"): Report of a Collaborative Study in Northern Ireland', *Ulster Medical Journal*, vol. 40 (1971), pp. 116–34
11 Dr J.F.T. Glasgow, personal communication
12 H.C. Kempe et al., 'The Battered Child Syndrome', *Journal of the American Medical Association*, vol. 181 (1962), pp. 17–24
13 Dr Heather Steen, personal communication
14 Dr Moira Stewart, personal communication

CHAPTER 4

1   Sir Ian Fraser, personal communication
2   'Robert Campbell in Queen Street 1897–1920: Day Surgery in the Belfast Hospital for Sick Children', *Ulster Medical Journal*, vol. 60 (1991), pp. 205–11
3   *Belfast Telegraph*, 23 February 1986
4   James Piggot, personal communication
5   *Ibid.*
6   *Belfast Telegraph*, 21 November 1994
7   N.C. Hughes, personal communication
8   R.S. Allison, *The Very Faculties* (Belfast 1969)
9   Medical Staff minutes, April 1950
10 W.D. Martin, personal communication
11 'The Development of Evoked Response Audiometry Services in Northern Ireland – The First Ten Years', *Journal of Northern Ireland Speech and Language Forum* (1979), pp. 39–45
12 *Ulster Medical Journal*, vol. 4, no. 2 (1945), p. 83
13 W.D. Pielou and I.D.F. Saunders, personal communications

CHAPTER 5

1   Sister Jean Kennedy, personal communication
2   Medical Staff minutes, June 1984
3   Medical Staff minutes, February 1985
4   Medical Staff minutes, February 1987

CHAPTER 6

1   Medical Staff minutes, June 1901
2   Dr J.F.T. Glasgow, personal communication
3   Dr J.F.T. Glasgow and Dr R.H. Taylor, personal communications

CHAPTER 7

1   H.G. Calwell, *The Life and Times of a Voluntary Hospital* (Belfast 1973), pp. 74–5
2   M.K. Robb, personal communication
3   John J. Walsh, former principal administrative education officer, Belfast Northern Group School of Nursing, personal communication

CHAPTER 8

1   Medical Staff minutes, May 1942
2   H.G. Calwell, *The Life and Times of a Voluntary Hospital* (Belfast 1973), p. 96
3   Letter from R.W. Harland to Dr Doris Odlum recorded in minutes of Child Guidance Subcommittee, August 1942

CHAPTER 9

1   H.G. Caldwell, *The Life and Times of a Voluntary Hospital* (Belfast 1973), p. 129
2   *Ibid.*, p. 130
3   Edward Butler et al., *Lissue Hospital History* (Belfast 1981)
4   Dr Roger McAuley, personal communication
5   Medical Staff minutes, May 1973
6   Jonathan Bardon, *A History of Ulster* (Belfast 1992), p. 532
7   Dr Roger McAuley, personal communication
8   Correspondence between Dr Elaine Hicks, Dr S.R. Keilty and the Eastern Health & Social Services Board, 1988
9   Dr Nan Hill, personal communication

CHAPTER 10

1 Medical Staff minutes, January 1936
2 Medical Staff minutes, July 1939
3 Medical Staff minutes, June 1936
4 T.W. Macfarlane, personal communication
5 M.G. Nelson, 'A History of Clinical Pathology at the RVH (1900–1980)' pp. 88–98
6 Medical Staff minutes, 1985–6

CHAPTER 11

1 Medical Staff minutes, December 1911
2 Medical Staff minutes, September 1934
3 Dr P.S. Thomas, personal communication

CHAPTER 12

1 Christine Hayden, departmental manager, personal communication
2 Janet Mercer and Ann Wilson, personal communication
3 Paper 10, Education and Training (Central Council for Education and Training of Social Workers 1975)
4 Patricia Donnelly, personal communication

CHAPTER 15

1 Medical Staff minutes, May 1976

CHAPTER 16

1 Letter from Sir Ian Fraser to Dr Martin Beare, chairman, Medical Staff Committee

CHAPTER 17

1 *Administrative Structure of Hospital Management Committees and Hospital Committees* (The Hawnt Report) (Belfast 1966)
2 Dr Mark Reid, chairman, Medical Staff Committee, personal communication

CHAPTER 18

1 Medical Staff minutes, June 1945
2 N.C. Hughes, personal communication
3 Donald Court and Anthony Jackson, *Paediatrics in the Seventies – Developing the Child Health Services* (London 1972), p. 30
4 Medical Staff minutes, April 1985
5 Rita Duffy, 'Strategy for Integration of Art within RBHSC' (1994); Sister Barbara Moneypenny, personal communication, 1996
6 *56th Annual Report of the Belfast Hospital for Sick Children* (1929)

INDEX

the official
fulham fc
annual 2012

Edited by Adam Reed
Content by Tom Brown & Scot Buckland

club honours

LEAGUE

Second Division/First Division
(now known as the Championship)
Champions: 1948–49, 2000–01
Runners-up: 1958–59

Third Division (South)/Third Division/Second Division
(now known as League One)
Champions: 1931–32, 1998–99
Runners-up: 1970–71

Fourth Division/Third Division
(now Known as League Two)
Runners-up 1996–97

Southern League First Division Champions
1905–06, 1906–07

Southern League Second Division Champions
1901–02, 1902–03

CUPS

FA Cup
Runners-up: 1975
Semi-finals: 1908, 1936, 1958, 1962, 2002

League Cup
Quarter-finals: 1968, 1971, 2000, 2001, 2005

EUROPEAN CUPS

UEFA Europa League
Runners-up: 2009–10

Anglo-Scottish Cup
Runners-up: 1975

UEFA Intertoto Cup
Winners: 2002–03

fulham fc

Craven Cottage, Stevenage Road,
London SW6 6HH

Main Number: 0843 208 1222
Ticket Line: 0843 208 1234

www.fulhamfc.com

contents

fulham

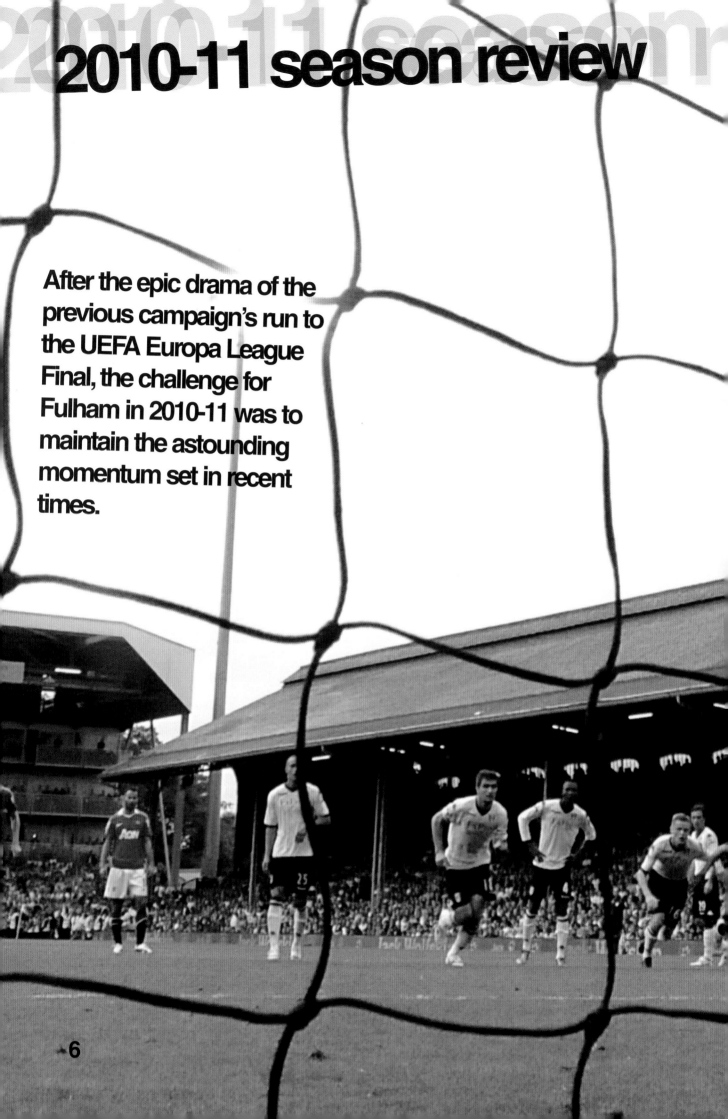

After the epic drama of the previous campaign's run to the UEFA Europa League Final, the challenge for Fulham in 2010-11 was to maintain the astounding momentum set in recent times.

Bobby Zamora made his England debut against Hungary.

August

One of the heroes of the previous campaign, Mark Schwarzer, was sidelined through injury as the new campaign kicked-off, but David Stockdale was ready to step into his shoes. The understudy proved he was up to the challenge, keeping two clean sheets and making a game-changing late penalty save against Manchester United which inspired the team to an equaliser (through Brede Hangeland) as the Whites achieved a deserved point against the reigning champions.

Meanwhile, Bobby Zamora was rewarded for his fine form in the previous season with a call-up to the England squad, and his first international cap, coming on as a substitute in the 2–1 win against Hungary.

However, despite some encouraging displays, aside from a 6–0 hammering of Port Vale in the Carling Cup in which new signing Mousa Dembélé picked up his first goal for the Club, by the end of the month the Whites were yet to win under new Manager Mark Hughes and sat 14th in the table with three points from the first three games.

Mousa Dembélé opened his Whites account against Port Vale in the Carling Cup

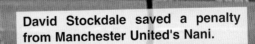

David Stockdale saved a penalty from Manchester United's Nani.

7

September

The first of Fulham's 11 victories of the season - a 2–1 win at home to Wolves – came at a cost as Bobby Zamora was stretchered off with a broken leg, which would put him out of action until late February.

With the previous season's top scorer out of commission, the team battled to draws away at Blackburn and at home to Everton which lifted the Club to seventh in the League table, but the Whites were knocked out of the Carling Cup by Stoke in a disappointing 2–0 defeat.

Disaster as Bobby Zamora broke his leg against Wolves.

Tottenham and Fulham players debated Tom Huddlestone's controversial strike.

October

Entering October, Fulham were one of only two teams in the Premier League to remain unbeaten, alongside Manchester United, but that record was ended by Tottenham, albeit controversially as William Gallas had appeared to be in an offside position when his team scored. However, after much debate between referee Mike Dean, his assistant, and the Tottenham players, the decisive goal stood.

In more pleasing news, Clint Dempsey began to prove that he was willing to take on the mantle of main goal scorer in Zamora's absence, netting three goals in four games, taking his tally to five in 10 league matches, and helping the Whites secure four points, in a 1–1 draw away to West Ham and a 2–0 home win against Wigan.

Despite losing for the first time in the season, come the end of the month Fulham remained in the top half of the table on 12 points after 10 games.

9

Brede scored a late equaliser at home to Villa.

November

November was always going to be a tough month, with fixtures against Manchester City and Chelsea, and so it proved.

Brede Hangeland won the Whites a point with a dramatic late equaliser at home to Aston Villa, but the team were narrowly edged out 1–0 at Stamford Bridge – where hot prospect Matthew Briggs made his first Premier League start – before a dispiriting 4–1 defeat at home to City, Carlos Tevez wreaking havoc before Zoltan Gera came off the bench to grab a consolation goal.

In a remarkably closely packed Premier League table, Fulham fell to 17th after collecting just three points out of a possible 15, leaving the Whites with just a one-point cushion from the relegation zone heading into December.

Youngster Matthew Briggs made his first Premier League start away to Chelsea.

Clint scored again in a 1-1 draw with Birmingham.

10

Chris Baird grabbed a crucial double against Stoke.

December

For the most part December was another month to forget, before an encouraging finale.

It began with a tough 2–1 defeat at Arsenal where two contenders for goal of the season by Samir Nasri cancelled out Diomansy Kamara's strike. Two winnable home games then returned just one point as a goalless draw against Sunderland was followed by a crushing 3–1 Boxing Day loss to struggling West Ham that took Fulham into the relegation zone for the first time in the season.

Christmas may have been ruined, but that defeat appeared to have a positive effect on the team who went out fighting two days later at Stoke, recording a first away win of the season thanks to two stunning Chris Baird strikes – his first and second for the Club. It felt like a turning point, and so it would prove.

Mousa completed the scoring in the 4-0 FA Cup win over Spurs.

January

A New Year's Day defeat at Tottenham was quickly forgotten as the Whites displayed vast improvement at the start of 2011.

West Bromwich Albion were put to the sword 3–0 at the Cottage, and Stoke were defeated 2–0 for the second time in a matter of weeks, this time thanks to a Dempsey double.

In the FA Cup Peterborough United were destroyed 6–2, with a Diomansy Kamara hat-trick, and Tottenham too were brushed aside 4–0 at the Cottage after a phenomenal first-half that saw Danny Murphy convert two penalties, and Mousa Dembélé net the goal of the season.

With the transfer window open too, the Whites strengthened with the loan additions of Steve Sidwell, Eidur Gudjohnsen and Gael Kakuta.

Clint Dempsey netted from the penalty spot against Stoke.

February

Fulham's form continued with a 1–0 defeat of Newcastle at Craven Cottage, Damien Duff scoring the only goal of the game against his former employers.

Creditable away draws at Aston Villa (2–2) and Manchester City (1–1) kept the points tally increasing, as did a goalless home draw in a Valentine's Day SW6 derby with Chelsea. Although Whites fans went home wondering what might have been had Petr Cech not saved Clint Dempsey's late penalty.

Having impressed again in place of Mark Schwarzer who had been on Asia Cup duty, David Stockdale became the second Fulham player of the season to be called up by England, and there was good news for the other, as Bobby Zamora was reintroduced to the squad after recovering from his broken leg.

His return wasn't all happy though as it coincided with the team crashing out of the FA Cup at the hands of Bolton Wanderers (0–1).

AJ and Clint were on the scoresheet at Villa Park.

Petr Cech saved Clint's late penalty.

13

March

A frustrating home game against Blackburn, that saw a dubious Rovers goal allowed despite an El-Hadji Diouf push on Mark Schwarzer, was settled from the penalty spot by none other than Bobby Zamora, with his first goal since returning from injury. The game ended 3-2 after Damien Duff's brace against another of his former clubs.

The home win was the highlight of an otherwise quiet month that saw only one other fixture, a 2-1 defeat at Everton where Clint Dempsey's second-half strike was not enough to cancel out Seamus Coleman and Louis Saha's earlier goals.

Bobby Zamora was back to scoring ways against Blackburn.

April

Fulham began to gain serious momentum as the season neared its end, and April featured three 3–0 victories, the first of which, at home to Blackpool, saw Bobby Zamora net two goals, to take his tally to six in only his seventh Premier League game of the season.

In a busy month, the Whites dropped just five points out of a possible 15 (a forgivable loss at Old Trafford, and a draw away at Wolves).

Three-goal victories over Bolton at home and Sunderland away accelerated the team to the safety of 45 points with three games left to play. The Bolton result also saw Clint Dempsey equal and then bypass Brian McBride and Steed Malbranque's record of 32 Premier League goals for the Club, writing his name into Fulham history.

Above: Simon Davies scored two at Sunderland.

Below: And Bobby bagged a brace against Blackpool.

Brede netted both in the 2–0 win over Birmingham.

And a successful season ended with a lively 2-2 home draw with Arsenal.

May

With safety assured, the Whites entered the final month in a comfortable mid-table position and with hopes of possible European football the following season through the Fair Play League.

A 5-2 loss at home to a revitalised Liverpool was not the result that fans had hoped for after two 3-0 wins in a row, but it seemed to spur Fulham on to another away win at Birmingham, thanks to a Brede Hangeland double.

Arsenal were visitors for the final game of the season, an entertaining 2-2 draw that saw Bobby Zamora and Steve Sidwell on target. The only sour note was a red card for substitute Zoltan Gera, which caused some to fear damage to the Fair Play ranking, but as things transpired, the Club ended the season in a more than respectable eighth place on 49 points, racking up 11 wins, 16 draws and a total of 49 goals whilst conceding only 43, and with a second UEFA Europa League campaign in two years to look forward to.

After a shaky start, it turned out to be the second highest league placing in the Fulham's history.

2010–11 results

Home games shown bold

Competition	Date	Against	Result	Scorers	Attendance
PL	14 Aug	Bolton Wanderers	0–0		20,352
PL	**22 Aug**	**Manchester United**	**2–2**	**Davies, Hangeland**	**25,643**
FLC2	**25 Aug**	**Port Vale**	**6–0**	**Gera 2, Dembélé, Zamora 2, Dempsey**	**9,031**
PL	28 Aug	Blackpool	2–2	Zamora, Etuhu	15,529
PL	**11 Sept**	**Wolverhampton W.**	**2–1**	**Dembélé 2**	**25,280**
PL	18 Sept	Blackburn Rovers	1–1	Dempsey	23,759
FLC3	21 Sept	Stoke City	2–0		12,778
PL	**25 Sept**	**Everton**	**0–0**		**25,598**
PL	02 Oct	West Ham United	1–1	Dempsey	34,859
PL	**16 Oct**	**Tottenham Hotspur**	**1–2**	**Kamara**	**25,615**
PL	23 Oct	West Bromwich Albion	2–1	Carson (og)	25,625
PL	**30 Oct**	**Wigan Athletic**	**2–0**	**Dempsey 2**	**25,448**
PL	**06 Nov**	**Aston Villa**	**1–1**	**Hangeland**	**24,000**
PL	10 Nov	Chelsea	1–0		41,593
PL	13 Nov	Newcastle United	0–0		44,686
PL	**21 Nov**	**Manchester City**	**1–4**	**Gera**	**25,694**
PL	**27 Nov**	**Birmingham City**	**1–1**	**Dempsey**	**24,391**
PL	04 Dec	Arsenal	2–1	Kamara	60,049
PL	**11 Dec**	**Sunderland**	**0–0**		**24,462**
PL	**26 Dec**	**West Ham United**	**1–3**	**Hughes**	**25,332**
PL	28 Dec	Stoke City	0–2	Baird 2	26,954
PL	01 Jan	Tottenham Hotspur	1–0		35,603
PL	**04 Jan**	**West Bromwich Albion**	**3–0**	**Davies, Dempsey, Hangeland**	**23,654**
FAC3	**08 Jan**	**Peterborough United**	**6–2**	**Kamara 3, Etuhu, Gera, Greening**	**15,936**
PL	15 Jan	Wigan Athletic	1–1	Johnson	18,820
PL	**22 Jan**	**Stoke City**	**2–0**	**Dempsey 2**	**23,766**
PL	26 Jan	Liverpool	1–0		40,466
FAC4	**30 Jan**	**Tottenham Hotspur**	**4–0**	**Murphy (2 pen.), Hangeland, Dembélé**	**21,829**
PL	**02 Feb**	**Newcastle United**	**1–0**	**Duff**	**25,620**
PL	05 Feb	Aston Villa	2–2	Johnson, Dempsey	35,899
PL	**14 Feb**	**Chelsea**	**0–0**		**25,685**
FAC5	**20 Feb**	**Bolton Wanderers**	**0–1**		**19,571**
PL	27 Feb	Manchester City	1–1	Duff	43,077
PL	**05 Mar**	**Blackburn Rovers**	**3–2**	**Duff 2, Zamora (pen)**	**25,687**
PL	19 Mar	Everton	2–1	Dempsey	33,239
PL	**03 Apr**	**Blackpool**	**3–0**	**Dempsey 2, Etuhu**	**25,692**
PL	09 Apr	Manchester United	2–0		75,339
PL	23 Apr	Wolverhampton W.	1–1	Johnson	28,825
PL	**27 Apr**	**Bolton Wanderers**	**3–0**	**Dempsey 2, Hangeland**	**23,222**
PL	30 Apr	Sunderland	0–3	Kakuta, Davies 2	39,576
PL	**09 May**	**Liverpool**	**2–5**	**Dembélé, Sidwell**	**25,693**
PL	15 May	Birmingham City	0–2	Hangeland 2	27,759
PL	**22 May**	**Arsenal**	**2–2**	**Sidwell, Zamora**	**25,674**

Key: PL - Premier Leage, FAC - FA Cup, FLC - League Cup

A s ever, the 2010/11 season was littered with memorable individual performances, making it all the more challenging to pick a Player of the Season.

Aaron Hughes was as consistent and reliable as ever, while his central defensive partner, Brede Hangeland, took his game to even greater heights – as if that was even conceivably possible. Chris Baird enjoyed arguably his finest period for the Club, while Damien Duff, Danny Murphy and Mousa Dembélé also caught the eye.

player of the season 2010-11

layer of the season

THAT BOY CLINT DEMPSEY

However, it was our fantastic American attacker that won the public vote in what can be best described as a season of unfailing inspiration and desire.

Wonderful goals and assists stood him out, while his tenacity, versatility and commitment to the cause earned yet more accolades. In the process, the 28-year-old became Fulham's record Premier League goal scorer as he eased the burden of the loss of three senior strikers.

Clint's 12 league goals alone won the team 13 points in one of the tightest seasons in Premier League history, underlining his contribution to our overall final placing of eighth.

A popular figure on the banks of the Thames since his arrival in January 2007, he has impressed and progressed to become one of the Whites' most important players.

This was a just reward for our longest-serving current player.

20

21

the boss

Martin Jol

Date of Birth: 16.01.1956
Birthplace: The Hague, Netherlands
Nationality: Dutch
Previous Clubs Managed: ADO Den Haag, SVV Scheveningen, Roda JC, RKC Waalwijk, Tottenham Hotspur, Hamburger SV, Ajax Amsterdam
Played for: ADO Den Haag, Bayern Munich, FC Twente, West Bromwich Albion, Coventry City, ADO Den Haag

The appointment of Martin Jol in June 2011 prompted much hope and excitement amongst Fulham fans, for in the experienced Dutchman the Club has one of Europe's most astute managers at its helm.

With a profound knowledge of the game and a shrewd tactical mind, he is both revered and respected. Off the field, despite a steely edge, he is recognised as one of football's genuine nice guys - a popular figure amongst players, colleagues and supporters.

An advocate of attractive football, over the years he has won many admirers for his approach and philosophy, while as a player, Jol was a forceful midfielder that was never afraid to put his foot in.

"Fulham is a very traditional club an really good feeling about this Club a

Back in English football after four years away having brought stability, ambition and belief to Tottenham Hotspur, his return to the Premier League was long anticipated. Having come close to taking over following the departure of Roy Hodgson a year earlier, for many his appointment makes for the perfect fit.

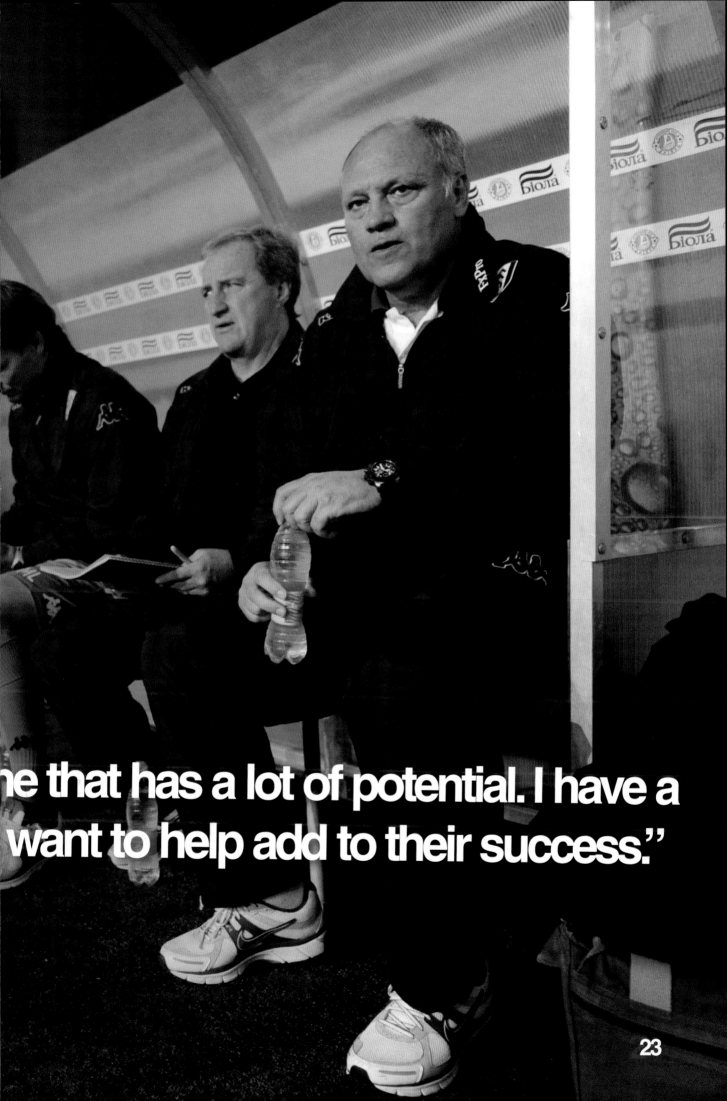

ne that has a lot of potential. I have a
want to help add to their success."

Pajtim Kasami

Squad Number: 10
Date of Birth: 02.06.1992
Birthplace: Struga, Macedonia
Nationality: Swiss
Height: 188cm
Weight: 90kg
Fulham Debut: v RNK Split (a) 28.07.2011
Previous Clubs: Bellinzona, Palermo

One of Europe's most highly-rated young players having earned a glowing reputation in Serie A with Palermo.

A player that can play anywhere across the midfield or off a front man, Pajtim (pronounced Pie-Tim) Kasami is confident on the ball, ambitious in possession and always looking to make things happen.

He was part of the Switzerland squad that reached the final of the 2011 European Under-21 Championships and a vital member of the side that won the Under-17 World Cup in 2009. He is hotly tipped to make a similar impact for the Swiss senior side too.

John Arne Riise

Squad Number: 3
Date of Birth: 24.09.1980
Birthplace: Alesund, Norway
Nationality: Norwegian
Height: 188cm
Weight: 82kg
Fulham Debut: v Crusaders (h) 21.07.2011
Previous Clubs: Alesunds, Monaco, Liverpool, Roma

One of Europe's most respected left-backs, Riise's summer 2011 capture was quite a coup for Fulham. A Champions League winner with plenty of international experience, he has been a consistent performer at the top for more than a decade.

Renowned for his unrivalled stamina and powerful shooting, Riise is also an accomplished player defensively. And having come close to joining Fulham in the past, he came here looking to finally show the Cottage faithful what he is capable of.

Csaba Somogyi

Squad Number: 22
Date of Birth: 07.04.1985
Birthplace: Dunaújváros, Hungary
Nationality: Hungarian
Height: 190cm
Weight: 80kg
Fulham Debut: N/A
Previous Clubs: Gyori ETO, Integrál-DAC, Héviz, Rákospalotai EAC

Csaba Somogyi became Martin Jol's first Fulham signing, joining as Mark Schwarzer's understudy.

The Hungarian stopper was well known to the Manager having spent time on trial at the Dutchman's former club Ajax. Despite a move failing to materialise, Somogyi impressed and, after completing a similarly successful period at Motspur Park, Jol moved quickly to bring him in on a full-time deal.

With a sound reading of play and excellent reflexes, he is sure to improve further during his time at Craven Cottage.

Marcel Gecov

Squad Number: 15
Date of Birth: 01.01.1988
Birthplace: Prague, Czech Republic
Nationality: Czech
Height: 182cm
Weight: 77kg
Fulham Debut: v Chelsea (a) 21.09.2011
Previous Clubs: Slavia Prague, Kladno (loan), Slovan Liberec

Fulham scouts had long monitored the development of Czech schemer Marcel Gecov (pronounced Gets-Off).

Having been named in the 2011 European Under-21 Championships team of the tournament, clubs from Germany and Holland began to circle. However, it was the Whites that moved swiftest, offering the young midfielder the chance to fulfil his dream of playing in the Premier League.

Primarily a box-to-box player, Gecov looks well suited to the demands of English football.

Zdenek Grygera

Squad Number: 26
Date of Birth: 14.05.1980
Birthplace: Prilepy, Czech Republic
Nationality: Czech
Height: 184cm
Weight: 80.2kg
Fulham Debut: v FC Twente (h) 15.09.2011
Previous Clubs: FK Svit Zlin, Petra Drnovice, Sparta Prague, Ajax, Juventus

Before he had even pulled on the white shirt Zdenek Grygera had already played a part in one of Fulham's finest moments.

The former Czech Republic international was a member of the Juventus side dumped out of the Europa League at Craven Cottage in March 2010. That night of drama would ultimately shape his future and strengthen his desire to play in the Premier League.

That wish has now been granted and having played in two European Championships, one World Cup, and a number of Champions League campaigns, Grygera arrived with plenty of experience.

Bryan Ruiz

Squad Number: 11
Date of Birth: 18.08.1985
Birthplace: Alajuela, Cost Rica
Nationality: Costa Rican
Height: 188cm
Weight: 79.8kg
Fulham Debut: v Blackburn Rovers (a) 11.09.2011
Previous Clubs: Alajuelense, KAA Gent, FC Twente

Costa Rican Bryan Ruiz's move to SW6 represented quite a coup for Martin Jol's side.

With some of Europe's leading clubs vying for his signature, including reported interest from Arsenal, Tottenham and Liverpool, Ruiz's deadline day signing was greeted with much excitement and rightly so for he is a game-changing talent.

A player that can play down either flank or through the middle, he scored for fun at previous club FC Twente whom he helped to the Dutch league title in 2010. However, there is more to his game than goals, with Ruiz chipping in with his fair share of assists too.

Orlando Sá

Squad Number: 9
Date of Birth: 26.05.1988
Birthplace: Barcelos, Portugal
Nationality: Portuguese
Height: 186cm
Weight: 89kg
Fulham Debut: v Chelsea (a) 21.09.2011
Previous Clubs: Braga, Maria Fonte (loan), Porto, Nacional (loan)

While few will have been too familiar with Orlando Sá before his deadline day free transfer from FC Porto, his transfer could represent a real bargain.

The former teen prodigy spent time on trial at Chelsea in 2008 and Martin Jol certainly believes he can add firepower to the Fulham attack, with the one-cap Portugal international both strong in the air and effective on the floor.

Physically imposing, Sá should relish the demands of English football.

craven cottage

Fulham's famous home on the banks of the Thames is one of the oldest standing football arenas in the world.

The stage for many a dramatic moment in Fulham and football history, the stadium dates back to 1896 and remains a true window into how football used to be, in an era when many of its contemporary grounds, such as the old Wembley and Highbury, have been torn down.

Fulham FC's spiritual home, it has also hosted some big events over the years, especially in recent times with international matches featuring Australia, Brazil, Republic of Ireland, Jamaica, Colombia and Ghana played out on the Cottage turf. UEFA also selected it as the venue for the 2011 women's Champions League Final. Even the football legend Pelé played and scored at the Cottage, in a 1973 friendly when Fulham defeated his club side Santos 2-1.

The capacity of the stadium today is 25,700, but the highest recorded attendance is almost double that at 49,335, reached in a game against Milwall on 8th October 1938 as the stadium used to have standing sections.

At the end of the 2001/02 season it was feared that Fulham would never play at Craven Cottage again because of regulations outlawing standing sections in top level stadiums, but happily, the Club returned in 2004 after a massive £8million was spent on refurbishment to bring the ground up to Premier League standards in time for the 2004/2005 season.

Craven Cottage Facts

- Current capacity: 25,700.

- Record attendance: 49,335 v Millwall. October 8th, 1938.

- Record modern attendance: 25,700 v Arsenal on Saturday 26th September 2009.

- The original 'Craven Cottage' was a royal hunting lodge dating back more than 300 years, and was located roughly where the centre circle is today.

- The stand on Stevenage Road celebrated its centenary in the 2005/06 season when it was renamed the Johnny Haynes Stand after the Club sought the opinions of supporters.

- Both the Johnny Haynes Stand and the Cottage are among the finest examples of Archibald Leitch football stadium architecture to remain in existence. Both are Grade II listed.

- Between 1980 and 1984, Fulham Rugby League (now Harlequins Rugby League) played their home games at the Cottage.

- The stadium features two statues. One, on Stevenage Road, of the Club's greatest ever player Johnny Haynes, and a second, on the Riverside, of pop legend Michael Jackson.

- Craven Cottage is the only ground in England to feature a dedicated section for neutral spectators.

the first team

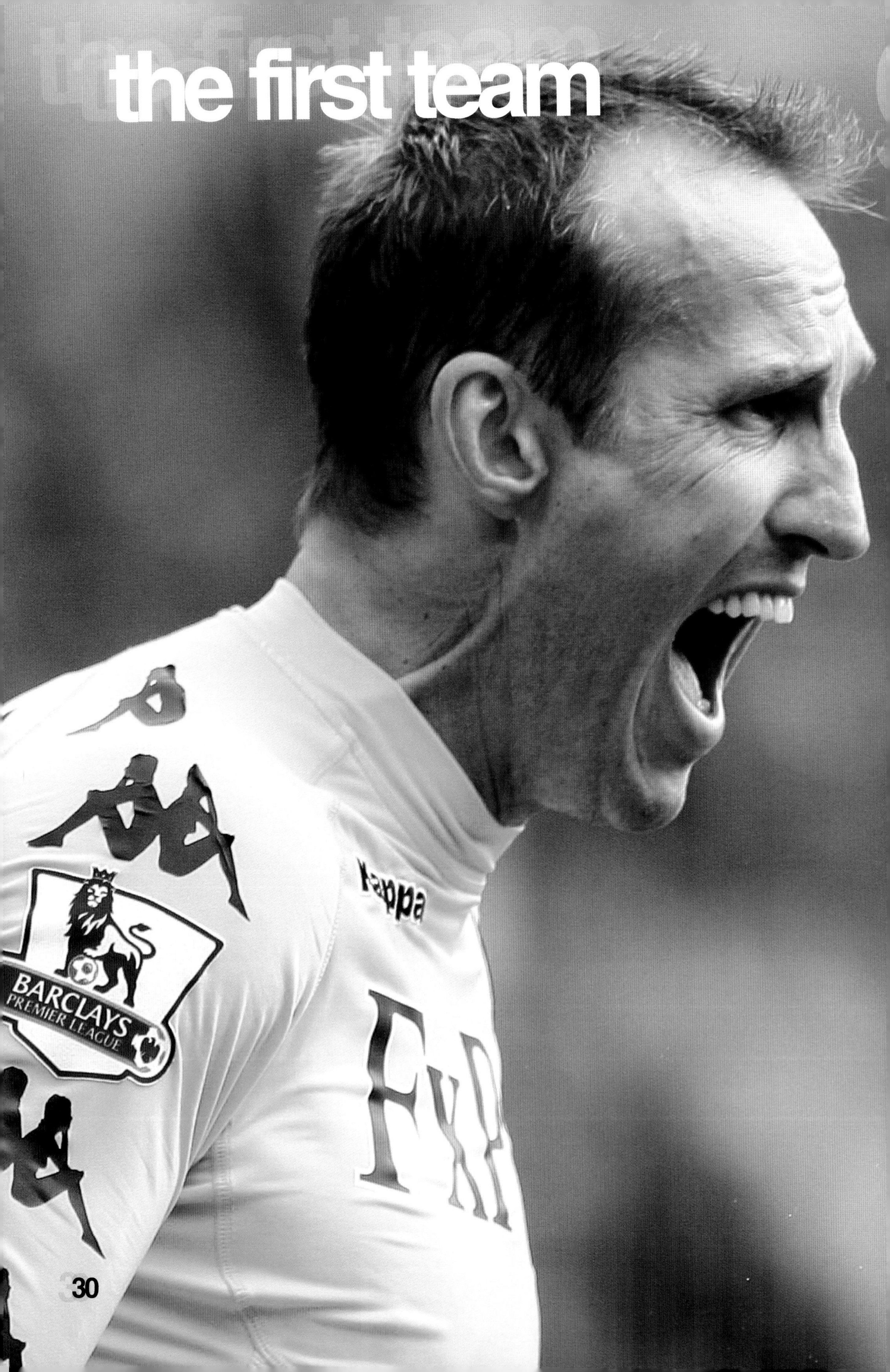

Neil Etheridge

Squad Number: 38
Date of Birth: 07.02.1990
Birthplace: Enfield
Nationality: Philippines
Height: 188cm
Weight: 90kg
Fulham Debut: N/A
Previous Clubs: Charlton (loan)

Fulham are blessed with a number of young goalkeeping talents, and Neil Etheridge is another chasing the number one shirt.

Despite representing England at youth level, it has been with his mother's home nation that he has made his greatest impression, with more than 20 international caps making him something of a Philippines star, before even making his First Team debut.

With number two David Stockdale on loan at Ipswich this term, Etheridge has stepped up to First Team squad duties on a regular basis.

Mark Schwarzer

Squad Number: 1
Date of Birth: 06.11.1972
Birthplace: Sydney, Australia
Nationality: Australian
Height: 195cm
Weight: 95kg
Fulham Debut: v Hull City (a) 16.08.2008
Previous Clubs: Marconi Stallions, Dynamo Dresden, Kaiserslautern, Bradford City, Middlesbrough

Now in his 16th season in English football, Mark Schwarzer is one of the top-flight's best, and his performances with Fulham have been nothing short of remarkable.

A free signing from Middlesbrough in 2008, his form in his first season at Craven Cottage saw him named Supporters' Player of the Year and contributed much towards the Club's record seventh place finish and qualification for the UEFA Europa League.

With a record breaking 91 caps for Australia (and counting), Schwarzer is a vitally important player for Club and country.

the knowledge

part one

1879 Fulham is the oldest of London's first class clubs with its foundations dating as far back as 1879.

25,700 The capacity of Craven Cottage – one of English football's most traditional and unique grounds.

1997 The year that Fulham Chairman Mohamed Al Fayed took over the Club.

5 Despite the fact he had bought a club playing in Division Three, the Chairman promised fans a return to the top-flight within five years. However, in a remarkable reversal of fortunes Fulham blazed a trail through the lower leagues and by 2001 the Whites had secured their place in the Premier League - in less than four years.

Did You Know?

When Fulham signed Paul Peschisolido for £1.1million and Chris Coleman for £2.1million they became the first club outside the top two divisions to pay a seven figure sum for any player.

2002 Fulham won the Intertoto Cup in the summer of 2002, beating Italian club Bologna 5-3 on aggregate with Japanese international Junichi Inamoto scoring once in the first leg and then three times in the second.

the first team

Stephen Kelly

Squad Number: 2
Date of Birth: 06.09.1983
Birthplace: Dublin, Ireland
Nationality: Irish
Height: 184cm
Weight: 82kg
Fulham Debut: v FK Vetra (a) 06.08.2009
Previous Clubs: Tottenham Hotspur, Southend (loan), QPR (loan), Watford (loan), Birmingham City, Stoke City (loan)

Kelly had long been linked with a move to Craven Cottage prior to his free transfer in 2009, and since his arrival the Republic of Ireland international has become a valued member of the squad.

An integral part of the Club's UEFA Europa League campaign the season before last, featuring in 10 of the 19 matches, he is sound defensively, ambitious going forward and capable of playing at both right and left-back.

Wherever he is deployed, Fulham know they will have 100 per cent commitment.

Brede Hangeland

Squad Number: 5
Date of Birth: 20.06.1981
Birthplace: Texas, USA
Nationality: Norwegian
Height: 199cm
Weight: 91kg
Fulham Debut: v Bolton (a) 29.01. 2008
Previous Clubs: Viking FK, FC Copenhagen

With strength and poise clear to see, Brede Hangeland has been as important to the Fulham cause as anybody in recent years.

With his unflappable demeanour and unexpected elegance, Hangeland embodies the team's transformation in recent seasons, and the £2.5 million that the Chairman paid in January 2008 now looks an absolute snip.

Comfortable on the ball, solid in the air and judicious in the tackle, his form and rise in recent seasons stand him out incontestably as one of the English game's most accomplished performers.

33

Philippe Senderos

Squad Number: 14
Date of Birth: 14.02.1985
Birthplace: Geneva, Switzerland
Nationality: Swiss
Height: 188cm
Weight: 82kg
Fulham Debut: v Sunderland (a) 30.04.2011
Previous Clubs: Servette, Arsenal, Milan (loan), Everton (loan)

A ruptured Achilles tendon a month after his 2010 arrival at the Club was far from the ideal start to life at Craven Cottage for Philippe Senderos.

But with that injury now fully behind him, the vastly experienced defender is ready to show what he can do and challenge for a place in the centre of the Whites defence.

A regular for his country, with more than 40 caps, he was part of Switzerland's 2010 World Cup squad and while wearing the red of Arsenal, won an FA Cup and played regular UEFA Champions League football.

Chris Baird

Squad Number: 6
Date of Birth: 25.02.1982
Birthplace: Rasharkin, Northern Ireland
Nationality: Northern Irish
Height: 181cm
Weight: 74kg
Fulham Debut: v Arsenal (a) 12.08.2007
Previous Clubs: Southampton, Walsall (loan), Watford (loan)

Every manager's dream, Chris Baird always puts the team's needs before his own desires, and the Northern Ireland international finally received the recognition that his performances and attitude rightly deserve in recent seasons.

Dubbed 'Bairdinho' by fans for his surging bursts from deep, raking passes and stinging strikes from distance, many have said that his two goals at Stoke City last season turned the tide on a season of unpredictability, into one of success.

He may not grab the headlines as much as others, but his selfless graft makes him no less worthy.

Aaron Hughes

Squad Number: 18
Date of Birth: 08.11.1979
Birthplace: Magherafelt, Northern Ireland
Nationality: Northern Irish
Height: 183cm
Weight: 78kg
Fulham Debut: v Wigan Athletic (a) 15.09.2007
Previous Clubs: Newcastle United, Aston Villa

Outside of Craven Cottage Aaron Hughes is one of the most underrated defenders in the top-flight. However, here at Fulham he is one of our undisputed heroes.

Very few read the game better, or are as composed and assured on the ball, and his faultless defending has given the team's attackers a solid platform to build upon.

The acquisition of the Northern Ireland captain in July 2007 for a reported £1million represents one of the shrewdest Fulham signings in recent years. His telepathic understanding with Brede Hangeland is also one of the country's finest.

Matthew Briggs

Squad Number: 28
Date of Birth: 09.03.1991
Birthplace: Wandsworth, England
Nationality: English
Height: 188cm
Weight: 78kg
Fulham Debut: v Middlesbrough (a) 13.05.2007
Previous Clubs: Leyton Orient (loan)

The youngest ever Premier League player when he debuted in May 2007 at the age of 16 years and 65 days, Matthew Briggs has had to be patient since, but in recent months the young defender has seemingly come of age.

Primarily a left-back, Briggs can defend, but he's also extremely comfortable on the ball, he has pace, can pass, is athletic and can get up and down the pitch.

The England Under-21 international started the current campaign in fine form, even scoring his first senior goal.

Rafik Halliche

Squad Number: 32
Date of Birth: 02.09.1986
Birthplace: Algiers, Algeria
Nationality: Algerian
Height: 186cm
Weight: 84kg
Fulham Debut: v Stoke City (a) 21.09.2010
Previous Clubs: Hussein Dey, Benfica, C.D. Nacional (loan)

Tough-tackling and commanding, Rafik Halliche is an important player for his country and showed his credentials when marking Wayne Rooney out of the game at the 2010 World Cup in South Africa.

As he looks to transform that form to his club football, Halliche will be hopeful of more chances than in his first Fulham season, perhaps in the UEFA Europa League, a competition he previously competed in with C.D Nacional.

quiz time

spot the ball

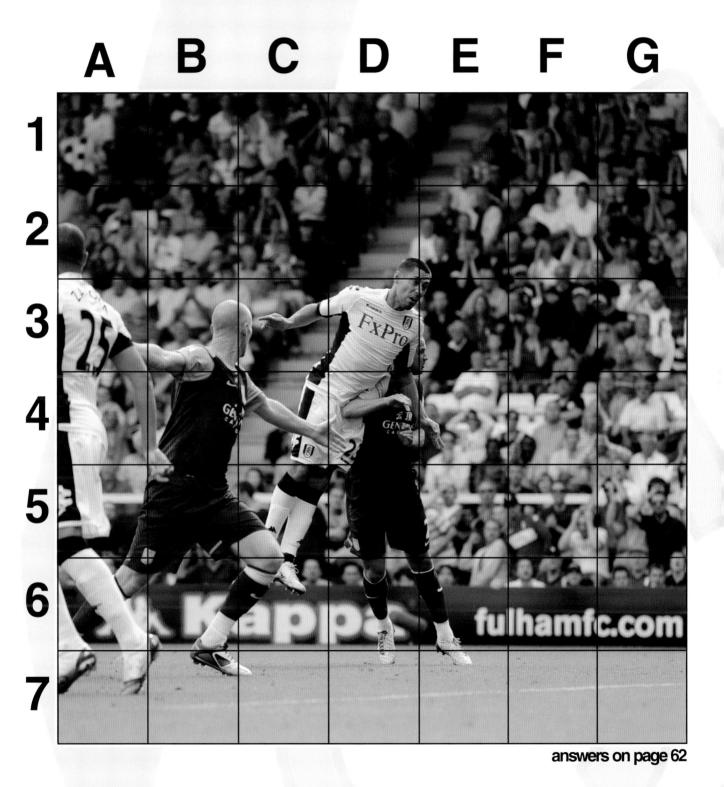

A B C D E F G

1
2
3
4
5
6
7

answers on page 62

what do you know about fulham?

1   Including 2011/12, for how many consecutive seasons have Fulham been in the Premier League?

. . . .

2   Who is Fulham's all-time top goalscorer?

. . . .

3   In which year did Fulham reach the Europa League Final?

. . . .

4   Which European trophy did Fulham win in 2002?

. . . .

5   Who is Fulham's famous Chairman?

. . . .

6   True or False, Fulham is the oldest professional football club in London?

. . . .

7   What is the real name of 'the Maestro' - Fulham's most famous ever player, who captained England and has his own statue outside the Cottage?

. . . .

8   Who is Fulham's all-time top Premier League goal scorer?

. . . .

9   In which year did Fulham reach the FA Cup Final?

. . . .

10   From which country is Fulham boss Martin Jol?

. . . .

answers on page 62

the numbers game

Test your mathematics skills by working out our Fulham FC equations... for example Chris Baird is number 6 and Steve Sidwell is number 4. Add them together and you get Pajtim Kasami who is number 10. Can you do the others?

1. Chris Baird + Steve Sidwell =

Pajtim Kasami

2. Orlando Sá + Bryan Ruiz =

3. Bjørn Helge Riise – John Arne Riise =

4. Stephen Kelly x Andrew Johnson =

5. Neil Etheridge – Marcel Gecov =

6. Aaron Hughes + Bobby Zamora – Danny Murphy =

7. Kerim Frei – Brede Hangeland + Pajtim Kasami =

8. Simon Davies – Dickson Etuhu + Damien Duff =

SQUAD LIST
1. Mark Schwarzer, 2. Stephen Kelly, 3. John Arne Riise, 4. Steve Sidwell, 5. Brede Hangeland, 6. Chris Baird, 8. Andrew Johnson, 9. Orlando Sá, 10. Pajtim Kasami, 11. Bryan Ruiz, 13. Danny Murphy, 14. Philippe Senderos, 15. Marcel Gecov, 16. Damien Duff, 17. Bjørn Helge Riise, 18. Aaron Hughes, 20. Dickson Etuhu, 21. Kerim Frei, 22. Csaba Somogyi, 23. Clint Dempsey, 25. Bobby Zamora, 26. Zdenek Grygera, 28. Matthew Briggs, 29. Simon Davies, 30. Mousa Dembélé, 31. Alex Kacaniklic, 38. Neil Etheridge

answers on page 62

word search

L	F	D	R	D	U	F	F	S	P	V	M
Z	K	E	L	L	Y	U	H	R	M	L	M
H	L	M	R	J	O	L	I	I	R	V	U
F	O	P	E	A	Z	H	A	S	L	C	R
G	Y	S	C	H	W	A	R	Z	E	R	P
R	I	E	O	P	A	M	A	A	P	A	H
U	S	Y	T	M	C	Y	G	N	M	V	Y
I	E	P	T	C	A	Y	R	M	J	E	T
Z	J	Z	A	M	O	R	A	I	O	N	U
I	G	F	G	J	O	S	M	O	I	Y	O
N	E	G	E	R	D	A	V	I	E	S	L
H	U	G	H	E	S	V	P	R	M	V	E

JOL	DUFF	HUGHES
FULHAM	ZAMORA	SA
CRAVEN	RUIZ	KELLY
COTTAGE	DEMPSEY	
SCHWARZER	RIISE	
MURPHY	DAVIES	

answers on page 63

clint dempsey

fulham

guess who

the knowledge

part two

11 The 2011/12 season is the Whites' 11th consecutive top-flight campaign. Only Arsenal, Aston Villa, Chelsea, Everton, Liverpool, Manchester United and Tottenham have enjoyed longer spells in the Premier League than Fulham.

7 At the end of the 2008/09 season Fulham recorded their highest ever top-flight finish of seventh place. Their 53-point haul was also their highest at the top too – not bad considering the Club finished 17th the season before and narrowly avoided relegation.

3 Three consecutive away league wins helped complete an extraordinary comeback during the 2007/08 season. Needing a win at Portsmouth's Fratton Park on the final day of the campaign to survive, Club Captain Danny Murphy popped up with a 76th-minute winner and sealed our top-flight safety.

Did You Know?

It took Fulham 18 games to reach the UEFA Europa League Final and in their nine home games the Whites were unbeaten at Craven Cottage with eight wins and one draw.

2 Despite not winning a major trophy the Club have reached two major finals – the FA Cup Final in 1975 (lost 2-0 against West Ham) and the UEFA Europa League in 2010 (lost 2-1 against Atlético Madrid).

62 The amount of games Fulham played in all competitions during the 2009/10 season – Mark Schwarzer featured the most, making 59 appearances.

45

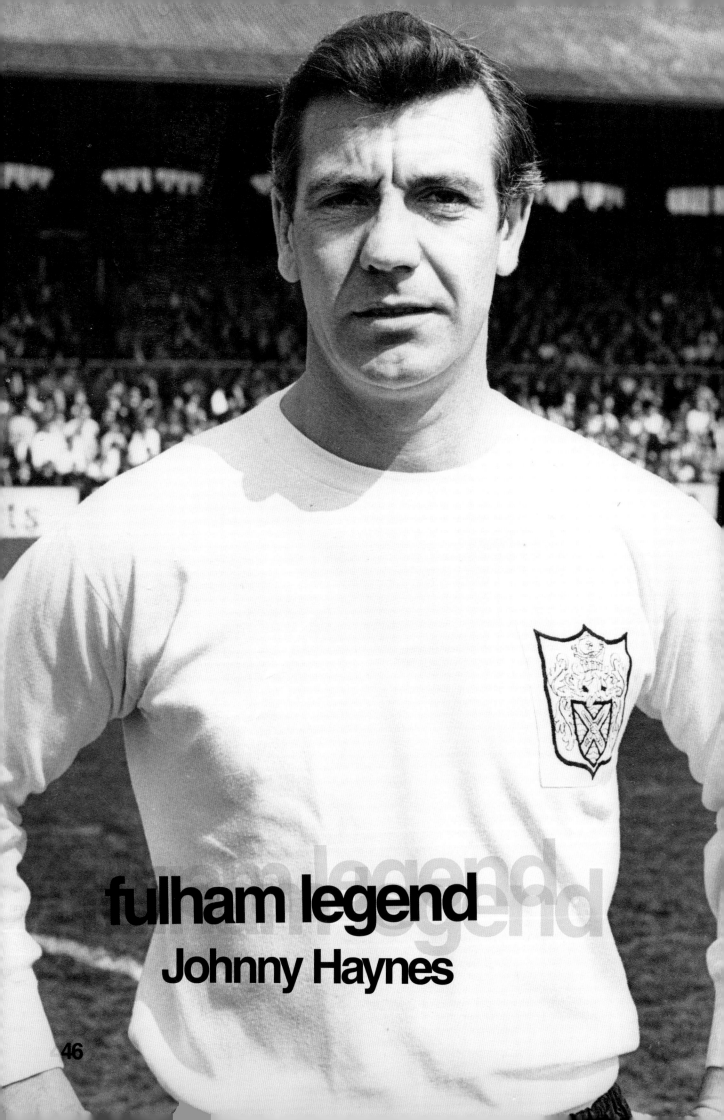

fulham legend

Johnny Haynes

46

Johnny Haynes was one of the star players of his generation and is recognised as Fulham's greatest ever.

In an era when the Club had a number of outstanding individuals, Haynes stood above them all. Naturally gifted, he added dedication and unrivalled commitment to his breathtaking composure and pinpoint passing. He knew where the goal was too, scoring 158 goals in a record 658 appearances for Fulham.

His nickname, 'The Maestro', was totally deserved, yet despite interest from a number of leading English clubs, as well as Italian giants AC Milan, Haynes spent his entire career at Craven Cottage – making his debut in 1952 and playing his last game 18 years later.

An inspirational figure not just for Fulham, but England too, he captained his country for 22 of his 56 caps.

Is it any wonder we built a statue of him at the front of our stadium?!

Did you Know...?

Haynes was the first footballer to appear for England at every level possible: Schoolboy, youth, Under-23 and 'B', before making his full international debut.

Brazilian legend Pelé once described Haynes as the "best passer of the ball I've ever seen".

Haynes became the first player to be paid £100 a week, immediately following the end of the £20 maximum wage.

Damien Duff

Squad Number: 16
Date of Birth: 02.03.1979
Birthplace: Ballyboden, Ireland
Nationality: Irish
Height: 177cm
Weight: 75kg
Fulham Debut: v Amkar Perm (h) 20.08.2009
Previous Clubs: Blackburn Rovers, Chelsea, Newcastle United

With his honest determination and vibrant edge, Damien Duff is blessed with an obvious attacking flair, rarely failing to catch the eye.

He is also a player that can fit into almost any tactical plan. After an indifferent three years at Newcastle, the left-footed winger was shifted to the right at Fulham, where his ability to cut inside added an extra dimension to the Whites' attack, with goals and assists aplenty.

Duff notched up his 500th league appearance last season, and his time at the top looks set to continue for a while yet.

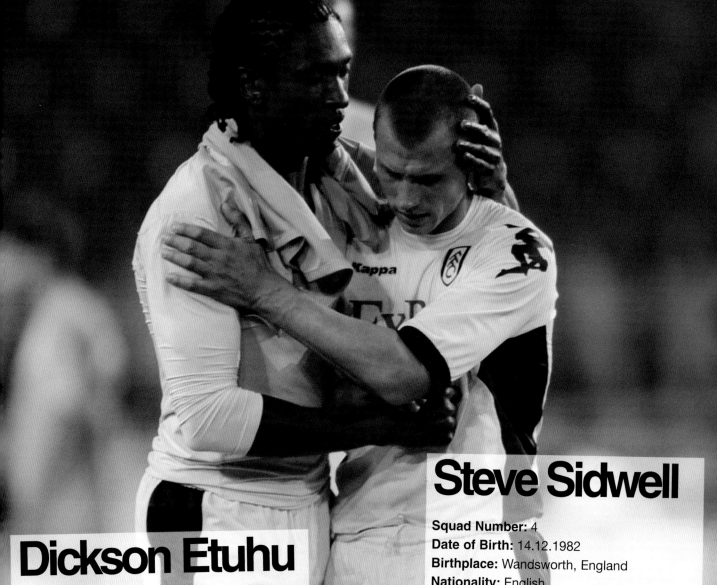

Dickson Etuhu

Squad Number: 20
Date of Birth: 08.06.1982
Birthplace: Kano, Nigeria
Nationality: Nigerian
Height: 189cm
Weight: 89kg
Fulham Debut: v Middlesbrough (h) 20.12.2008
Previous Clubs: Manchester City, Preston NE, Norwich, Sunderland

Another who has progressed considerably at Fulham, Dickson Etuhu's presence in the centre of the park is a key component of the team's formation.

Since his arrival from Sunderland at the start of 2008/09, his athleticism and raw power have complemented the craft of his fellow midfielders, and provided protection for the defence.

The Nigerian international performs an often selfless role, but while he has impressed greatly as our resident midfield 'enforcer', there is much more to his game and there were moments throughout 2010/11 when he broke free from his defensive shackles and emerged as a genuine goal threat.

Steve Sidwell

Squad Number: 4
Date of Birth: 14.12.1982
Birthplace: Wandsworth, England
Nationality: English
Height: 183cm
Weight: 80kg
Fulham Debut: v Stoke City 22.01.2011
Previous Clubs: Arsenal, Brentford (loan), Beveren (loan), Brighton (loan), Reading, Chelsea, Aston Villa

Another who has reignited his career at Craven Cottage, Steve Sidwell has impressed since joining the Whites, initially on loan, in January 2010.

The 'Ginger Iniesta' brings more refined elements to the Fulham midfield, with the timing of his passing and shooting adding much to the team's range of play.

Ambitious and determined, he is constantly probing, making bursting runs from deep, and having missed a lot of football in recent years, the 2011/12 season is an important one for the midfielder.

49

Danny Murphy

Squad Number: 13

Date of Birth: 18.03.1977

Birthplace: Chester, England

Nationality: English

Height: 177cm

Weight: 79kg

Fulham Debut: v Wigan Athletic (a) 15.09.2007

Previous Clubs: Crewe Alexandra, Liverpool, Charlton Athletic, Tottenham Hotspur

With his name already etched into Fulham folklore, Danny Murphy's influence in the heart of the Whites' midfield is constant.

Now in his 19th season as a professional, the talisman still holds the same enthusiasm for the game as he did when he first broke through as a 16-year-old at Crewe Alexandra.

His CV has since been updated by time spent at Liverpool, Charlton and Tottenham (where he worked with Martin Jol), and decorated by nine England caps and a sum of trophies including the FA Cup, League Cup and UEFA Cup. But, it is perhaps his time at Craven Cottage that has served as his most rewarding.

Bjørn Helge Riise

Squad Number: 17
Date of Birth: 21.06.1983
Birthplace: Alesund, Norway
Nationality: Norwegian
Height: 173cm
Weight: 73kg
Fulham Debut: v FK Vetra (a) 30.07.2009
Previous Clubs: Alesund, Viking FK (loan), Standard Liege, Brussels (loan), Lillestrøm, Sheffield United (loan), Portsmouth (loan)

Now in his third season at Craven Cottage, Bjørn Helge Riise is back from a spell on loan at Sheffield United and hopeful that he can recapture his early Fulham form.

Comfortable on either flank, the younger brother of defender John Arne Riise is noted for his endeavour going forward, which appeals to Martin Jol's attacking sensibilities.

A useful outlet, Riise keeps the ball well and offers pin-point delivery. In fact, he finished third in the UEFA Europa League's assist table in 2009/10.

Simon Davies

Squad Number: 29
Date of Birth: 23.10.1979
Birthplace: Haverfordwest, Wales
Nationality: Welsh
Height: 178cm
Weight: 76kg
Fulham Debut: v Stoke City (h) 27.01.2007
Previous Clubs: Peterborough United, Tottenham Hotspur, Everton

A central figure ever since he signed from Everton in January 2007, much has transpired in that time and Davies has certainly played his part - from two relegation battles to our highest-ever top-flight finish and march to the Final of the UEFA Europa League where he scored in both the Semi-Final and Final.

The image of Davies in full flow with the ball at his feet has been one of the more familiar on-field sights of the recent era. He is an intelligent player who uses the ball wisely, and whose accuracy from the flanks has provided many assists.

Clint Dempsey

Squad Number: 23
Date of Birth: 09.03.1983
Birthplace: Texas, USA
Nationality: American
Height: 187cm
Weight: 84kg
Fulham Debut: v Tottenham Hotspur (h) 20.01.2007
Previous Clubs: Furman University, New England Revolution

In his High School yearbook, Clint Dempsey was asked where he saw himself in five years. His reply? "Playing soccer in Europe." Several years later that young hopeful now stands as one of the most respected players, not just at Fulham, but in the Premier League.

Many of the American's exploits will live long in the memory, with his goals last season taking him to the top of the Club's all-time Premier League goal scoring chart.

Pleasing on the eye, there is, however, more to Dempsey than just tricks and flicks, with technique, high energy, toughness and fearless direction coursing through his game.

classic season

1974–75: The Road to Wembley

Fulham may have made it to the Semi-Finals of the FA Cup on six occasions, but only once have they made it all the way to Wembley. And we did it as a Second Division (now Championship) club.

Fulham being Fulham though, we had to do it the hard way, taking the longest and most difficult possible route to the Final. Every one of the five ties was won away from the Cottage, and no club, before or since, has played as many matches to get there.

This was back in the days before penalty shoot-outs, when a draw meant a replay, and there were no limits on the amount of replays that could be played.

It took three games to dispose of Hull City in the Third Round, then four to get past Nottingham Forest in Round Four. Imagine trying to fit in all those cup matches around the League fixtures. Especially considering there were 24 teams in our division back then!

Fulham fans before the 1975 FA Cup Final.

Fulham's John Mitchell, Bobby Moore, Alan Mullery and Viv Busby look optimistic about their chances in the FA Cup Semi-Final as they board the team coach on the day before the match.

53

Viv Busby scores the sensational winner at Goodison Park in 1975.

Mitchell and Busby celebrate after the Fifth Round defeat of Everton.

After making such hard work of overcoming two teams from the same division as ourselves, bizarrely it only took one attempt for us to knockout Everton, who were top of the First Division at the time, in Round Five, Viv Busby taking his Cup tally to six with a third double in the competition. But the shock success also owed as much to the superbly organised defence in which Alan Mullery and Bobby Moore were outstanding.

In the Quarter-Final there was a long trip to Carlisle, then enjoying their only season as a First Division club. Les Barrett grabbed the only goal in a 1-0 victory, but goalkeeper Peter Mellor was the star.

Onto the Semi-Final, and the Whites were drawn against their third opponents from the top-flight, Birmingham City. Fulham had the better of the play at Hillsborough and led through a splendid goal by John Mitchell, but unfortunately the team let their opponents back into the tie and had to settle for a 1-1 draw. The replay, at Manchester City's old home, Maine Road, saw the ending of the Club's Semi-Final jinx that dated back nearly 70 years.

It is doubtful whether any of Mitchell's other 59 Fulham goals were as scrappy as the one in the 119th minute of the replay against the Blues, but certainly none were as joyously received nor as significant. Against all the odds the Whites won through to Wembley, with a team of veterans, modestly priced journeymen and homegrown talent.

John Mitchell's dramatic last gasp extra time winner in the Semi-Final replay.

Unfortunately, the Final itself was anti-climatic, West Ham winning a match played in an abnormally good spirit 2-0. If it was true that the Fulham players felt as many of the supporters did, that being there was the achievement, no Fulham fan blamed them, but regardless, the team played very well and did the Club proud.

The FA Cup had undoubtedly taken centre stage, but the team finished in a respectable 9th place out of 24. And despite some big names like George Best and Rodney Marsh joining England stars like Alan Mullery and Bobby Moore at the Cottage a couple of years later, it would be a long while before the Club got close to such success again.

The Duke of Kent meets the players at Wembley.

1974–75 Division Two League table

Manchester United	42	26	9	7	66	30	61
Aston Villa	42	25	8	9	79	32	58
Norwich City	42	20	13	9	58	37	53
Sunderland	42	19	13	10	65	35	51
Bristol City	42	21	8	13	47	33	50
West Bromwich Albion	42	18	9	15	54	42	45
Blackpool	42	14	17	11	38	33	45
Hull City	42	15	14	13	40	53	44
Fulham	**42**	**13**	**16**	**13**	**44**	**39**	**42**
Bolton Wanderers	42	15	12	15	45	41	42
Oxford United	42	15	12	15	41	51	42
Leyton Orient	42	11	20	11	28	39	42
Southampton	42	15	11	16	53	54	41
Notts County	42	12	16	14	49	59	40
York City	42	14	10	18	51	55	38
Nottingham Forest	42	12	14	16	43	55	38
Portsmouth	42	12	13	17	44	54	37
Oldham Athletic	42	10	15	17	40	48	35
Bristol Rovers	42	12	11	19	42	64	35
Millwall	42	10	12	20	44	56	32
Cardiff City	42	9	14	19	36	62	32
Sheffield Wednesday	42	5	11	26	29	64	21

West Ham United captain Billy Bonds (left) shakes hands with his Fulham counterpart Alan Mullery (right).

The 1975 FA Cup Run

Round	Opponent	Result	Score	Fulham Scorer/s
Third Round	Hull City (h)	D	1-1	Jim Conway
Third Round Replay	Hull City (a)	D	2-2	Viv Busby 2
Third Round 2nd Replay	Hull City (n)	W	1-0	Alan Slough
Fourth Round	Nottingham Forest (h)	D	0-0	
Fourth Round Replay	Nottingham Forest (a)	D	1-1	John Dowie
Fourth Round 2nd Replay	Nottingham Forest (h)	D	1-1	Alan Slough
Fourth Round 3rd Replay	Nottingham Forest (a)	W	2-1	Viv Busby 2
Fifth Round	Everton (a)	W	2-1	Viv Busby 2
Sixth Round	Carlisle United (a)	W	1-0	Les Barrett
Semi-Final	Birmingham City (n)	D	1-1	John Mitchell
Semi-Final Replay	Birmingham City (n)	W	1-0 aet	John Mitchell
Final	West Ham United (n)	L	0-2	

Andrew Johnson

Squad Number: 8
Date of Birth: 10.02.1981
Birthplace: Bedford, England
Nationality: English
Height: 172cm
Weight: 67kg
Fulham Debut: v Bolton (h) 13.09.2008
Previous Clubs: Birmingham City, Crystal Palace, Everton

Fulham's signing of Andrew Johnson in July 2008 was a statement of real intent. For the Whites had secured the services of a player of renowned goal scoring ability, searing pace, high-level work rate, cunning movement and eight England caps.

A dependable source of goals wherever he has played, he has more than 100 in English football, and Johnson will be looking to add to that tally for Fulham in 2012.

forwards

56

Bobby Zamora

Squad Number: 25
Date of Birth: 16.01.1981
Birthplace: Barking, England
Nationality: English
Height: 187cm
Weight: 85kg
Fulham Debut: v Hull City (a) 16.08.2008
Previous Clubs: Bristol Rovers, Bath (loan), Brighton, Tottenham Hotspur, West Ham United

Few players had better 2009/10 seasons than Bobby Zamora, but similarly, few had a more frustrating 2010/11 – with the striker absent for the majority of the campaign following a cruel leg break.

The England striker has undoubtedly become one of the team's most important players, bringing much to the Whites' front line – including an unrivalled ability to hold up the ball, intelligent link-up work and the foresight to bring others into play.

From open play or set pieces, he is the scorer of a wide variety of goals.

Mousa Dembélé

Squad Number: 30
Date of Birth: 16.07.1987
Birthplace: Wilrijk, Belgium
Nationality: Belgium
Height: 185cm
Weight: 82kg
Fulham Debut: v Manchester United (h) 22.08.2010
Previous Clubs: Germinal Beerschot, Willem II, AZ Alkmaar

In Mousa Dembélé Fulham unearthed quite a find, the Belgium international emerging with such an illuminating gift for the game that people have not failed to notice.

After his arrival in SW6 in the summer of 2010, Dembélé was regularly a talking point in an impressive debut season.

A captivating on-field presence who exudes an enthusiasm rarely seen outside of the school playground, he plays the game today as he always has done. Players of his ilk have always been appreciated at the Cottage – the Fulham faithful have long held a soft spot for a showman - and Dembélé is no exception.

young professionals

Keep an eye out for these young talents...

Dan Burn

A towering central defender who joined the Club in the summer of 2011 from Conference side Darlington where, despite only being in his teens, he had become a key player. Comfortable on the ball and a threat from set-pieces, Burn is more than just an accomplished stopper, with comparisons already being made with Chris Smalling.

Alex Kacaniklic

The Swedish youngster is now in his second season at Fulham having joined the Whites from Liverpool alongside fellow Development Squad team-mate Lauri Dalla Valle last summer. Kacaniklic regularly catches the eye with his direct and often game-changing running, chipping in with goals and assists too.

Kerim Frei

With his hard work, dazzling tricks and ability to beat his marker, the Swiss youth international is one of Fulham's most promising young players. A real talent who was rewarded with his First Team debut in this season's UEFA Europa League, and ripped Chelsea apart in the Carling Cup, a bright future beckons.

Tom Donegan

One of a number of new additions to the Fulham squad in what proved to be a very busy summer transfer window. The teenage midfielder was signed for the future, having impressed with Everton's Academy, but such is his promise, he was promoted to First Team duties, making his senior debut in the UEFA Europa League.

the knowledge

part three

Did You Know?

Defender Matthew Briggs became the Club's and the Premier League's youngest ever player at 16-years and 65-days when he made his First Team debut against Middlesbrough in May 2007.

6 The Whites have reached the Semi-Final of the FA Cup on six occasions – the last of which came in 2002 and ended in a narrow 1-0 defeat against Chelsea.

658 The legendary Johnny Haynes made the most appearances for the Club, featuring 658 times.

178 Gordon Davies is the Club's all-time top scorer with 178 goals.

33 Before the start of the 2011/12 season, Clint Dempsey became Fulham's leading Premier League goal scorer with 33 top-flight goals.

10 The Club's biggest top-flight victory came during the 1963/64 season when they beat Ipswich Town 10-1.

11 Bobby Zamora became the 11th Fulham player to represent England in a full international. The list may not be as long as some clubs' – but not everyone can boast two former England Captains in Johnny Haynes and Alan Mullery, and a World Cup winner in George Cohen amongst their former players!

Did You Know?

Fulham have nine official international members' clubs, in Australia, Denmark, Finland, Italy, Netherlands, New Zealand, Norway, Sweden and USA.

future fulham

future fulham

Central to the Club's current and future plans, the Fulham Academy made significant progress during the 2010/11 season, in which the Under-18s were crowned champions of their respective league and made the National Play-Off Final.

As a result, there were many impressive results and performances, as those on the outside of the Club really took notice of former Fulham defender Kit Symons' young side – and rightly so.

But while the Under-18 age group may have grabbed all the headlines, there was success too across the Academy in general, as all age groups demonstrated winning football and wholesale progress.

Most important though is the development of young players for the First Team, and the Club was delighted to see Matthew Briggs break through, and the likes of Neil Etheridge and Danny Hoesen named on the senior squad bench.

Following them in early 2011/12 we've already seen Kerim Frei make his mark, while there were also opportunities for Lauri Dalla Valle and Tom Donegan.

After such an impressive 2010/11, with solid foundations for success in place, the Fulham Academy continues to build for a bright future, with more young hopefuls tipped to make an impact in the coming years.

junior members' club

Fulham FC Junior Members receive a range of exclusive, fantastic benefits, for **just £10**!

Get the cheapest tickets going at Craven Cottage with exclusive Junior Members offers. Including £5 **discounts on matchday tickets** for at least four B and C grade games.

Receive a special Members only Membership Pack!

Your very own dedicated Junior Members' Club Magazine, **Halftime**

Get a 10% discount on **holiday soccer courses** with the Fulham FC Foundation!

£10 off your first in-store purchase of £50 or more at the Fulham FC Club shops.

You could even be invited to the **Junior Members Christmas party**, where lots of surprises await!

And gain entry to the ballot, which is reserved for Season Ticket Holders and Members, to **become a ball boy or ball girl** at a Fulham match!

Fulham FC Junior Membership is available to any fan under the age of 16. If you have any questions or would like to sign up, ask a parent or guardian to phone **0843 208 1234 (option 2)** or check out **www.fulhamfc.com/members**

61

quiz time answers

quiz time answers

spot the ball - page 37

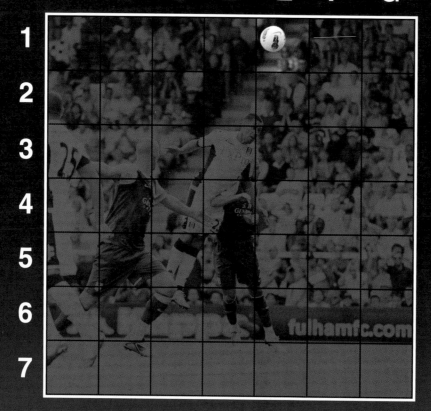

A B C D E F G

1 2 3 4 5 6 7

fulhamfc.com

what do you know about fulham? - page 39

1. 11; 2. Gordon Davies; 3. 2010; 4. The Intertoto Cup; 5. Mohamed Al Fayed; 6. True; 7. Johnny Haynes; 8. Clint Dempsey; 9. 1975; 10. The Netherlands

the numbers game - page 39

1. Pajtim Kasami, 2. Dickson Etuhu, 3. Philippe Senderos, 4. Damien Duff, 5. Clint Dempsey, 6. Mousa Dembélé, 7. Zdenek Grygera, 8. Bobby Zamora